FORBIDDEN TASTE

Catherine could not bring herself to heed the warnings whispering through her. Just for this moment, she vowed, then never again. Tomorrow Collier would be her enemy the same as before.

Lightly, he trailed his fingers up her neck, then down again.

A strange tremble skipped through her. She had never been touched as he touched her, but she could not find it in her to stop him—not even when he lifted her chin and found her mouth in the dark.

Wine. That was how Collier tasted. Heady. A slow trickle that kindled her senses and warmed places she had not known were cold.

"I won't lose you again," he spoke against her lips.

Books by Tamara Leigh

Misbegotten
Unforgotten

Published by HarperPaperbacks

Unforgotten

⋈ TAMARA LEIGH ⋈

HarperPaperbacks
A Division of HarperCollins*Publishers*

HarperPaperbacks
A Division of HarperCollins*Publishers*
10 East 53rd Street, New York, N.Y. 10022-5299

ISBN 0-06-108448-4

HarperCollins®, ®, HarperPaperbacks™, and
HarperMonogram® are trademarks of HarperCollins*Publishers*,Inc.

Cover illustration by Jon Paul

First printing: March 1997

Printed in the United States of America

Visit HarperPaperbacks on the World Wide Web at
http://www.harpercollins.com/paperbacks

❖ 10 9 8 7 6 5 4 3 2 1

To my sister, Teresa Annette, for showing me God through her eyes: Your faith is my inspiration, little one. Keep shining, and let no one take your light from you.

Unforgotten

Prologue

Northern England, May 1464

She had seen her death. Though every eve this past sennight the dream had come to her, this time it had seemed so real. So vivid.

The bodice of her chemise was moist with the sweat of fear as Catherine reached under the bed, fumbling until her fingers closed around the dagger's hilt. Blessedly.

Each night before attempting a few precious hours of sleep, she felt for it, its presence lending her a sense of security. But this night was different, for the dream grew a need in her to have the dagger in hand. She gripped it tighter and settled her head back to the mattress. Try as she did to resist sleep and the terrible dream awaiting her, fatigue dragged her back to its depths.

Suddenly, her enemies were upon her—before, behind, and beside her. They were faceless, all of them, though she certainly did not need to see their faces to know them for the traitors they were. The stench of their bodies burned her nostrils, their breath stirred the fine hairs along her arms, their taunting voices filled her ears. Though Catherine knew her defense of the gatehouse would be for naught, never would she surrender.

Straining beneath the weight of her sword, she raised it as the one with leering eyes jumped forward. In the next instant, those same eyes turned disbelieving as she sank her blade into the man's arm.

For a long, slow moment, there was silence, then it burst. With a roar of pain and anger, the man dropped his sword and lunged for her. She saw his mouth, moldering teeth bared, bottom lip lathered with saliva. The devil himself.

Catherine stumbled back against the portcullis winch and tried to raise her sword again, but it was too late. The man tore the weapon from her hands and, without a moment's hesitation, turned it on her. His face was above hers now. Though she could never remember it upon awakening, she saw his features contort as he drove the blade through her. Then, issuing a triumphant laugh, he lurched back.

Catherine looked down to the blood spilled from the middle of her. In the next instant, pain radiated through her like the sear of a hot iron. It dragged a cry to her lips, but she held it in with the last of her strength. Then, her battle finally over, she crumpled to the floor.

Lord, if only she had her life to live over.

1

London, March 1997

Collier Morrow slammed the receiver down. "Bastard," he said with a growl as a vision of his older brother rose before him.

James would be smiling that maddening smile of his, with his feet propped on the edge of the desk, an unlit cigar jutting between his lips. And he had every reason to wallow, for the acquisition of Strivling Castle was no small conquest. Indeed, there was no conquest beyond it.

Collier kneaded the tense muscles of his neck. The rivalry between him and his brother went back years, encouraged by their father who had seen it as a means of ensuring they followed in his footsteps and that it could never be said he'd produced weak-kneed off-spring. The lessons Winton Morrow had taught his sons had not died with him six years ago. Indeed, the rivalry was still very much alive. If it wasn't James scrambling to snatch a property from Collier, it was Collier retaliating on the next go-around. Always some higher stake to ascend to. Always some way to better the other. Until now.

It had been their father's greatest desire to recover Strivling Castle, which had been held by the Morrows from the fifteenth century until the nineteenth when it had been sold to raise the family out of financial difficulties. Having failed in that endeavor, his sons had regarded it as the ultimate prize, with the victor never to be outdone.

Collier's defeat too great and pain too real, he drew a deep breath and slowly exhaled. He still ached—his neck, arm, and ribs. A painful reminder of the injuries he'd sustained a year ago.

Realizing where he was heading, he struggled against the need, but a moment later thrust a hand into his pocket and closed it around the vial. Just two, he promised himself. No more than three.

"Your home is lovely," a voice intruded on his torment.

He swung around.

Aryn Viscott stood in the doorway—the woman whom Collier intended to marry, though she didn't yet know it. Her shoulder-length auburn hair framing her face and startling blue eyes unwavering on him, she smiled.

"Not exactly the reception I was expecting," she said and stepped forward.

Telling himself he felt neither pain, nor anger, Collier released the vial and strode from behind his desk. "It's good to see you."

"Is it?"

"You know it is, darling."

The doubt in her eyes said otherwise. "You were going to meet me at the airport."

He had been, but then the phone had rung. Although he had felt a pang of guilt at sending his driver for her, he'd had no choice. Not when something as important as Strivling was at stake. "I apologize," he said. "An important call came in."

"Anything serious?"

Collier tensed. The last thing he wanted to do was talk about it. "No." He pulled Aryn into his arms.

She hesitated, then dropped her handbag and leaned into him.

Collier gathered her nearer and claimed her mouth. God, he wanted her. It had been more than a month since they had been together, and he could think of no better way to spend the remainder of the afternoon than making love to her. And perhaps he would have, if the phone had not rung.

He knew he ought to let it ring, but pulled back. "I've got to get it." He turned from the disappointment in Aryn's eyes and snatched up the receiver. "Morrow here."

"Hello, brother."

Grateful his back was to Aryn, Collier locked his gaze on the clouds gathering in the sky outside. "James."

"Have you heard?"

"I have."

"Then I won't keep you." The line went dead.

Collier settled the receiver back in its cradle. Though part of him wanted to rage, he could not have Aryn see what the loss of Strivling meant to him.

"What's happened?" she asked. "Why did James call?"

Her knowledge of the discord between he and his

brother was limited to the little he told her, and that was enough. "Nothing you need worry about." Collier took her arm. "I'll show you about the manor now."

Aryn resisted his pull. "You have to end it, Collier. This thing between you and your brother cannot continue. Look what happened with—"

"It's under control," he said, the vial pressing urgently against his thigh.

Her eyebrows pinched together. "You're sure?"

Until three weeks ago his dependence on the painkillers *had been* under control, but when the bid for Strivling had started going James's way, he had begun to feel the pain again. Though he had fought the yearning, in the end, he had turned to the only thing capable of alleviating his suffering. But he could quit. After all, he'd done it once before.

"Of course I'm sure," he said. "Now would you like that tour, or should we continue where we left off?" He thumbed her bottom lip.

The doubt was a long time disappearing from Aryn's face. "Much as you tempt me," she finally said, "I think a tour would be more fitting for this time of day."

Collier's strained mouth fell into a grin that felt almost genuine. "Sometimes, Aryn, you are more proper than the English."

She made a face. "It's because I've been spending too much time with you. Shall we go?"

Collier closed the door of his bedroom and drew Aryn into his arms, but that was as far as he got.

"How unusual," she said, staring past his shoulder. "Is it a woman? Ah, yes. I see her now."

Thwarted, but telling himself it would take only a few minutes to satisfy her curiosity, Collier turned to the portrait above the mantel. At first glance, the mash of colors made no sense, making it appear more a piece of modern art than a portrait commissioned in the fifteenth century. But it did belong to that time, as did the woman who was revealed here and there through the landscape painted over her during the sixteenth century.

"Who is she?" Aryn asked.

"It's believed to be Catherine Algernon. The picture was brought out of Strivling Castle in—"

"Strivling." She frowned. "Didn't it once belong to your ancestors?"

Once, and now again, but now it belonged to James. Collier forced down emotions that threatened to reveal him. "Yes," he said, then returned to the previous topic. "The picture was thought to be nothing more than a landscape."

"Then no one knew what lay beneath?"

"Not until it had hung in the library of this manor for twenty-five years with the morning sun on it. It was then that the top layer of paint began to peel away."

"But why would anyone paint over her?"

"She was never completed." Collier gestured to a gape in the scenery which revealed the outline of hands, the only color coming from the red rose clasped between them. "See?"

Aryn nodded.

"As the portrait would have been thought useless in its unfinished state, the landscape was painted over it—a not uncommon practice with paintings that were never completed, or later deemed inadequate."

Aryn stepped to the mantel. "Aren't you curious to know what, exactly, she looks like?"

"I've always been curious."

"Then why not have the portrait restored?"

"It's been attempted. Unfortunately, the landscape gives up only what it wishes to."

"As if it guards a secret, hmm?" Aryn fingered the frame. "Why do you think it was never completed?"

Collier lifted his gaze to the blue eyes staring out from the canvas. "If it is, in fact, Catherine Algernon, then her sudden death would account for it."

Aryn looked over her shoulder. "How did she die?"

Collier fixed a teasing smile on his face. "You would know if you were English," he said, though the truth of it was that the legend of Catherine Algernon had died long ago. Only the generations of Morrows kept it alive.

Aryn raised her eyebrows. "Well, since I am American, you'll just have to tell me, won't you?"

Collier liked the way her eyes sparkled with the light of good humor. It was one of the many things that had attracted him to her in the first place.

"Was she a significant figure?" Aryn asked.

Collier braced an arm against the mantel. "No. It was her death that put her name on men's lips."

"Which brings us back to the question of how she died."

"Have you heard of the Wars of the Roses—the House of Lancaster against the House of York?"

Aryn offered an apologetic shrug.

"It was a civil war waged for the throne of England. Catherine Algernon supported the Lancasters"— Collier indicated the red rose the lady held—"whereas the Morrows supported the Yorks whose badge was the white rose."

"Hence, the Wars of the Roses."

He nodded. "In 1461, the Yorkists overthrew King

Henry the sixth and installed Edward the fourth on the throne. In an attempt to subdue the northern barons who continued to support Henry, Edward sent a man by the name of Montagu to lay siege to their castles. There was resistance, but eventually surrender. Edward's policy being one of conciliation, he restored the castles to their Lancastrian lords. Then, in 1464, they revolted again, but with the same result. Among the last to fall was Strivling. It was in the final engagement that Catherine died."

"Go on."

"Legend has it that, following the death of Lord Somerton and his son—Catherine's betrothed—she took control of the castle's defenses."

Aryn's smile widened.

"Let me guess, this is the part you like?"

She laughed. "Of course. It's nice to know not all damsels were in distress. So then what happened?"

"Montagu pledged that the man who succeeded in opening Strivling would be awarded the castle. Being a landless knight, my ancestor, Edmund Morrow, accepted the challenge. Unfortunately, he and the others who offered their services that day were defeated, and those not killed were captured and imprisoned—Edmund among them."

"And then?"

"On the day following his capture, Edmund led an escape from the dungeon. He and his followers had just captured the winch room when—"

"Winch room?" Aryn asked.

"It's where the winches that control the portcullis and drawbridge are located," Collier explained, then continued. "Suddenly, Catherine appeared with sword in hand to defend it. This one." He touched the blue-black hilt of the sword that rested on the mantel.

Aryn's face reflected surprise. She'd been too engrossed in the portrait to notice it. "This very sword?"

Collier nodded.

"Did she actually use it?"

"Yes, but though she had the passion for fighting, she had none of the skill. The sword was turned on her and she was slain."

"Edmund killed her?"

Collier shook his head. "The man's name was Walther—a mercenary knight—the same as Edmund. Catherine cut his sword arm and, in his fury, he killed her.

Indignation rolled into Aryn's eyes. "Chivalrous! Her life for a few drops of blood."

Collier chuckled. "I'm sorry to be the bearer of bad news, but regardless of how your Hollywood portrays knights, chivalry was often forgotten when there was blood to be shed and booty to be had—especially when a man's pride had been trounced as much as Catherine trounced Walther's."

"Hmm." Aryn glided a finger down the blade.

"Careful," Collier warned. "The edges are as sharp as the day they last drew blood."

She turned her blue eyes on him. "So with Catherine dead, her enemy was let in and your ancestor was awarded Strivling Castle."

"Actually, Edmund was granted the barony of Highchester. Strivling is one of its three castles."

"My," Aryn murmured. "And what of Walther?"

"Edmund awarded him charge of one of the lesser castles. Thereafter, the mercenary fell into obscurity."

"Not soon enough for my liking."

Collier grinned. "It's more than five-hundred years in the past. Nothing can be done about it now." He pulled Aryn toward him.

She held on to her indignation a moment longer, then wound her arms around his neck.

Collier covered her mouth with his, kissed her long and hard, trailed his lips to her ear. "It's been too long," he whispered.

She arched against him. "I love you, Collier."

Uncomfortable with her declaration, he pushed it to the back of his mind, then slowly proceeded to explore the vulnerable places he'd learned during this past year and a half of courting her.

"Your mind is somewhere else," Aryn murmured. She slid a hand over Collier's abdomen and played her fingers through the fine hairs covering his chest. "Is it James?"

She had been silent for so long that Collier had begun to think she'd drifted off to sleep—had prayed she had. Clasping his hand over hers so she would not feel what he was going through, he lowered their joined hands to the mattress between them. "Where else would my mind be?"

The moonlight on her upturned face reflected a wry smile. "I was hoping it would be on me."

Collier closed his eyes. The strain of holding in his emotions all these hours was overwhelming. After he and Aryn had made love this afternoon, they'd gone downstairs to supper, and afterwards had talked for hours. Now, nearing midnight, he was still denied the relief he had vowed he would not seek until after she was asleep. Feeling as if he was going through withdrawal all over again—first yawning and perspiring, and now his flesh peaking in goose bumps and the muscles beneath beginning to twitch—he wondered how much longer before he could put an end to his torment.

"Forgive me, Aryn." He released her hand and dragged another blanket over him. "The day just started off bad."

"But got better, I hope," she said with a smile in her voice, obviously fishing.

He tensed as his ribs joined with the pain in his neck and lower back. "It did."

"I'm relieved. Now tell me what happened."

"Tomorrow. It's past midnight and we've an early start to make in the morning if you want to see all of London."

"I'm not tired. Really."

Which meant she was not likely to go to sleep until he told her. "The property I lost to James was Strivling," he said with as much matter-of-fact as he could manage.

"Strivling? But that's your ancestral home. It . . ." Her words drifted into silence. "You didn't tell me you had a chance to purchase it."

He'd hurt her by not confiding in her, but it was business—nothing to do with their relationship. "Yes, a chance, but that was all." He flexed his shoulder which ached so fiercely it felt on fire.

"I'm sorry, Collier. I know it must have meant a lot to you. What do you think James will do with it?"

Collier tried to block the pain that shot from shoulder to hip. "He intends to take up residence there."

Aryn sighed. "I suppose it could be worse. He might have transformed it into one of those castle hotels."

Her words rattled Collier. Had he been wrong in thinking to carry out the plans for Strivling which had first been conceived by his father? For certain, his brother's decision to maintain it as a private residence had been a strong factor in his acquisition of it. No, he rejected the idea. The cost of maintaining the castle as a private residence would be exorbitant. If James did not wish to bankrupt himself, he would eventually have to sell it or develop it.

Doing his damnedest to relax the tension from his body, Collier looked into the shadows where Aryn lay. "It's midnight," he said. "We should get some sleep."

"All right." She levered onto an elbow, lowered her head, and murmured against his lips, "I love you." But rather than finish the kiss, she drew back. "Are you coming down with something? You feel warm."

Warm, yet so damned cold. "I'm fine. Good night."

Aryn's silence was excruciatingly long, her suspicion tangible, but then she lay back down. "Good night."

As Collier lay still beside her, he turned his thoughts to the phone calls that needed to be made before dawn, to the day he would spend with Aryn, to anything other than that which called more loudly to him with each passing moment. But it was no use. A half hour later he lay awake.

Silently swearing, he tossed back the covers and rose.

The vial skidded across Collier's desk and fell to the floor. Dragging his attention from the phone discussion, he looked at where the vial had spilled its contents onto the carpet, then swiveled his chair around.

From the doorway, Aryn stared at him with accusing eyes. She knew.

"I'll call you back," Collier interrupted the man on the other end of the line, and hung up.

"You lied to me," Aryn said. "You told me it was under control."

He could lie to her again, but he wouldn't. She would just have to understand. "It *was* under control."

"But?"

He rose from his chair. "I needed them again."

"Strivling?"

Though he knew she sought more than confirmation, that was all he gave her. "Yes."

She swung away.

"Aryn!"

She looked over her shoulder. "I'm leaving."

Not just leaving, but walking out of his life. "Stay," he said, his voice strangely choked.

She shook her head. "I can't."

"It has nothing to do with you."

"Doesn't it?" Her smile was sorrowful. "Those pills shut me out, Collier—not that I wasn't out before, but at least I was beginning to reach you. But you don't want that, do you? You can't stand anyone getting that near."

His pride kicking and screaming all the way, Collier said, "I want you, Aryn."

"Want me, but don't trust me—"

"Of course I do." It was an automatic response. He knew it the moment he said it. He *didn't* trust women—not since his mother had walked out on his tyrannical father and never once looked back at the young sons she left behind.

"No, you don't trust me," Aryn said. "If you did, you would have told me about Strivling."

"It's business. That side of my life I keep separate from the personal."

Clearly, she didn't believe him. "Can you even say you love me?"

All of him stiffened. *Did* he love her? Was that

what he felt? "I want to marry you, Aryn." That ought to be enough.

She quickly shuttered her surprise. "And what of love?"

She was pushing him. Wanting something he couldn't give. "I want to marry you," he repeated.

She shook her head. "You *do* love me." Her eyes were bright with tears. "You just can't see past those damned pills and this incessant drive of yours to outdo your brother to realize it."

Though he wanted to take her in his arms, he clenched his hands. "If you believe I love you, why are you leaving?"

Bitter laughter parted her lips. "Because I'm not supposed to have to tell you what you feel, Collier. It's for *you* to tell *me*." She drew a shaky breath, crossed the room, and brushed her mouth across his cheek. "Good-bye." She turned and walked out the door.

He wanted to go after her and—damn it!—tell her he loved her if that was what it took, but he couldn't. He turned to the window and, a short while later, watched Aryn step into a cab.

As the car wound down the driveway, Collier vowed he would get her back. All Aryn needed was time. All he needed was a way out from under the pills that lay crushed beneath his feet.

Staring into the clouds the plane rose through, Aryn tried to swallow the lump in her throat, but it was no use. The muffled sob came, and behind it another. She turned to the window and let the tears fall.

She cried for the first time she and Collier met, for the first time they made love, and a hundred other "firsts."

But mostly, she cried for the climbing accident which had been the beginning of the end of them. The large dosages of painkillers prescribed to ease Collier's suffering had caused marked changes in his personality—so much that, six months following his accident, she had issued the ultimatum that if he did not break his dependence on them, their relationship would end. Where Collier had gone wrong was in believing he could handle the withdrawal without professional help. . . .

Feeling a sudden tightness in her chest, Aryn opened her purse and fumbled inside. Had she packed it in her suitcase? she wondered with rising panic. Beginning to cough, she dug deeper and, a moment later, found the inhaler. Thankfully, she had not misplaced it as she sometimes did. She put her mouth around it and dispensed the metered dose. A short time later, it was as if the asthma attack had never happened. But still there was Collier.

Hurting so much she wanted to cry aloud, Aryn squeezed her eyes closed.

A hand settled on her shoulder. "It will all work out, my dear," the elderly woman beside her said.

No it wouldn't. Her battle for Collier was lost as surely as Catherine Algernon's battle against the Yorkists. Perhaps another time. Perhaps another place, but—

"Another time, another place," the elderly woman added.

Startled, Aryn looked into her softly wrinkled face. Her eyes sparkled like moonlight on snow, her mouth curved gently, and over her brow fell a dark lock of hair that contrasted with the silvered confection crowning her head.

The matron's smile widened. "You will see." She settled back and closed her eyes.

2

Aryn was dead.

Like a demon rising out of him, Collier bellowed
first his fury, then his pain, and lastly his grief. But it
was not enough. Never would it be enough.

He crumpled the letter and hurled it into the fireplace that had not known an ember for more than six
weeks—six weeks of hell to gain heaven, and now
that heaven had been snatched from him in the words
penned by the trembling hand of Aryn's mother: Her
daughter had passed away following respiratory failure brought on by an acute attack of asthma.

His head pounding furiously, every muscle in his
body beginning to shake with the collapse of his emotions, Collier shouted, "Aryn! God, Aryn."

It was not calm, contained Collier Morrow who
shook his fist at God and cursed Him. It was not
proper, thoroughly English Collier Morrow who
swept his arm across the top of the bureau and sent a

vase shattering to the hearth. It was not even the Collier Morrow who, until six weeks past, had sought relief in the viciously comfortable world of painkillers. This Collier Morrow was borne of agonizing loss. A man who had never known love before Aryn and would never know love again.

The admission stilled him. Love. Yes, he finally admitted it, he had loved Aryn.

Wishing her back to life, but knowing it was useless, he toppled a chair, raked books from shelves, flung a framed photograph and the bedside lamp against the door, and sent the fire irons clattering to the carpet. But he found no relief. Nothing to deliver him from the truth that Aryn was lost to him forever.

In his search for something else to lay hands to, Collier's gaze was drawn to the picture above the mantel. Thinking to rend Catherine's secret on the stone hearth, he strode forward, but as he reached for the picture, the gleam of finely-honed steel caught his eye.

He seized the sword. Barely feeling the blade as it dug into his hands, he caught his distorted reflection in its silvered length: Collier Morrow, a man with whom business had always come first. A man who had given only the leavings of the emotions he poured into his work to any who dared try to make a place for themselves in his life.

He closed his hands more tightly on the blade. As the blood flowed between his fingers, he forced himself to acknowledge the truth: He was to blame for Aryn's death. Had he not driven her out of his life with his refusal to give back any of the emotions she had spent on him, it was likely she would not be dead now. If only he hadn't waited so long to realize the depth of *his* emotions.

Believing there was a chance to get her back, a month after she had left him, Collier had finally admitted himself for treatment. But too late.

"Sir?" an uncertain voice spoke from the opposite side of the door.

It was an aching journey up from the depths Collier had descended to, but finally he identified the voice as belonging to his housekeeper.

"Leave me," he ordered.

"Are you well, sir?"

"I am." Never would he be well again.

"Do you require a physician?"

Although he was tempted to loft the sword at the door, he suppressed the desire. "I do not need anyone. Leave me!"

A moment later, he heard the shuffle of retreating feet. Only then did he begin to feel the pain. As if awakening, he looked at the sword, and in the next instant released it.

He stared at his lacerated hands. God, what had he done? This would not bring Aryn back. Nothing would bring her back—excepting a miracle. And he didn't believe in miracles. For that matter, he hardly believed in God.

With his old injuries beginning to ache, his mind crept to the one thing capable of giving him relief. Although this afternoon when he'd driven away from the treatment facility he had thought it all over with, Aryn's death threatened to break him. To undo the six-week battle he had thought won.

Sweat breaking upon his brow, Collier dropped his head back. "Another chance," he said. "One . . . more."

The ceiling overhead stared blankly at him, mocking him for his pleading.

Collier squeezed his eyes closed. Never again would he hold Aryn, make love to her, nor see himself reflected in her laughing eyes. Never again would she tease him out of a mood, curl her naked body against his back, nor awaken him with kisses and caresses.

"I . . . love you, Aryn," he murmured the words she had so longed to hear, but would never hear now.

It did not register at first, the fluttering against Collier's brow, but then it brushed his cheek, neck, and hands. He opened his eyes.

There, swirling down around him like leaves dancing on the wind, were flakes of color: some vibrant, others pale. Thinking it a hallucination brought on by grief, he followed the fall of flakes upward.

Was he going mad? he wondered as he watched the paint peel away to reveal what had been hidden for more than five hundred years. It couldn't be. He stepped forward. "Aryn?"

Barely had he spoken her name when something thrust him forward. But at the moment he should have collided with the mantel, he was lifted off his feet. Seeing the portrait rush toward him, he threw an arm up before his face, but it was not necessary. The portrait fell ahead of him into myriad brilliant colors that a moment later came all around him. Then he was pulled backward.

Thinking he must have lost consciousness, Collier cursed himself for the weakness and attempted to struggle his way back to the surface. But he could find no release from the insistent pull. The colors swirling around him began to lose their brilliance, and a moment later he was enfolded in darkness. Then there was nothing. No movement, just a great still for his tormented mind to plod through.

He would come to soon, he told himself. When he did, the portrait would be as it had been before the aberration. Everything would be as it had been— meaning Aryn would still be dead.

Suddenly, air rushed past him as if he fell from a great height, and the clamor of metal rose to his ears. Then he slammed back to earth.

His body wracked by the fall, he struggled for his first breath. It choked its pervasive odor up his nostrils—musty and old. Then the chilly air began to seep through him, followed by an awareness of something that dug into his shoulders, back, buttocks, and thighs.

He opened his eyes. The ceiling flickered as if with candlelight. This was not his bedroom. Abruptly, he sat up, giving rise to the clatter which had preceded his return to consciousness.

Or *had* he regained consciousness? Looking down his front, he followed the course of intricately linked metal that clothed him from shoulders to knees, and which was responsible for his discomfort. He wore a hauberk—shabby, but, nevertheless, chain mail. And encasing his legs above the cuffs of crude leather boots was . . . hose?

Something hard at Collier's hip drew his regard. The sword and the sheathed knife alongside it were as unfamiliar to him as the medieval garb he wore. No, he could not have come to his senses.

Wondering how much longer it would be before reality returned, he stood, and with him rose the thousands of links that must have lent twenty-five or more pounds to his frame. The hauberk seemed so real, but then, this dream was unlike any he had ever had. Not at all like the indistinct images he was accustomed to.

Collier clenched his hands. Pained, he raised them and stared at the injuries he had inflicted on himself when he had grabbed the sword. But no more than he deserved. Aryn lay cold in the ground and all he did was bleed.

He looked down the torch-lit corridor. Ahead was a door, and another beyond that. Although he knew he must soon awaken, curiosity drew him forward. He passed the first door, but when he reached the second, he pushed it inward.

The room was lit by what appeared to be firelight in the night outside. Dancing and jumping over the walls, it revealed to him the figure that lay facedown across the bed—a woman, her shadowed curves familiar to him even through the garment she wore.

Aryn.

Collier allowed himself to be deceived only a moment, but by then he was halfway across the room. This was nothing more than an illusion, he told himself. His mind had placed Aryn in this dream with him. Still, if he could have her only in his dreams . . .

He lowered himself beside the bed. The dark head resting on the mattress edge was crowned with hair of a length that far exceeded Aryn's. But it was her.

Aching to touch her—to look upon her—Collier lifted a hand to brush the hair from her face. He was allowed no nearer.

She lunged up from the mattress. "Traitor!" she screamed, and swept her arm toward him.

Collier saw the light streak across the blade she held and jerked back, but it was not enough. The dagger grazed his lower jaw, then continued downward where it was stopped short by the chain mail.

"Murderer!" she cried.

Though the truth of her accusation struck him to the core, this time when she carried the blade toward him, Collier was prepared. He caught her arm, dragged her to her knees, and forced her back. She fell beneath him onto the yielding mattress.

The feel of her was so incredibly real Collier forgot she was merely the workings of his grieving mind. Forgot she was dead.

"Nay!" she shouted. "Severn!"

Nay? Severn? Collier glimpsed fear on her face as she thrashed side to side and strained her dagger-wielding arm where he pinned it above her head. Collier called to her, "Aryn, it's me—Collier."

At first, she seemed not to hear, determined as she was to escape, then she stilled. Her eyes wide amid the hair flung across her face, she stared up at him. Then she resumed her struggles. "Severn!" she screamed louder.

Collier grasped her chin and pulled it around. Even in the dim light he saw the hate shining from her eyes. "Aryn," he said, "stop this. I only want to—"

The door slammed against the wall, bringing a rush of light into the room.

Collier swung his head around and settled his gaze on the large man barreling toward him, then the half-dozen others coming behind. The instinct for survival rushing adrenaline through his veins, he seized the dagger from Aryn, lunged back onto his knees, and threw it. Though he had the distance, he hadn't the aim. The dagger fell to the floor.

And still the great man came.

Collier pulled his sword from its scabbard.

"Severn!" Aryn cried, struggling against the straddle of Collier's thighs.

Knowing she might be hurt if he didn't release her,

Collier vaulted down from the bed, and an instant later threw up his sword deflecting the blow of the other man's blade. Then once again. But it was purely defensive on his part, for other than the fencing classes he'd taken at university ten years past, he knew nothing of swordplay. This was real, with no gentlemanly rules to govern it, and carried out with a weapon far heavier than the saber he had once been proficient with.

The man's next thrust would have sliced Collier's head from his neck had Collier not caught it mid-blade. He stared at his opponent through the angle of their met weapons. Though the man was not as tall as Collier, all of him was thick as a bear. He would weigh at least three hundred pounds to Collier's two-hundred-ten.

Suddenly, the man heaved that great weight of his forward.

It was Collier's undoing. He stumbled back and lost the defensive as the others closed around him.

"Do not kill him," Aryn shouted in an accented voice that was not at all American. "I would have him alive."

English, Collier thought as he was wrestled to the ground, but not his English.

Though one of the soldiers quickly relieved him of the dagger on his belt, Collier resisted when another attempted to take his sword from him.

"Give over," the man said with a snarl.

Collier wasn't about to.

A moment later, the man slammed his fist into Collier's face. It gained him the sword, and Collier a mouthful of blood from a nose that felt broken. Then Collier was dealt another blow, this time to the ribs— the same as those injured in his climbing accident a year ago.

The pain! It swept him like fire, but Morrow pride allowed no more than a grunt past his lips.

"Stand back," a deep voice commanded.

Collier was dealt several more blows before the command was repeated.

"I say again, stand back!"

With obvious reluctance, the soldiers complied.

The bear of a man who appeared over Collier stared hard at him, then looked over his shoulder. "You are well, my lady?"

My lady?

Aryn stepped alongside him, her hands on the belt of the robe she had donned. She looked at where Collier lay. "Aye, Sir Severn."

Then this was the one she had called to, Collier realized. Sir Severn, meaning he was a . . . knight?

"The bastard did you no harm?"

"No harm," she assured him.

Though it was difficult to think past his pain, as Collier stared at Aryn—seeing the torchlight turn in the auburn tresses falling over her brow—he thought she had never looked more lovely. Nor more untouchable. Why? The Aryn he had known would have been on her knees beside him long ago to soothe his pain.

"Though methinks had you not come when you did," she added, "the cur would surely have violated me."

Her words jolted Collier, leaving him speechless.

Lower jaw jutting, face darkening with anger, Severn pressed his sword to the juncture between Collier's legs. "You know the penalty for rape, York lover?"

Considering his reception thus far, Collier could well imagine.

"Enough," Aryn commanded.

Grudgingly, Severn withdrew his sword.

"He speaks strange," Aryn said.

His speech *would* seem strange to her, Collier thought. The English she spoke sounded older than his. Middle English?

"No doubt a mercenary brought from abroad to fight Edward's battles for him," Severn said.

York lover. Mercenary. Collier searched both through his mind, but before he could make sense of either, Aryn spoke again.

"He called himself Collier, and me . . . Aryn."

Severn grunted. "Yorkist trickery, my lady."

Though the light was poor, Collier thought he saw uncertainty flicker in Aryn's eyes.

"Aye, trickery," she agreed.

"He should die, my lady."

She shook her head. "First I would know how he came into the keep."

Why did she not seem to know him? Nor her name? Collier wondered. Why had she accused him of attempting to rape her when she knew he would never do such a thing? "Aryn," he said, "I do not mean you any harm. I—"

Severn planted his booted foot hard in Collier's side. "You will not speak unless spoken to," he growled, "and if our lady addresses you, you will answer her 'my lady.' Understand?"

Refusing to double over, Collier gripped his side and lifted his gaze to Aryn.

The torchlight glanced off her watchful eyes, from which no compassion shone.

"Answer me," Severn demanded, "else I'll not wait 'til you have divulged all you know."

"I understand," Collier said.

Severn smiled. "Nay, not yet, but soon you will."

He turned to Aryn. "I will take him to the tower now, Lady Catherine."

Catherine.

Collier jerked as if struck. Catherine, not Aryn. It was the key that flung open the doors to this madness, and which reminded him that being here with Aryn was only imagined. A fantastic dream.

He recalled the paint floating down around him. Looking up and seeing the lady in the portrait revealed. Seeing Aryn. It was grief that had caused Aryn and this place to arise from Catherine Algernon's portrait. Grief that had transported him back to what must be the year 1464—the year Montagu had triumphed over Strivling Castle. As real as Aryn seemed, as real as she had felt in his hands, and as real as he wanted her to be, she was not.

Rough hands gripping Collier beneath the arms reminded him of the injuries done him. He clenched his hands against the ache of his bruised body.

"He will talk this night," Severn said.

"Nay." Aryn—or was it Catherine?—shook her head. "Morning comes soon enough."

"But—"

"You will get naught from him this night. He is too beaten. Let him think on his injuries these few hours ere dawn."

"Aye, it comes soon enough," Severn reluctantly conceded, and nodded to the soldiers. "Bring him."

As Collier was forced past Aryn, he looked one last time into her intensely blue eyes. They were cold, but still they were eyes he had known well. In the next instant, he was struck by the realization that they were the same as those which had gazed out from Catherine Algernon's portrait all these years. Yet never had he noticed a likeness between Aryn and Catherine—

No. This was all part of the game his mind was playing. None of it was real.

"Move," a soldier snarled and thrust Collier forward.

Collier subdued his anger with the reminder that he was restrained, weaponless, and seriously outnumbered.

Out of the room and through the corridor he was led, then down spiraling stairs that opened onto the Great Hall. Though the layout was roughly the same, it was not Strivling's twentieth-century hall which Collier had stepped into less than a year ago. Five hundred years and a siege stood between this and the one he had known.

Considering the confusion of bodies vying for sleeping space, filth among the rare inches of floor, and a cloying stench, it could only mean the castle folk's retreat to the keep was a result of Montagu's forces having broken through the outer wall. Which also meant it was past the middle of May. Thus, if this which his mind had conjured followed history as laid down over five hundred years ago, Strivling had only a few days remaining before it fell. Or less.

Outside, Collier was struck by the cold air that carried the scent of the sea upon it. It chilled him—as if this truly was northern coastal England.

As he was hastened down the stone steps, he searched the bailey. Although the stronghold's inner walls kept out Montagu's forces, the ravages of the siege were everywhere to be seen. Most of the inner buildings were only blackened remains, and those yet standing were not without damage of some sort. Rubbish littered the ground, and without regard to where they caught their few hours of sleep, soldiers curled up amongst it.

Surprised at the vividness of his imagination that had conjured all this from his limited knowledge of Catherine Algernon's resistance, Collier swept his gaze to the wall-walk where soldiers moved carefully between the battlements, then to the tower where he was to be imprisoned. He knew it, for it was not so long ago he had been given a tour of this place that had once held Montagu's men. Amazing how real it all seemed.

"Guard," Severn called as he stepped into the tower ahead of Collier.

The guard appeared. "Escaped capture this morn like the other, eh?" the man said, eyeing Collier.

The other? Collier wondered.

Severn nodded. "'Twas in Lady Catherine's chamber we captured him. He was trying to violate her."

The guard's face darkened. "Ye probably cannot wait to question him, then. I'll ready the room for you."

"Nay," Severn clipped. "'Twill wait until morn."

"Best done now, Sir Severn."

Severn's hands closed into white-knuckled fists. "Lady Catherine says otherwise."

The guard shrugged. "I should put him with the others?"

"Aye." Severn turned to Collier. "First light," he said, then strode from the tower.

"Remove his hauberk and boots," the guard ordered.

Reminding himself that none of this was real, Collier stood unmoving while the soldiers dragged the mail and boots off him. Soon he would regain consciousness, he assured himself, then all that would remain of this would be a vague memory.

Nothing left to him but the shirt falling past his knees and the hose beneath, he was ushered into the stinking bowels of the tower, past cells from which no sound issued, and into a large, open room. Collier looked to the metal door set in the floor. It was in the pit below that Montagu's men had been kept. Although Collier had not gone down into it when he'd visited Strivling Castle, he had shined a flashlight on it and seen the crudely set stone walls and the earthen floor fifteen feet below.

The guard heaved the door back.

Although Collier knew he ought to resign himself to the remainder of this dream, when the soldiers dragged him forward he found himself reacting as if it were real. He wrenched an arm free and slammed an elbow into the gut of one of the soldiers. The man yelped, but did not release him. A moment later, Collier was thrust into darkness.

Unfortunately, his mind did nothing to protect him from the imagined pain he felt when he hit the ground—imaginings that were not unlike what he'd experienced when his addiction to painkillers had been at its worst. Every ache he had ever had jarred, he growled out a string of profanity. Damn it, he was tired of this!

He sat up and looked about the dim pit, but all that was revealed to him was darkness against greater darkness, and even that was stolen from him with the slamming of the trapdoor overhead.

"Are there any others left?" someone asked.

"Others?" Collier repeated.

"Who were not captured this morn with the rest of us."

"I saw no others."

"What is your name?"

"Collier."

There followed a long silence, and then the man said, "I am Morrow. Sir Edmund Morrow."

3

Edmund Morrow.

Collier stared into the darkness. It certainly followed that he would meet his ancestor in this dream, but Edmund's presence here also meant that with the new day's rising he would lead the others in an escape that would see history made in the winch room. The room where Catherine Algernon would give her life to defend a castle already fallen.

Realizing it also meant that Griffin Walther, her murderer, was amongst the men in this pit, Collier wondered when his imagination would reveal the man to him.

"Come nearer," Edmund beckoned.

Although Collier wanted to throw off this dream and the pain accompanying it, he moved toward Edmund's voice. A moment later, his foot brushed his ancestor's leg.

"Morrow?" he said.

"Sit beside me."

Lowering himself back against the wall, Collier grimaced as the moisture seeping through the stones wet him through his shirt. Still, the support of the wall was a comfort to his aching body.

"What did you learn?" Edmund asked.

What *had* he learned? Only that this dream borne of grief and a fertile mind he had not known he possessed, had made Catherine Algernon into the image of the woman he had loved and lost. But that was not what Edmund wished to know.

Very well, Collier thought, he would play the dream out to its end. "They are nearing starvation," he said, drawing on his knowledge of history. What he had seen supported it. "The well is near dry, and there is talk of surrender."

Edmund was silent a long moment, then said, "You speak strange, my friend."

Although Collier's dream had provided him with the garb of these medieval times, his English had remained modern. But as Edmund was from these Northumbrian lands which, to go farther north would see one stepping foot in Scotland, Collier decided it would be easiest to explain his speech away as simply a different dialect. "I come from Wessex," he said, naming an area of southern England.

"Cannot say I have ever heard one from Wessex talk as you do," someone farther down the wall said.

"Aye," piped another. "Mayhap you were sent down here to ferret out Montagu's plans."

"Or you were," Edmund countered.

The man grumbled, but said no more on the matter.

"The same is said of each man who is thrown down after the others," Edmund explained. "Before you it was Walther who, like you, escaped early capture. He made it to the winch room ere being apprehended."

So, Griffin Walther was the "other one" the guard had referred to.

"I would have had the drawbridge down had that big bastard not come when he did," a voice opposite said.

It had to be Walther.

"You speak of Severn?" Collier asked.

"Aye, that's the name of Catherine's dog. He and his men beat me when I would not tell him what I knew. Upon my life, he is the first I shall kill when I escape."

"'Twill happen soon enough," Edmund assured him. "Now get some sleep. You shall need it."

Had Edmund already laid his plans for escape? Collier wondered.

"You were questioned, Collier?" Edmund asked.

"I was not." Though he might as well have been for the beating he'd taken. Collier felt his nose and discovered it was not broken as he'd first believed. "Ar—" She was not Aryn, he reminded himself. "Lady Catherine ordered the questioning done in the morning."

"Then it is night?"

"It is."

"Where were you captured?"

"Lady Catherine's room."

"Her bedchamber?" Edmund said, incredulous.

"Yes."

"Then you had planned on using her to gain Montagu his entrance."

That explanation was more believable than the truth. "Yes, but Severn and his men showed up."

"How is it you made it into the keep unopposed?"

What would his ancestor's reaction be if he told him he had dropped out of the sky and exchanged a jogging outfit for hose, tunic, and chain mail? Collier wondered. Undoubtedly, it would not be appreciated. "Though the passages are guarded, the soldiers have grown too weary to keep watch," he said. From what he had seen, it was likely the truth. "I had no difficulty getting past them."

Collier sensed the turning of Edmund's mind.

"We must leave here soon," Edmund said.

"What do you plan?"

"*That* I keep to myself, friend. You understand."

Edmund was as suspicious as the rest of them.

"Let us get some sleep," Collier's ancestor said. "Morning comes soon."

Would it? His beaten body exhausted, Collier closed his eyes and sought the sleep that would surely return him to his own world.

Catherine's dream came again. Menacing. Frightening. Yet this time when she swung her blade toward the one with leering eyes, another appeared. It was into his flesh she sank her sword. Into this one whose face she saw clearly. The one who called himself Collier and her Aryn.

As she stumbled back against the winch, she raised her sword, but Collier lunged forward and wrested it from her. A moment later, she felt the moisture seep through her gown. Knowing what she would see, she looked at the crimson spreading across her bodice. How odd she felt no pain. . . .

"My lady?" a voice sharp with concern swept the last of Catherine's dream from her.

Opening her eyes, Catherine stared into the

rumpled sheet she lay facedown on. She was alive, she assured herself. Though cold and shaking, she breathed. But though the dream was gone the same as the others, what was not gone was the face of the man who suddenly impressed himself upon her memory. The man who had slain her in her dream. The same who had tried to violate her yester eve.

Why had the dream changed? Why was it not the one with leering eyes who had killed her?

"My lady?" the old maid said again. Gently, she shook Catherine's shoulder.

Catherine lifted her head and looked at Tilly whose wizened face was revealed by the bare light of dawn. "I am awake. Is it time?"

"Aye, Sir Severn says to make haste."

Catherine released the dagger she gripped beneath the pillow—leaving it so she would not alarm Tilly. "Tell him to proceed. That I shall join him shortly."

"Would you not have me assist you?"

"'Twill not be necessary." For what use a lady's maid when there was not much of the lady left about her? She would wash her face and hands, dress, and make her way to the tower. "Go now and deliver my message."

Tilly turned, but at the door looked over her shoulder. "How are your dreams, my lady?"

It was the same question the old woman was wont to ask from time to time, as if she knew they were more than just dreams. But she couldn't possibly know, for Catherine had never told anyone of them—other than her father.

Shortly before being sent to live at Strivling, she had come to him with tale of a dream in which she had seen an army come against the king's. Her father had grown very still, and afterward made her promise to never again speak of it or any of her dreams. He had warned her that people would not understand, and might even think her a witch. Thus, she hadn't told anyone else, not even years later when Hildegard, her betrothed's mother, had mentioned the Duke of York's first attempt to steal the throne from King Henry. The year, 1452, had coincided with the dream Catherine had told her father of.

Catherine met Tilly's gaze. "You know I can hardly ever remember my dreams upon awakening."

Tilly stared at her a moment, then stepped into the corridor and closed the door.

Catherine lifted the pillow from the dagger. The blade evidenced the blood she had drawn from the man who had come into her chamber yester eve, the same who had slain her in the dream Tilly had awakened her from. The memories spinning renewed fear through her, she shuddered.

Her dreams were a curse—had always been a curse. Against her will, she recalled the one she'd had two years ago during the first of Edward's sieges upon Strivling. In it, she had foreseen the death of the woman who was to have been her mother-in-law, and on the following day, Hildegard's troubled heart had released her from life.

Remembering the older woman breathlessly gripping her chest, and her headlong flight down the stairs, Catherine swallowed hard. If only Hildegard were here now. . . .

Catherine had been only seven when sent to be raised by her betrothed's mother. At first she had feared the woman who had imposed all manner of rules and propriety on her, but though strict and domineering, Hildegard had not been cruel. She had only been determined that the woman who wed her guileless son grow to be as strong as she, herself, was for her husband. Thus, Catherine's fear had eventually turned to respect and a strong desire to please. And unapproachable Hildegard had grudgingly come to care for this daughter who was not of her womb. But all for naught.

Despair slipping in, moisture gathering in her eyes, Catherine bowed her head.

You must be strong, Catherine, the voice of Hildegard spoke to her as if from the grave. *There is no one else to do it. No one to turn the usurper from these walls.*

Catherine drew a deep breath. Aye, she would be strong—unlike Lambert, her betrothed, who had been weak, and his father who had been weaker. Both dead from the first days of the siege: one consumed by a ball of burning pitch, the other impaled by an arrow.

"I will not fail you," Catherine whispered. Although Strivling's food and water supplies would soon be depleted, talk of surrender was more and more heard from the castle folk, and the barony's lesser castles had yielded to King Edward—including the one held by her father—she would not allow the usurpers to take what did not belong to them. She would defend Strivling with the last of her breath. Just as Hildegard had done. Just as she, herself, did in her dreams.

Another chance. One more. The words echoed through Collier as he looked upon himself where he stood in his bedroom with head bowed. Then the paint began to flutter down around him. . . .

Awakening suddenly, Collier opened his eyes.

However, it was not his bedroom he found himself in. The pit continued to hold him, the stench to assail him, and the cold to creep over his lightly clad body. He had not escaped the dream.

Or was it a dream? He rubbed a hand across his brow, then shoved his fingers through his hair. If he were still on painkillers, he might have blamed this on them, but he had been six weeks without them, and even during the worst days of withdrawal, never had anything like this happened. Pain, intense yearning, and throbbing discomfort had tormented him that first week, not hallucinations. Not dreams so real he could touch them.

Still, it would be utter madness to accept this as reality. Not at all the logical Collier Morrow his father had raised him to be. This was nothing more than his fascination with Catherine Algernon, coupled with his need for another chance with Aryn. Wasn't it?

He dropped his head back against the wall. Imagined or not, what had he to lose by treating it as if it were real?

Suddenly, the door overhead whined open, filtering light into the pit that showed Collier the shadowed figures of those who shared this place with him. There were, perhaps, a dozen men.

A rope ladder was lowered into the pit. "Collier!" a man shouted down. "Come forward."

He pushed off the wall, but before he could stand, a hand landed to his shoulder.

"If you live, friend," Edmund whispered, "I will take you with me when I go."

Collier picked out the sparkle of his ancestor's eyes. "I will live."

Edmund dropped his hand away.

All the aches and pains of Collier's beating having

stiffened him these past hours, he rose and walked to the ladder. Rung after rung he climbed until, nearing the top, a lantern was thrust into the pit. Blinded by its terrible brilliance, he jerked his head away.

"'Tis him," Severn growled. "Bring him up."

Grasping hands dragged Collier out of the pit.

"There," Severn ordered.

Squinting, Collier discerned his destination only a moment before he was forced back against the wall. Then his arms were wrenched upward to meet steel manacles.

They intended to chain him to the wall, he realized, but not if he had any say in it. He had only begun to struggle when Severn's shadow stole the light from his eyes.

Malice was etched in the curl of the big man's upper lip, the hitch of his nostrils, the folds of flesh around his sunken eyes. He pressed his dagger between Collier's legs. "If you prefer, I will do it now."

Collier stilled. What could be more real than this?

When the soldiers had finished fastening the manacles around his wrists, Severn stepped back. "A fool thing to value for a man who will never use it again." He dipped his eyes to that which he had threatened.

Anger tightened Collier's body, but he turned it back with the reminder that if he had truly journeyed backward in time, it was not to die at this man's hands. No, whatever had brought him to the fifteenth century had done it for a purpose. And if none of this proved real, it didn't matter what Severn did to him. Eventually, he would awaken.

The trapdoor dropped closed, its meeting with the metal frame vibrating across the floor and up the wall at Collier's back.

"Leave us," Severn ordered.

The soldiers disappeared into the shadows of the dimly lit corridor of cells.

"Your name?" Severn asked.

His eyes adjusted to the light, Collier met the knight's gaze. "Collier."

"All of it."

As he could not be Collier Morrow in this past of Edmund Morrow's, he searched for another. His middle name, then. "Collier Gilchrist."

"Gilchrist," Severn echoed, a frown folding his brow.

However, before Collier could guess at his confusion, it was defined for him.

"Collier Gilchrist," Catherine said in a voice that would have been Aryn's if not for the English accent. "'Tis not usual for a man to refer to himself by his Christian name."

Collier had forgotten that surnames were more prominently used in these times than one's first name—it being reserved for intimates.

"Especially to those he does not know," she added.

But he knew her—at least, the image of her. Collier settled his gaze on Catherine where she stood just inside the room.

Wearing a nondescript gown, and a veil over her hair, she stared at him out of a face that appeared years younger than Aryn's twenty-six. But though she did not look more than eighteen or nineteen, her eyes were older than Aryn's—eyes which were as unfeeling upon him this day as they had been the night before.

"You are a mercenary," she said, stepping forward.

As he had already been named a Yorkist, then that of mercenary seemed as good a role as any. "I am."

"Though not even a knight."

His poor display of swordsmanship on the night

past had not escaped her attention, for no true knight would have fought as he had. And though he was descended from Edmund Morrow, he could not claim his ancestor's noble blood. Not for many centuries. "I am a soldier."

Catherine halted before him. "How did you gain entry?"

Her nearness calling back too many memories of his days with Aryn, Collier found himself slipping further into the belief that this was, indeed, reality.

"How?" she demanded.

"I came over the wall with the others."

"And for a day and night were amongst us?" She shook her head. "Believable only if there is a traitor in our midst. One who hid you, then let you into the keep." She took a step nearer. "Who aided you?"

"No one."

Her eyes grew colder. "You lie."

What had hardened her so? Collier wondered. This siege? Or did it go beyond that? Was this who Catherine Algernon had always been? Or was this truly Aryn shaped by a different age, a different environment, a different set of circumstances? Maddening. "No one aided me," he maintained.

"You would give your life for a man not even worthy of scraping dung from King Henry's boots?"

"Henry is no longer king," Collier pointed out.

Catherine's eyes flashed with anger. "Albeit your precious Edward sits the throne now, come summer all that will remain of him is rot."

She was so wrong. It was she who would give her life for a king who had years ago lost what little mind he had ever had. "The battle is over with," Collier said.

Her chin rose. "Yours, perhaps, but not mine."

Collier stared at her willful countenance and wondered if she was the second chance with Aryn he had pleaded for. No, he must be going mad—if he was not already.

"He is mine?" Severn asked.

Catherine dropped her gaze to the floor.

"My lady?"

"Not yet. First I would speak with Morrow again. He knows Montagu's weakness. I am certain of it."

"He is as stubborn as this one, my lady. Let us be done with both of them."

"I have spoken," Catherine said.

He stared at her a long moment, then shouted over his shoulder, "Guards."

They came immediately, and in silence removed the manacles from Collier's wrists. Taking a firm hold on him, they pulled him toward the trapdoor.

Collier glanced at Catherine standing near the entrance. Her back to the room, shoulders squared, and arms crossed over her chest, she was as still as one already dead. What went through her mind? he wondered. What thoughts and fears haunted her in these last hours?

"Climb down," Severn said.

Knowing that if he did not comply he would be thrown in, Collier lowered himself back into the pit.

"Morrow!" Severn shouted.

Collier stepped to the ground and turned to the dark figure beside him.

"Be prepared," Edmund spoke low, then reached for the ladder.

As Edmund neared the top, Collier was allowed a glimpse of his ancestor. However, it was too momentary to discern more than Edmund's figure—tall and broad. Then the ladder was pulled up and the trapdoor dropped closed again.

Knowing that very soon Edmund would overpower these men and lead the others out of here, Collier stepped to the wall. However, in the next instant he straightened.

What of Catherine? Had she been present during Edmund's escape and fled only to confront him and the others in the winch room? Or had Collier's presence effected change in this past? If so, then perhaps it was not in the winch room Catherine would die, but in the room above.

How was he to save her—if he was to save her? If this was all real? Collier clenched a fist on his thigh. Only if the past was not yet disrupted by his presence could he do anything to help her. For now, it was in Edmund's hands.

4

"*My lady, make haste!*"

Catherine looked over her shoulder. "Montagu?" she asked, her heart pounding with sudden knowing.

The soldier's gaze slid past her to Severn, then to Morrow who was being led to the manacles. "Aye, my lady. 'Tis thought to be a mine."

Montagu was tunneling. Drawing a steadying breath, Catherine met Severn's gaze. "Proceed with the questioning," she said. "I shall return shortly."

He nodded.

Catherine lifted her skirts and followed the soldier up from the dungeon. Outside, the morning mists swirled around her feet. It was quiet, she thought as she hurried toward the northern tower. So quiet, she could hear the roll of the sea on the rocks below Strivling. Too quiet.

She looked to the men-at-arms who manned the wall-walk. Some looked back at her, bewilderment dragging at their brows as they silently asked the same question she did: Why had the day's siege not begun? Each day that passed, Montagu heralded first light with a barrage of flaming arrows, balls of burning pitch, and siege engines that steadily weakened Strivling's walls. What did his silence mean?

The end is near, Catherine's inner voice warned. Digging her nails into her palms, she shook her head against the images which had visited her on the night past. She would not think on it now.

As she entered the northern tower, she was confronted by half a dozen soldiers who looked upon her with defeat dulling their eyes. They knew.

Though it was not necessary for her to gain a closer look at the bowl of water set on the floor, she knelt beside it and stared at the rippled surface caused by the vibrations not yet felt underfoot.

Montagu was tunneling beneath the wall, and not one of these soldiers needed her confirmation of it. How long ere the king's man brought the tower down?

Catherine squeezed her eyes closed. *What now, Hildegard?* she begged the silence. *What am I to do?*

She sat back on her heels. They could begin a countermine, and perhaps break into Montagu's mine, but the hand-to-hand combat that would follow in the underground gallery would surely see Strivling's men fallen beneath the greater number of Montagu's.

Wanting badly to cry, but knowing Hildegard would not have approved, Catherine stood. "Return to your stations," she said.

As she looked from one man to the next, she saw the glimmer of hope extinguish from their eyes. They were tired of defending a castle they could not possibly hold against the usurping Edward. Nevertheless, their loyalty would stand them by her to the end.

From out of Catherine's depths rose a part of her that cried for these men—a part of her that Hildegard would have scorned as weakness. Her refusal to submit to Montagu could mean their death. As she watched them file out of the tower past her, she determinedly pushed herself aside and once again assumed the demeanor of Hildegard. It was time to question Morrow.

Light rushed into the pit, followed by the ladder.

"Hurry," Edmund shouted.

A moment of surprised silence answered him, followed by the clamor of men staggering up from the walls.

Collier made it to the ladder first and led the way up out of the pit. At the top, he came face-to-face with his ancestor.

"Collier?" Edmund asked, offering him his hand.

Collier was momentarily stunned by this man who hardly resembled the portrait made of him at a later age. But it was more than the ravages of the pit. More than the bruised jaw and cheek. In the portrait, Edmund Morrow's features had been smoother—refined—making him appear far more handsome than he really was. Undoubtedly, the artist had taken great license, especially in overlooking the puckered skin that ran from the underside of Edmund's jaw to the neck of his tunic. Scarred, as if by fire.

Collier accepted Edmund's hand. "Yes," he said, "I am Collier Gilchrist."

Edmund heaved him up into the room, then nodded to those he had overpowered. "Choose your weapon."

Collier looked to where Severn sat crumpled against the far wall, then to the guards who lay unmoving nearby. Thankfully, there was no sign of Catherine, but it only meant that it was in the winch room they would meet again.

He crossed the room and knelt beside Severn. Trying not to think too deeply on what he did, he closed his fingers around the knight's dagger, but as he pulled it from its sheath, a large hand fell to his arm.

Swinging his gaze up, Collier saw that Severn had dropped his head back against the wall. He was far from dead, but of no immediate threat—his chest bloodied and eyes bare slits in his fleshy face.

Edmund had done this, Collier realized, and likely had not thought twice about shedding blood to gain his end. He—

Suddenly, someone leapt forward, pulled Severn's sword from its scabbard, and impaled him on it.

Collier jerked his head around and looked up at the triumphant stance of the one who stood over his shoulder.

"Bastard," the man spat from a cruelly curling mouth.

Griffin Walther. Collier was sure of it. "The man was of no threat," he said, surging to his feet.

Walther landed his foot to Severn's chest. "But not dead." Using the man's body for leverage, he pulled his sword free. "By your own sword, you bastard." He eyed the blood on the blade, then chuckled.

Before Collier could act on the impulse to slam his fist into Walther's face, Edmund intervened.

"We go now!" he shouted.

Collier and Walther turned.

As if sensing the tension between them, Edmund looked from one to the other, warning in his eyes.

Now was not the time for discord, Collier conceded. If Montagu was to be let into Strivling, keeping to the course of history as closely as possible, then they must go now.

His sword before him, Edmund hastened from the room.

The others scrambled up from the pickings of the dead and hurried after the one who had made himself worthy of being called their leader.

"You with us?" Walther asked, his tone challenging.

Collier looked into the eyes of the ruthless man whom fate had chosen to take Catherine Algernon's life. A man who would have no regrets except for the spilling of his own blood. A true mercenary. "I am with Morrow," he said.

Walther's scant eyebrows arched high. "Poor choice," he said, then turned away.

Wondering how he was to keep this man from taking Catherine's life, Collier followed. One after the other, they crept the narrow stairway, but upon reaching the landing above, Edmund tossed all caution aside.

Collier knew it only from the grunts and thuds that drifted down the stairway. When he came after Walther into the guard's station, two more of Catherine's men lay dead.

"Lower the bar," Edmund ordered, then retrieved a ring of keys from the guard who lay at his feet. "The winch room," he said, seeking Walther's gaze.

Walther held out a hand for the keys. "I will show you."

Edmund shook his head. "Strivling is mine."

The others—Collier included—stilled to see which of the men was the stronger-willed.

"Do we stand here long enough, 'twill not even be an issue, will it?" Edmund reminded Walther of the precious time he wasted.

The mercenary's jaw ground side to side. Then, grudgingly, he acquiesced. "'Tis this way." He stepped around Edmund and walked to the back of the guard's station.

"Gilchrist," Edmund called.

Collier strode forward.

"I want you at my back," Edmund said.

Not if he were told that the one he was entrusting his life to was not the soldier he pretended to be, but a man from the twentieth century who had never killed as Edmund had. Still, there was none with a greater stake in keeping Edmund alive than he, for without him, Collier could not be born—providing this was not the dream he had previously been so certain it was. "I will protect it," he said.

Edmund nodded, then crossed to where Walther awaited the turning of the key that would gain them passageway to the winch room.

A torch in hand, Walther passed through the door, followed by Edmund, Collier, and the others. As they turned off one flight of stairs onto another, ahead cracked a beam of light from beneath a door.

"'Tis it," Walther said, and set the torch in a wall sconce.

Edmund rasped over his shoulder, "Weapons at the ready."

As Collier looked upon his dagger, he wondered whether he was prepared for blood. Even to save his ancestor's life, could he take another's? Was he capable of killing?

A moment later, light flooded onto the stairway.

Four to their twelve. That was all Montagu's men

had to contend with in their quest to take the winch room. Quickly, they cut their way through Catherine's men who barely had time to draw their swords before death carried them to the floor.

Walther was among those who slashed through life as if it were wheat to be harvested, but though Edmund looked prepared to do battle himself, it was over too soon.

The deaths Collier had witnessed raw upon his memory, he stared at the triumphant soldiers. Killing was enough a part of these men's lives that they had long ago turned a blind eye to the horror of what they did—just as Collier had accepted the atrocities of the twentieth century.

As Edmund straightened from one of the fallen soldiers, he shouted, "Secure the door." He looked to Collier. "Your sword, Gilchrist." He tossed the weapon he had unclenched from the dead man's fingers.

Collier caught it.

"Edgar . . . Walther," Edmund called, "man the portcullis winch. Gilchrist, assist me with the drawbridge."

Collier slid the dagger and sword beneath his belt and stepped behind one of two large mechanisms upon which chain was spooled.

"The rest of you," Edmund said, "stand at the ready lest our battle is not yet done."

And it was not done, for suddenly there came the sound of booted feet on the stairs.

Collier took hold of the lever on his side of the winch and followed Edmund's lead in lowering the drawbridge. As the clatter of chains merged with the din of the portcullis chains, the door crashed inward.

Like a swarm of angry bees, Strivling's men-at-arms

surged into the room. Montagu's men eagerly engaged them, but the defenders proved worthier of sword than the first who had had only the chance of God to turn back the besiegers. And God must have been sleeping.

"Walther!" Edmund shouted.

Collier looked up and saw that the mercenary and the other man had abandoned the portcullis to engage in the battle.

"Hurry, man," Edmund urged Collier.

When the drawbridge finally met the ground, Collier and Edmund started toward the portcullis winch, but then three of Strivling's soldiers broke through the line of Montagu's men.

Edmund drew his sword and leapt forward.

Though Collier followed suit, once again his use of the sword was strictly defensive. Fifteenth century or not, he was no killer.

Although his opponent was a man smaller than he, the soldier was of a speed that had Collier's breath jerking from him as he strove to keep his flesh from the other's blade. Then he heard Edmund's shout of pain.

Collier stole a sideways glance and saw that his ancestor was pressed against the far wall by two of Strivling's soldiers. Blood was slowly spreading down the shoulder of his tunic.

"Hell!" Collier growled. What he did next likely went against knightly training, but then, he was no knight. He slammed his fist into his opponent's face.

The man's eyes wide with disbelief, he stumbled back and dropped to the floor.

Wondering why he had not thought to use his fists sooner, Collier ran to where Edmund appeared to be losing his battle—a battle which Collier's presence

had likely effected change in, for history as he knew it
had brought Edmund out of this without mishap.
As he approached, one of the soldiers upon Edmund
swung around.

Collier allowed only one crossing of their swords
before landing his fist.

The soldier stumbled back against the wall.

"Finish him," Edmund growled.

Collier looked to his sword. No. Still, there was a
way to ensure the man did not soon rise. Collier dealt
him another blow.

The remaining soldier swung toward Edmund's
belly, gaining himself a few links of mail. And likely
he would have gained more had he not glanced at
where Collier advanced on him.

Edmund embraced the opportunity, and a moment
later felled his opponent. A hand to his injured shoulder, he looked at Collier. "I cannot say I approve of
your fighting technique, but I thank you, friend."

Collier looked past him to the battle being waged
against those who sought to take back the winch
room. Up off the stairs they continued to come,
though almost to the man they were cut down the
moment they set foot inside the room.

What of Catherine? Collier wondered. When
would she make her entrance into this nightmare?

"The portcullis," Edmund said.

However, there was yet another man determined
they would not raise it. The soldier put his sword
through Montagu's man and charged Edmund.

Collier met Walther's calculating gaze. Thinking it
would have been so easy for the mercenary to have
stopped this one who sought Edmund's blood, and
understanding why he had not, he stepped into the
advancing soldier's path.

*   *   *

It would not budge. Warning ringing through her, Catherine tried again, but still the door held—as if barred. "Guard!" she called.

No answer.

She swung her gaze to the gatehouse. And knew. "The winch room," she cried. "They have escaped."

A half-dozen soldiers drew their swords and ran toward the castle's last defense, but before more could join them, Montagu's siege began afresh.

The first of the arrows found its mark among the battlements. With a cry, the stricken soldier toppled from the wall-walk. Then a ball of burning pitch fell to the roof of the smithy.

Her world crumbling all around her, Catherine stood rooted to the spot—fully aware that the next missile might find her. It didn't matter. All that mattered was the winch room, but though she was drawn to it, she was also repulsed. There lay her death. She knew it as surely as she breathed.

The air feeling suddenly heavy upon her lungs, she looked heavenward. Where there had not been clouds a short time ago, they now blew in with the urgency of a storm upon the sea.

Catherine took a step toward the gatehouse, but that was all. In the next moment she dropped to her knees. Turning her face to the dark, lowering sky, she pleaded, "Father, deliver us."

The clouds continued to roll in, each trying to find a fit over Strivling Castle. Then a drop of rain fell to Catherine's cheek, and like a tear, coursed a slow path downward. Her answer.

She dropped her chin to her chest. "What am I to do?" she whispered.

As always, Hildegard was with her. *Be strong, Catherine. There is no one else.*

Holding the words to her, hardening herself with the strength of the woman who spoke them, Catherine lifted her head and looked to the gatehouse. She would defend it with the last of her breath. She flung the raindrop away with the back of her hand, stood, and ran forward.

The stairs of the gatehouse were littered with the bodies of the slain, of which only two belonged to Montagu's men. All of the others were of Strivling. Murdered.

Anger trembling through her, Catherine looked up at the doorway of the winch room. It stood empty but for the soldier fallen across the threshold.

They were up there, she knew, but what did their silence mean when it should be filled with the clatter of chains? Did they wait for her?

With her last breath, she reminded herself as fear crept over her anger.

She knelt beside a soldier whom she would not allow herself to put a name to, turned his fingers back from his sword, and closed her own around it. As she gained her feet, her gaze fell to the man's sightless eyes. Eyes that minutes ago had been lit with life.

"So sorry," she whispered. "If only—"

There was no time for regrets. Reminding herself of the duty she owed Strivling—and Hildegard—Catherine slid her gaze from the sharply honed point of the sword to the blue-black hilt. "God help me," she said, then began picking her way over the strewn bodies.

5

Blood was everywhere. Although the larger portion belonged to Catherine's men, the blood of Montagu's soldiers pooled with those they had fought. Which left only five.

Edmund, Walther, Collier, and two of the others who had come out of the pit with them, looked at one another.

For Collier, it was a grim moment of silence, evoking images of the man he had turned from Edmund's path only to send him back into Walther's. It was then the mercenary had slain the soldier. Savagely.

Collier clenched his hands. God, what he had seen this day.

Walther's triumphant laughter broke the silence, and a moment later the two remaining soldiers joined him.

Edmund smiled, but that was all. He knew the only victory worth celebrating was complete victory, and it had yet to be attained.

It would be his, though, Collier knew, and the

barony of Highchester his reward. All that was left to do was raise the portcullis. But what of Catherine? She had not come, as legend had said she would. Thus, if all this was truly happening—and Lord, it seemed abominably real—then his presence must have affected the events that had led up to her defense of the winch room.

"Montagu awaits," Edmund said as he positioned himself at one end of the portcullis winch.

Collier stepped forward to assist him, but it was Griffin Walther who reached the winch first.

"Ready," the mercenary said. If he could not outdo Edmund—or see him dead—then all that was left to him was to further his reward.

And he could have it for all Collier cared. He wanted out of this dream . . . this time warp . . . whatever it was. Somehow he would deal with Aryn's death, but not this way.

As the great chains were drawn up, above the din a woman's voice screamed at what they did.

Collier jerked his head around in time to witness Catherine's entrance into the winch room. It was just as he had hundreds of times imagined it—though without the face of Aryn upon this medieval woman.

Wielding a sword, she stepped over the one who lay in the doorway. "Traitors!" she shouted, then joined her hands on the sword hilt and lunged forward.

Forgetting this time and place, and seeing only Aryn, Collier leapt after her. As if in slow motion, he saw the two soldiers coming behind her. And before her, Walther. The mercenary released the winch lever, stepped back, and drew his sword.

Collier hardly heard the slamming of the portcullis as it fell. All he could think of was Aryn. He had to reach her first. Had to stop Walther.

"Aryn!" he shouted, but she didn't seem to hear.

His heart pounding, Collier watched as Walther raised his sword against Aryn's. A moment later, their blades met. Though the impact forced Aryn back, she quickly recovered, but only to have the next blow propel her against the winch.

Walther was toying with her. He had proven himself too well-versed in swordplay to allow Aryn more than the one blow—if that. But that was good, for it gave Collier the time he needed to reach her. And he must reach her.

Knowing all she did was for naught, Catherine lifted the unwieldy sword as the one with leering eyes stepped nearer. It was the terrible dream all over again, though this time it was real. It had given her enemies faces to hold their murderous eyes, mouths to breathe the breath that stirred the hairs along her arms, and bodies to reek their taste upon her tongue. Very soon she would be dead.

With the leering one's sword reaching for her, Catherine jumped to the side and swung her blade down—and would have had the mercenary's flesh had another not appeared. Gilchrist. Still, she was not to be denied her small victory.

With Gilchrist's shout of pain straining her ears, she bent back against the winch and raised her sword once more. However, true to her dream, he lunged forward, drove his body hard against hers, and trapped the sword between them.

"Give over," he said between clenched teeth.

Futile though it would prove, Catherine held to the hilt with all the strength she had left. It was not enough. A moment later, Gilchrist's hand supplanted hers.

Although Catherine knew it ought to be fear racing

through her, relief filled her instead. She had done all she could.

"Aryn," he called her that name again.

Looking into his intense gray eyes, she could have sworn concern shone out of them. Was it possible he regretted what he was about to do? Suddenly, she felt moisture through her bodice. Knowing what she would see, she looked down her front. Blood. How odd she felt no pain.

Crumpling into darkness, Catherine sighed as the comforting arms of death enfolded her. It was done.

She thought it her blood, Collier realized as he caught Aryn against his chest, but it was not hers. The injury she had dealt him had bled out upon her gown. She must have believed herself dead. But considering she had died once before in this room, she had good reason to think it.

That last thought jolted Collier back to reality. This woman was not Aryn. Aryn was dead, and though Catherine Algernon ought to be, he had come between her and death. Or so it seemed.

The doubts beginning to rush through him again, he thrust them aside and dropped the sword he had wrested from Catherine. Then, lifting her slack body, he turned from the winch.

Walther stepped into his path. "She was mine!"

Bloodthirsty bastard. "Once," Collier said, "but no more."

The mercenary's nostrils flared. "You have wronged me, Gilchrist."

Collier stared at him. "Then we will certainly meet again, won't we?"

"I pray for the day."

"Enough!" Edmund erupted. "'Tis Montagu you keep waiting with your bickering."

Fury smoldering in his eyes, Walther grabbed the winch handle.

Collier resumed his stride. Where he was going, he didn't give any thought to. All he wanted was to be away from this place that smelled of a slaughterhouse.

The drawing up of chains loud behind him, he stepped over the one on the threshold. Though to negotiate the bodies on the stairs was no easy feat carrying Catherine, he managed it without mishap, and at the bottom paused. Before him was the open doorway leading out onto the bailey. It stood empty but for the drizzling rain.

Collier glanced at Catherine—or was it Aryn? Her weary face gentled, her lashes heavy upon the dark circles beneath her eyes, her vulnerable mouth a mouth he had kissed hundreds of times, he felt a surge of protectiveness.

God, he prayed to the one he was forever questioning the existence of, *if this is real, let me find Aryn beneath the anger and hatred of this woman.*

In the bailey beyond, the triumphant shouts of those coming beneath the portcullis was met by the din of others determined to defend Strivling to the death. For Catherine.

But perhaps there was a way to gain their surrender, Collier thought. If Strivling's people were shown Catherine had been taken, their reason for defending the castle might be lost. Of course, if all this proved real, he would be tampering with time. What he did might effect changes in this world that would impact upon the world to come—but then, hadn't he already done so in returning Catherine's life to her?

Deciding there were enough deaths this day, and all the days before, for Strivling to make its mark on the history of the Wars of the Roses, he stepped into the rain.

With the tormented shouts and cries of Strivling's men resounding wall-to-wall, heads began to turn and faces to fall. Montagu's men also paused to heed Collier and the woman he carried. Then they resumed their advance on those who had suddenly lost their taste for battle.

As Collier watched, one after another of Strivling's soldiers lowered their swords.

"You are like no mercenary I have ever known," Edmund said as he came alongside Collier.

Collier looked into his ancestor's face. "I shall take that as a compliment."

Arching an eyebrow, Edmund opened his mouth to reply, but in the next instant something caught his regard. "My reward," he murmured, then strode toward the gateway through which a heavily armored knight rode before a mass of others.

Lord Montagu, Collier guessed. The man's shining armor and the fine stallion beneath him belonged to no ordinary knight.

A moment later, there came another who sought his audience. Walther. He threw Collier a narrow-eyed look, then hastened to where Montagu had halted his mount to receive Edmund.

Collier gazed after Walther's back. If he stayed in this time and place, eventually he and the mercenary would clash. After all, Collier had stolen Catherine's life from the other man, and though Walther couldn't know it, he certainly felt its loss.

Montagu conversed a few minutes with Edmund, then urged his mount forward. "You are Gilchrist?" he asked.

"I am," Collier said.

Montagu's eyebrows snapped together. "Mercenary you may be, but you will afford me my title."

Collier was not accustomed to bowing to anyone. Even when his father had been a dominant force in his life, the two of them had clashed repeatedly over Winton Morrow's staunch belief that, regardless of whether he was right or wrong, he was owed respect and unquestioned agreement. Not that he had earned it, but that it was his due—bought through the opportunities he had given Collier.

"Yes, my lord," Collier grudgingly allowed Montagu his form of address.

The nobleman jutted his chin toward Catherine. "Whence does this blood flow?"

Collier glanced at her tainted bodice. "It is my own," he said, then added, "my lord."

"Drawn by Lady Catherine herself," Griffin Walther said with satisfaction.

Knowing the mercenary meant to shame him for having been wounded by a woman, Collier looked sharply at the man who stood near Montagu. What would Walther say to be told that before this new past had been cut out of the old it had been *he* who had felt the edge of Catherine's blade? He could not say it, though.

But Edmund could. "Ah, but had Gilchrist not interceded, 'twould surely have been your arm she would have cut, Sir Griffin."

Fury swept the man's face. "And I would have slain her!"

None but Collier—except, perhaps, Walther—knew how true were the words he spoke.

"Enough," Montagu snapped. He sidled his mount alongside Collier and looked down at Catherine. "She will not thank you for saving her life, Gilchrist."

No, he didn't imagine she would. Had she any

regard for her own life, she would not have continued this senseless battle. And most certainly she would not have ventured into the winch room to confront soldiers sure to strike her down.

"She would be better off dead," Montagu muttered.

Meaning what? That her punishment for defying King Edward would be worse than death? Collier tightened his hold on Catherine.

. . . *better off dead*. The words slipped into Catherine's awakening consciousness, then slipped away as an awareness of the cold and wet seeped through her. Were there not fires for the eternally damned? Did it rain in hell? Shivering, she huddled deeper against the warmth at her side. It felt as if she were being held. So comforting.

"Ah, she awakens," someone said, his voice familiar from years past. Terribly familiar.

Nay, it could not be. She was dead. Wasn't she? Fear unfolding, Catherine opened her eyes and focused on the face above her. But it did not belong to the one who had spoken. Rather, it was Gilchrist who looked back at her. The man who had taken her life. Or had he?

Not understanding, but knowing she had to get away, she thrust her hands against his chest. "Unhand me!" she cried.

He lowered her to the ground. "It's all right," he said, as if to soothe her.

She stumbled back. Nay, it was not all right. Nothing was right. She was supposed to be dead—unless this was, indeed, hell.

Clenching her jaws to prevent her teeth from chattering, she looked down her bodice and saw the faint stain which the rain had all but washed away. She passed her hand across the front of her gown. There was no rent in the material to attest to the sword she thought to have been put through her, and no pain as must surely be felt.

She looked back at Gilchrist and saw the injured arm he held against his side. His blood upon her, then? It had to be. Blood which she had drawn.

But if she were alive, then it meant she had only lost consciousness. Fainted. But why? The mere sight of blood? The thought of death? Knowing Hildegard would have held such weakness in contempt, she berated herself. No greater shame could there be.

"Hello, Lady Catherine," the voice which had first awakened her spoke again.

Her heart leaping, she turned.

John Neville, or better known as Lord Montagu, looked down at her from his war horse, the visor of his helmet pushed back to reveal his cutting smile. Here was the man who had two years past stormed Strivling's walls in the first of the sieges meant to assert Edward's wrongful right over England. Strivling's defiance had lasted three days, though only because Hildegard's heart had failed. Against Catherine's protests, the baron and his son had surrendered. Then Montagu had come inside the castle walls, just as he had done again.

Nay, she was not dead, Catherine thought, but that did not mean she was delivered from hell.

Montagu nudged his mount nearer. "Do you remember me, Lady Catherine?"

She did, as if only yesterday. She had been barely sixteen, and he an arrogant warrior bent on humbling those he conquered. She remembered the satisfaction in his eyes when he had looked upon Hildegard's shrouded body, the way he had treated Lord Somerton and her betrothed, and the hand he had laid to her cheek. She had bitten him, and only Lord Somerton's swift intervention had saved her from his wrath. "How could I forget you?" she asked, raising her chin.

A corner of Montagu's smile jerked. "Indeed, though you were still something of a child." He swept his gaze over her. "But no longer."

Catherine felt as if she'd been touched by his vile, Yorkist hands. It was a struggle to hold her arms at her sides when what she wanted was to cover herself. "Nay, a child no longer," she forced past the constriction in her throat. How she hated this man and every one of those who followed him and his king.

"You should not be so free with your emotions," Montagu said. "No good ever comes of allowing the enemy to know one's true feelings. And we *are* enemies, are we not?"

Rain streaming down her face, she stared at him.

He nodded. "You see your people?" He swept a hand before him.

With foreboding, she looked behind. Though her gaze fell first to Gilchrist, she quickly looked beyond to where Strivling's soldiers were surrounded by Montagu's men. The two dozen men-at-arms and remaining knights stared at her with defeated eyes. Severn was not among them, but then Catherine had known he would not be. Had he lived, the traitors would never have made it to the winch room.

"And there." Montagu indicated those who had been ushered out of the keep onto the steps. The villagers who had retreated to the castle ahead of Montagu's advance on Strivling stood forlorn alongside the household servants.

Her people. Beaten.

"They have surrendered," Montagu said. "What of you, Lady Catherine?"

She met his gaze. "You know I cannot."

Though he had surely known that would be her answer, he shook his head as if deeply disappointed. "What am I to do with you, hmm?"

"No doubt what best pleases you."

His eyes narrowed. "No doubt." Without warning, he reached down and cupped her chin in his palm.

Catherine jerked out of his grasp. "Do not touch me!"

Anger squared Montagu's soft chin and turned his hands into fists. He was tempted to strike her, but something—likely his audience—prevented him from doing so. "You test me sorely, Lady Catherine," he growled.

"Be thankful I did not bite you."

His jaw ground side to side. "You are a woman. Thus, I must needs make allowances for you. But I warn you, do you ever again defy me, not even God will be able to save you."

Did God even enter into this? If so, where was He? "As He saved me this day?" Catherine dared again.

Montagu's nostrils flared. "Though I give you back the life you forfeited in refusing King Edward your fealty, I shall take it do you not soon learn your place."

"Never will I—"

"You forget something. 'Tis not only your life that belongs to me, foolish woman, but your people's. Have a care for them if not yourself."

As much as it sickened Catherine, she had no choice but to yield.

"Do you understand?" Montagu asked.

She nodded.

"Speak it!"

"I understand."

Still he was not satisfied. "You will show me the respect due my station."

For Strivling's people she would do it. "You have bought it, Lord Montagu."

Although he was obviously displeased with what she yielded, he did not press it further. "Remember this day, Lady Catherine." He guided his mount around.

That was all? As dear as her sacrifice in having submitted to the king's man, surely her punishment was to be greater than this. She choked down her hate. "Lord Montagu," she called.

He stilled, as did all the others. "Lady Catherine?" he said, keeping his back to her.

Another indignity. "What is to be my place at Strivling?"

He looked over his shoulder. "Patience. You will know soon enough, and I promise 'twill be more than fitting." He dismounted and started up the steps of the keep.

Foreboding burrowing deeper, Catherine stared after him.

"We feared you were lost to us, my lady," Tilly said, suddenly appearing at her side.

"As I did myself," Catherine murmured. In the next instant, something drew her gaze past the old woman. There stood the one with leering eyes who, in those first dreams, had murdered her, and a short while ago had appeared to have every intention of doing so true to the dream. But then Gilchrist had come between them. . . .

"Come," Tilly urged, "you are needed in the hall."

"The hall?"

"Still you are the lady of Strivling."

Catherine shook her head. "No longer. Strivling belongs to Edward now." Although his policy of conciliation had seen these lands returned to the Somertons following the first siege, with the old man and his son dead, her place was no longer here. And even had she and Lambert spoken vows, and a son been born of their union, she did not believe Edward would be so lenient this time. Instead, one of his supporters would be awarded Strivling, and nevermore would the usurping Yorkist trouble himself over it.

"You are needed, my lady," Tilly urged. "The castle folk will draw strength from your direction."

When Montagu had come the first time he had allowed his men to overrun the hall and harass the women. For certain, it would be worse this time. Although the thought of serving him and his men settled like a stone in her belly, Catherine nodded. "I shall do it."

Tilly squeezed Catherine's hand. "First I will tend to your needs."

Until that moment, Catherine had not considered her appearance. She slid her gaze from her stained bodice to her soiled skirts. Well she could imagine what the rest of her looked like—face besmirched and wet hair straggling past her shoulders as if she were a trollop rather than a lady.

"Come." Tilly turned toward the keep.

Although Catherine knew she ought to ignore the sensation she had felt throughout her exchange with Montagu, she glanced behind her.

With the others dispersing around him, Gilchrist remained unmoving, his eyes searching her for something.

What did he want with her? Revenge for what she had done to him in the winch room? Nay, it went beyond that. It went back to the night he had come into her chamber. Fearing him, Catherine turned on her heel and hurried after Tilly.

To look upon Catherine in her defeat had been far more difficult for Collier than he had expected. Try as he did to separate her from Aryn, he could not. He clasped a hand over his bloodied arm and watched her ascend the steps.

"We must needs talk," Edmund said, coming alongside him. "But first, Montagu."

His reward. "Of course," Collier said. He clenched his hand tighter on his wound.

Edmund looked to it. "'Twas not meant for you," he murmured, but in the next instant shrugged. "Come, we will find a fine needle to stitch us both." He started across the bailey.

Following, Collier wondered at the state of medical knowledge in the middle ages. As his wound was deep, it would, indeed, require stitches. However, the thought of an untrained person pushing a primitive needle through his skin did not appeal to him. Setting his teeth against thoughts of what lay ahead, Collier entered the keep.

6

She ought not to be alive, Catherine thought for the tenth time. And once again, she reflected on the events which should have led to her death.

It was the last dream which had come to pass. The one in which she had cut Gilchrist and he had wrested the sword from her. All had been exactly as she had foreseen it. Except her death. But then, in the dream with Gilchrist she had felt no pain as she had when the one with leering eyes—Walther—had put the sword through her. Too, she had only just noticed the blood upon her when Tilly had awakened her this morn. Had it been the mercenary's blood all along?

She looked beyond the throng of soldiers to the high table which the arrogant Montagu had taken for himself. Opposite the king's man sat Gilchrist—a man of lowly birth among the noble, and yet looking as if he belonged. But he didn't belong, something told her. Regardless of his station, he was very much out of place. Why?

A strange feeling swept Catherine—that this man who had stepped between her and Walther was going to change her life. But then, had he not already?

Abruptly, she halted her churning thoughts. Change her life? Nay. No man, and most especially this mercenary, would ever have such influence over her. And that included Montagu.

Collier felt watched. His pain growing more insistent with each passing moment, he gripped his tankard tighter and looked around.

As intoxicated by victory as they were by drink, Montagu's men straddled benches, sang raucous songs, swilled ale from slopping tankards, and sent servants scurrying to do their bidding. Catherine moved among them.

Obvious in her attempt to keep distance between herself and Montagu, she directed the castle folk from across the hall and ventured near only when Montagu's men attempted to pay the serving women undue attention. Surprisingly, her sharp words and scolding stares were heeded. Conquered as she was, she still commanded respect.

Collier pressed his injured arm hard against his side. As the knights were tended to before the soldiers, he had yet to be seen by either of Montagu's physicians.

Bloody fifteenth century, he silently cursed. In his twentieth-century world there had always been something to alleviate suffering. Such as painkillers . . .

"I like you, Gilchrist," Montagu spoke above the din.

Collier looked across the table to where the man reclined in an ornately carved chair. "I am honored, my lord," he said, though he found little more liking for this man than he did for Walther.

"Your manner of speech does puzzle me, though. Wessex, you said?"

Collier inclined his head.

"Hmm," the nobleman murmured, but before he could comment on it further, a serving wench appeared to refill his tankard.

Battling the weakness of his injury, Collier ground his jaws together.

"For you, sire?" the girl asked, wrongly assuming he was also of the privileged class. But then, he was the only soldier invited to sit at table with Montagu. All others were knights.

He nodded. Though his first taste of the wickedly bitter brew had tempted him to spit it from his mouth—it was unlike any ale he had ever tasted—his need to wet his parched throat had made him swallow down the entire contents of his tankard, and still he was thirsty.

"Tell me, Morrow," Montagu said, turning his attention to Edmund, "what be your reward for opening Strivling?"

Collier wasn't sure if it was relief that Montagu had abandoned the subject of his speech which swept him, or the alcohol he had consumed on an empty stomach. Both, he decided as his pain began to ease. Although nowhere near as effective as painkillers, the strong brew offered relief that had him carrying the tankard to his lips once more.

"As you surely know, my lord," Edmund began, "I am a landless knight of noblest blood, but the third of four sons. Thus, it was to seek my fortune that I turned mercenary. Though I have amassed a goodly sum fighting the battles of others these past five years,

I wish more than coin to see me to the end of my years."

Montagu's eyes reflected understanding. After all, he also had a reward coming to him, Collier knew. Having crushed the Lancastrians in the decisive battle at Hexham a week earlier, the king would very soon name him the Earl of Northumberland, and though it was not yet done, Montagu must know it would be.

"To the man who lowered the defenses, you promised Strivling, my lord," Edmund continued.

Montagu looked around the miserably shabby hall. "You wish charge of this castle?"

"Charge?" Edmund repeated. "Nay."

Montagu frowned. "Then what is it you seek?"

Walther's restless shifting drew Collier's gaze to where the mercenary knight sat farther down the table. The enmity in his eyes said he knew what Edmund was asking for—likely the same he, himself, would have asked for had he been the one responsible for opening Strivling.

"If it pleases you, Lord Montagu," Edmund said, "I would have this Northumbrian barony for myself."

Montagu raised his eyebrows. "You are asking to be made Baron of Highchester?"

"Aye, my lord."

Montagu leaned back in his chair. "'Tis a grand price you put on opening Strivling. From mercenary to baron . . ." He shook his head.

"The blood I have given to this siege and at the battle of Hexham is worthy of a barony."

"And you say you have the coin to set it right?"

"I do, my lord."

"As you know, 'tis King Edward who must bestow the title upon you. I can but recommend you to him."

"That is all I ask."

Montagu pondered this, then smiled. "'Tis done."

Although Edmund must have been elated, he controlled his emotions. "I thank you, my lord."

Collier wondered if he was the only one who felt the coursing of Walther's anger.

"However," Montagu continued, "ere I can return to London to address the king on this matter, I must first secure the lands farther north. Would you join me, Sir Edmund?"

In Edmund's hesitation, Collier sensed his ancestor would have preferred otherwise. "If it so pleases you, my lord, but what of Strivling? Someone must begin putting it back to order."

"Either of these men would serve you well." Montagu indicated Walther and Collier.

Edmund considered Walther briefly before turning his gaze on Collier. "Would you be agreeable, Gilchrist?"

Walther's bench scraped loudly as he thrust back. A moment later, he stalked across the hall. That he, a knight, had been passed over for a mere soldier was an offense he would not soon forget.

"Methinks Sir Griffin does not approve of your choice," Montagu said.

An understatement, Collier thought. Had it been Walther in the alternate past who had remained behind at Strivling? Was this how the mercenary knight had earned himself charge of the lesser castle held by Catherine's family? And if he, Collier, were to accept Edmund, what impact would it have on the past? What of Catherine?

He looked to where she stood across the hall. With her long hair confined beneath a veil, she was the very image of Aryn.

"Gilchrist?" Impatience edged Montagu's voice.

Collier looked back at him. "I am a mercenary, my lord. A soldier."

Montagu smiled. "And therein lies your reward for your part in opening Strivling. Many are the men I have knighted in battle. Do you accept?"

Collier stared at him. Knighted? He could hardly swing a sword other than to deflect the stroke of another's, he knew far more of money, investments, and real estate than of arms and fighting, and thought nothing of the ruthless business dealings he engaged in every day, but found the taking of another's life reprehensible. Collier Morrow a medieval knight? Ludicrous, and yet . . . if, beneath Catherine's hard exterior, he might find Aryn, then having knighthood conferred upon him would bring him that much closer to her world.

"I accept," he said.

Montagu looked to Edmund. "Gilchrist will stay in your stead."

Edmund nodded. "I thank you, my lord."

Next, Montagu turned to the topic of their northward journey.

Collier glanced over his shoulder to the blazing fire which had yet to knock the chill from the hall. Though he'd never thought much about central heating, he now realized how much of a luxury it was. But at least the hall wasn't as drafty as he had read they were, likely due to the multitude of tapestries hung about the walls.

A short while later, one of the physicians appeared at Collier's side. "I will sew you now," he said, and nodded to a bench against the wall.

Feeling the deepening effects of the ale, Collier set the tankard down and crossed to the bench.

The physician unwound the cloth bound around his

arm. "'Tis gone deep," he said as he probed the tender flesh. "It will need to be seared to prevent infection."

The very thought turned the ale in Collier's belly to acid. What else awaited him in this godforsaken time and place?

The physician straightened. "Once that is done, it can be stitched closed."

"Will it heal?"

The man shrugged. "Possibly . . . possibly not. But soon we shall know."

And if it didn't heal? What, then? Amputation? Again, Collier cursed the backwardness of this time. A year ago, his body had been broken, and yet he had emerged from his accident whole—or nearly so. Were this the twentieth century, he would be quickly stitched, and within the month using his arm again. Now he might lose it completely.

"Show me your hands," the physician said.

Collier turned his palms up, revealing the cuts slashing horizontally across them—insignificant compared to his arm, yet both dealt by Catherine's sword. The same sword he had left in his own time only to come against it in the fifteenth century. Was it still in the winch room?

The physician ran his thumb over the caked wounds. "These will heal," he pronounced, then looked over his shoulder. "Girl, come hither."

The serving wench, who looked as if she had yet to reach puberty, faltered. "B-b-but sire," she stammered, her eyes wide with fear, "I know naught of t-tendin' wounds."

The physician glowered. "Do you argue with me?"

"Ah, nay, sire. 'Tis j-just that—"

"I will assist him, Sara," Catherine said, appearing at the girl's side. "Return to the kitchens."

Eagerly, the wench scurried across the hall.

Catherine clasped her hands at her waist and turned her cool regard on the physician. "What is it you require?"

Untouchable, Collier thought. Catherine Algernon had no intention of allowing anyone past her defenses—

It was the same thing Aryn had accused him of the day she had discovered he was still dependent on painkillers. Ironic that it was he on the other side of the fence now, hoping to get in when the sign clearly read KEEP OUT.

The physician regarded Catherine a long moment, then nodded. "I will need a basin of boiled water, clean linen strips, and the whites of four eggs to dress the wound."

She turned away.

How it must pain her to tend the enemy, especially one she herself had wounded, Collier thought as he watched her cross the hall.

The physician began arranging his bottles and implements on a nearby table. It was a fascinating array, but what captured Collier's regard were the needles the man unwrapped from a piece of linen. They were long and fine, but more, they looked clean.

At least he knew something of sterilizing, Collier thought, though it was still not much consolation.

Shortly, Catherine returned with the items requested and set them out on the table.

The physician thrust a piece of wet linen toward her. "Cleanse the wound," he said.

Her lower jaw set harder.

Would she refuse? Collier wondered. He didn't think so, for in coming to the young girl's aid she had accepted the responsibility for herself.

Catherine eyed the linen, then took it and stepped to Collier's side. "Your arm," she said, her gaze frigid.

He propped it atop his thigh.

Considering her height, it would have been easier for her to kneel. However, as if in doing so she might surrender her dignity, she bent over him. Her touch impersonal, though not harsh, she quickly set about cleansing the wound.

Near enough to touch, Collier thought as he stared at the top of her veiled head, but forbidden. He drew a deep breath. She smelled like Aryn. Nothing distinct—just that soft, womanly smell that had filled him every time he held Aryn. Would he ever hold her again?

As if hearing his unspoken question, Catherine lifted her head, and in that moment of unguardedness, Collier saw questioning in her blue eyes. Then, abruptly, she drew back.

"'Tis clean," she said.

The physician uncorked one of his bottles and wet a cloth with its contents. "Stay near," he said, and looked to Collier. "Lay back."

He was to be administered anesthesia, Collier realized. Although he could certainly use the relief it offered, he had to know what it contained. "What is in it?" he asked.

Annoyance flickered in the man's eyes. "'Twill allow you to sleep through the cauterizing and stitching."

"Yes, but what does it contain?"

Although his tolerance looked to be sorely tested, the physician said, "Mandragora bark, henbane root, opium . . ."

Collier heard no more past the last. Opium. The painkillers he had become addicted to had been a derivative of that drug. What would happen if he allowed this man to administer him a dose in this medieval form? Would his desire for painkillers return greater than it already had?

When he had previously resumed taking the drug without Aryn's knowledge, it had been with the intention of only taking one, but within hours it had become more than that and he had needed another. And another. What of withdrawal? Would he have to go through that hell all over again for just this once? And Aryn . . . ?

He glanced at where Catherine Algernon stood with her arms folded across her chest and gaze trained across the hall. It wouldn't matter to her, but it had meant everything to Aryn Viscott.

Collier shook his head. "I will not require it." Out of the corner of his eye, he saw Catherine start. She was listening, then.

The physician stared at Collier a long moment, then growled, "Your bravery has already been noted, soldier. Naught more is required of you."

"I will bear your ministrations without benefit of your medicines," Collier maintained.

The physician regarded him a long moment. Then, as if deciding Collier deserved the agony he brought on himself, he turned to Catherine. "Bring me a fire iron," he snapped, "and a piece of kindling."

She crossed to the hearth and soon returned with the items.

The physician thrust the kindling into Collier's hand. "Lay down and bite on this."

Knowing he was going to regret not having accepted the anesthesia, Collier clamped the wood between his teeth and stretched out on the bench.

The physician accepted the iron from Catherine, then instructed her, "Hold his shoulders down."

Again, Collier witnessed her internal struggle, but in the end she put her hands to his shoulders and leaned her weight onto him.

The physician lifted the iron. Its tip glowed orange.

Collier looked up at Catherine.

"You are a fool of a man," she whispered.

As he already knew.

What followed words could not possibly describe. The pain was excruciating, and all in the hall sober enough to look beyond their noses knew it. Though Collier splintered his mouth on the piece of wood, and bit it in two, somehow he remained conscious.

7

"You are not of Wessex," Edmund said in a low voice.

Collier looked over his shoulder and met his ancestor's gaze. No, he was not fooled. "I am not," Collier conceded.

Edmund's eyebrows arched. "I would ask where 'tis you *do* come from, but I do not think you would tell me, would you?"

Collier turned from the fire that provided all the warmth there was to be had in the hall, and with the exception of a few torches, all the light now that Montagu's men had bedded down for the night. "If I told you, you would not believe me," he said, his voice hoarse from the shouts he had suppressed when the physician had applied the hot iron and needle.

"Neither are you a mercenary."

Beneath the blanket draped over his shoulders,

Collier shifted his bandaged arm in its crude sling. "Am I not?"

"A man who uses his fists when the fight is more easily won with weapons? Who takes the sword intended for another that he might deliver our king's enemy to safety? Who calls Catherine Algernon a name not her own as if he knows her by it?" He shook his head. "You do not fit, Gilchrist, and yet there is this feeling I know you. I do not understand it."

For a fleeting moment, Collier entertained telling him the truth, but just as quickly abandoned it. "I do not understand it myself," he said.

Edmund was silent a long moment, then asked, "Who are you?"

Feeling beaten and weary beyond his years, Collier looked into the dying flames. "Your ally," he said, there being nothing else to call himself.

Edmund sighed. "That I know. You saved my life, for which I am deeply indebted."

Had he saved Edmund's life? Collier wondered. Who was to say whether or not Edmund would have fended off the events of an altered past?

"We will talk again," Edmund said, and turned and strode back toward the bench he had claimed for the night.

Collier watched him disappear among the shadows. Then he lowered himself into the chair before the fire.

It had been a long day. In fact, he couldn't remember one ever having been longer—and still there were hours left before dawn. With the sun's rising, would it bring the end of a very long and painful dream? he wondered. Or further proof that this was no dream?

He closed his eyes. Though he still doubted, he had

a feeling that if ever he found sleep this night he would awaken to find himself in the fifteenth century.

And Catherine Algernon would still hate him.

Catherine flattened herself against the wall and waited. Although she'd had to strain to hear Morrow's exchange with Gilchrist, she had caught most of it. It disturbed her, but then she was already troubled by this man who had put himself between her and Walther.

Recalling Gilchrist's refusal to accept the physician's offer of relief, Catherine saw again the pain contorting his face and the determination in his eyes that he would not shout out his suffering. Though beneath her hands she had felt his inner raging, he had endured every sear and stitch done him, and when it was over with, had risen from the bench and walked away.

Nay, as Morrow said, Gilchrist did not fit. However, to listen in on the conversations of her enemies was not the reason she had ventured out of her chamber. There was something far more important she must do.

Trying to be patient, Catherine counted off ten minutes, then peered around the tapestry at the man positioned before the hearth. Gauging by the slight rise and fall of Gilchrist's shoulders, he had drifted off to sleep.

She shifted her gaze to the corridor that led to the storeroom. The guard, leaning against the wall with his chin resting forward on his chest, looked to pose no threat, and neither did any of the others. Too much ale did that to a person.

Thinking how harsh Hildegard's punishment

would have been for any of Strivling's soldiers found
in such a state, Catherine stepped from behind the
tapestry. She was careful to avoid those who made
their beds on the floor, but once clear of them, quickened her step.

She was halfway there. Now if only the guard was
no more alert than Gilchrist—

Suddenly, a hand clapped over her mouth and
wrenched her back against a solid chest.

Catherine could not prevent the scream that rose
from her, but the man's hand captured it and kept it
from awakening those in the hall.

"Which passageway?" he rasped near her ear.

Gilchrist.

"Which one?" He held her hard against him with
the one arm.

He knew of the secret passages within the walls of
the keep? Catherine wondered. Or was he only guessing this was the means by which she had made it past
the guard Montagu had posted outside her chamber?
Either way, she had no intention of telling him. She
shook her head.

"God bless it!" he muttered.

It was an expression Catherine had not heard
before, but from his tone, she knew it must be a
curse.

"Listen to me," he whispered. "Unless you wish
Montagu to know of your venture, you will keep
silent. Understood?"

Why *didn't* he raise the alarm? What did he
intend? Could it be any worse than Montagu's wrath?
Worse than exposing the existence of the wall passages to Edward's dog?

Gilchrist lowered his mouth to her ear. "Lady
Catherine?"

His breath upon her sent a disturbing sensation spiraling up her spine. Telling herself it was only fear, she grudgingly nodded.

Slowly, Gilchrist lifted his hand from her mouth, but did not release her. Then, gripping her arm, he turned her around.

Although Catherine could barely pick out his shadowed profile as he looked beyond her, she sensed his searching gaze. Did he know? she wondered. The hall was rich in tapestry, and though the wall hangings served to keep the great room free of drafts, the primary purpose of three of them was to conceal the walled passages.

And it seemed Gilchrist *did* know of one of them. Pulling Catherine after him, he started toward the tapestry to the left of the lord's high table. Now she understood how he had moved undetected through the keep last eve. What she had yet to know was who had told him of the passageway in the first place. Even so, he had chosen wrong. That one led to the lord's solar where Montagu slept. But he knew that, didn't he?

"Nay," she gasped. "'Tis the wrong one."

He halted. "Then show me the one you used."

And if she did not, what then? Would he awaken the hall, or worse, drag her up to where Montagu slept? "'Tis behind the garden tapestry," she yielded. "Right of the hearth."

Collier looked to where he had risen from the chair to intercept her. Though it made sense Catherine would not have passed so near him had she not needed to, as there were more than a dozen tapestries hung around the walls, he had decided on the only passage he knew of. Not that he knew where it led, for when Strivling Castle's twentieth-century owners had shown it to him, he had not thought to inquire into it. At the time it had seemed so trivial. . . .

Retaining his hold on Catherine, Collier started back toward the hearth. Shortly, they stepped behind the tapestry.

"Open it," he said.

She tugged at her arm. "You will have to release me."

He didn't trust her, but with his injured arm he could not hold onto her and also search out the access to the inner stairs. He released her.

Catherine hurriedly moved away. "I do not require your escort," she said. "I can make my way to my chamber alone."

No doubt, Collier thought, but it was an opportunity to speak with her which might not come his way again. "Open it," he said.

Her resentment seethed across the space separating them. Fortunately, it was no place to argue.

Collier heard the whisper of her hands as she ran them down the paneling, followed by a barely audible click, and then a cool draft of air.

Catherine brushed against him as she stepped ahead of him into the unlit passageway.

She was not waiting for him, Collier realized as the sound of her feet on the stairs drifted upward. He searched out the first footing, then hurried up after her.

Damn arm! he cursed it for slowing him. For certain Catherine would lock him out if he didn't reach her first.

A soft glow of light fell onto the stairs as the door above was thrust open, then Catherine stepped through it.

Collier took the last of the stairs in one bound, but

barely had he set foot in Catherine's chamber when she slammed the door against him. He put a shoulder to it, ignored the jarring pain of his injured arm, and used his greater weight against Catherine's.

She stumbled back, regained her balance, and darted out from behind the tapestry.

Collier followed. "Catherine," he said, "I mean you no harm. I only wish to talk to you."

She straightened from beside the bed and swung around. In her hand was the dagger she had used on him the night before. "Get out," she said, her eyes large and angry through the auburn hair fallen over them.

He took another step toward her.

"I shall scream!" She thrust the dagger before her.

"No, you won't."

"I will!"

Reminding himself that she believed he had tried to rape her, and that she must think he would try to do so again, Collier halted. "And how would you explain how I came into your room?"

She glanced toward the door behind which Montagu had surely stationed one of his men—no doubt dozing as those in the hall did. She reminded Collier of a cornered animal. "I wish you to leave," she said.

As much as she hated, and as much as she dared where few men would, Catherine Algernon also feared. If only she didn't fear him. "Have you ever trusted anyone?" Collier asked.

She seemed surprised by his question. Then her eyes hardened again. "Never a man."

"I know you believe me to be a Yorkist—"

"Are you not?"

Collier considered her question for a moment. He

certainly was no Lancastrian, for the weak King Henry was not a man he would ever have supported. "I suppose I am a Yorkist," he admitted, "but not as you believe me to be."

"A Yorkist is a Yorkist. Vile traitors to the crown!"

Collier, having always been fascinated with English history, especially this time period, could easily have argued medieval politics with her, but this was neither the time, nor place. "I am not your enemy, Lady Catherine."

A forced laugh parted her lips. "Of course you are."

He shook his head. "If that were the case, I would not have put myself between you and Walther."

The dagger wavered in her hand. "I did not need your help."

"No? Walther would have killed you."

"You do not know that."

"I do. And you know it, too, don't you?"

This time she hadn't enough anger to overcome the fear. Her eyes growing wide, she slowly lowered the dagger. "Who are you?"

Collier stepped forward. How much could he tell her? And would she believe any of it? No, it was too soon. For certain, her medieval superstitions would label him a sorcerer or such, and he had no desire to be burned at the stake. Keeping an eye on the dagger, he halted before her.

When Catherine turned her face up to his, it reflected the same vulnerability he had seen on Aryn's face the day she had walked out of his life. Without thinking, he laid a hand alongside her face.

She drew a sharp breath, but did not pull back. "Who?" she asked again.

Though he knew he was pushing the bounds, he

caressed her cheek with a thumb. "A man who has come a very long way to find you."

She frowned. "What do you want of me?"

Collier lowered his gaze to her mouth. Near enough to kiss, but forbidden. "Only for you to trust me."

She gasped. "Trust you? But you are my—"

"No," he said sharply, "I am not your enemy."

Startled, she stared at him with familiar blue eyes. Aryn's eyes. But that wasn't all that was familiar about her.

Collier was struck with remembrances of the first time he had kissed Aryn. She had been angry with him, but out of that anger had come a passion he had never before experienced with a woman. Like fire and ice they had come together. Burning one another with their needs. Melting.

"Gilchrist?" Catherine said, uncertainty in her voice.

Her use of his surname reminded Collier that this was different. Very different. But it did not prevent the stirrings of his body.

Again, he looked to Catherine's mouth. Did she feel what he did? Did she want his arms around her as he wanted hers around him? He was trespassing, he knew. Every moment he stood so near her he risked her fury—and the dagger at her side. However, knowing it and paying it heed were two different things. She was Aryn. Had to be.

Seeking, he grazed her lower lip with his thumb.

A tremble went through her and she swayed toward him.

Collier slid his hand around the back of her neck and lowered his head. Though her lips tasted of Aryn, it was as if she were untried—as if no man before him had kissed her. Was it possible? Had

Catherine's betrothed never sampled what was to have been his?

He heard the dagger fall to the floor. Then, a small sound escaping her throat, Catherine pressed her breasts against his chest.

Aching, Collier deepened the kiss, and a moment later, Catherine parted her lips. But barely had he touched his tongue to hers when she stiffened.

With a gasp, she jerked back and landed her palm to his cheek. "Cur!"

His skin was fiery hot where she had struck him. Collier met her gaze. The vulnerability was gone, and in its place the anger, hatred, and bitterness of Catherine Algernon.

He touched his cheek. Damn, but he knew better than to do what he had done—especially considering how inexperienced she seemed. She had every right to be angry.

"Trust!" Catherine spat. "'Tis all you want? Why, you are worse than Montagu."

"I am truly sorry," he said. As he turned away, his booted foot sent the dagger skittering across the floor. He bent and retrieved it.

Her anger tempered by sudden wariness, Catherine glanced from him to the dagger.

And still she believed him capable of atrocities. Knowing it was likely a losing battle to find Aryn in this woman, Collier tossed the weapon atop her bed. "Should you need it," he said. "Good night, Lady Catherine."

He stepped behind the tapestry and into the passageway. Barely had he begun his descent when he heard the sharp click of the door behind, then the scrape of a key as Catherine secured the door against him.

Collier negotiated the last of the stairs in darkness,

and at the bottom quietly reseated the secret panel behind him. His arm beginning to ache anew, he crossed to the hearth. Though this past half hour he had all but forgotten about his pain, it seemed more than willing to make up for lost time. It was going to be a very long night.

Breathless, Catherine stepped out from behind the tapestry. Lord! Why had she let him touch her like that?

In her search for an explanation, she saw him again and heard the words he had spoken to her: *Walther would have killed you.* He had known, as assuredly as if he had seen into her dream. It was that which had unsettled her and left her vulnerable. Then he had touched her. As if under a spell, she had allowed him to trespass where no man had ever trespassed.

Catherine laid fingers against her lips and drew a ragged breath against them. Though his was the first kiss she had ever known, there had been something strangely familiar about Gilchrist's mouth on hers. Something pleasing about the press of her breasts against him. She had . . . liked it.

Catherine was sickened by the admission. "Damn you, Gilchrist!" she cursed. He had set out to seduce her, and had he not broken the spell by touching his tongue to hers, she might well have laid down for him. As if she were a common trollop.

Knowing how Hildegard would have berated her for such behavior, Catherine condemned herself over and over until, finally, she convinced herself she had not liked Gilchrist's touch—that she had hated every moment of it. Nay, never would she have laid down for him. He would have had to rape her.

But he is no rapist, a small voice whispered to her.

Catherine removed her mantle and dropped it atop the chest at the foot of her bed. It was then she remembered what she had set out to do.

Thwarted, she thought as she looked at the men's breeches and tunic she had earlier donned. All the more reason to hate Gilchrist. But tomorrow she would try again to reach the storeroom—providing she was allowed another day at Strivling.

8

The winch room was silent. A tomb for those who had fought to hold Strivling.

Collier's throbbing arm reminded him he had also shed blood here. He looked to the fallen men. In this, the fifteenth century was no different from the twentieth, he thought wryly—men who gave their lives for another's gain. Although Edward's claim to the throne was certainly stronger than Henry's, and he was far worthier, it was a waste of life.

Stepping into the room, Collier saw that the sword lay where he had dropped it yesterday. He strode to the winch and bent down. It was his blood on it, not Walther's, but was it the same sword that had sat on his mantel all these years? He lifted it into the light.

So it was. He knew by heart its slender blade, the Latin inscription beneath the cross guard proclaiming it "indomitable," the hand-and-a-half grip, its heavy pommel.

Although his first thought had been to leave it to find the fate which had delivered it into his hands five hundred years from now, his next was that it no longer mattered. Without Catherine's death attached to it, the sword was without significance.

Carrying it before him, Collier picked his way among the bodies that still lay upon the stairs. As he stepped out into the first light of day, a group of soldiers approached and entered the gatehouse he had exited. Under Montagu's orders, they were to remove the dead, Strivling's to be tossed into a communal grave, Montagu's to be given "proper burials."

Laughter turned Collier's attention to the tower which had held Strivling's prisoners. Sharing a joke between themselves, two soldiers emerged carrying one of the guards Edmund had slain when he had come out of the pit. A moment later, they were followed by two others bearing another's body.

Had they already brought Severn out? Collier wondered.

"Gilchrist!"

Collier looked around.

His stride brisk, Edmund advanced on him. "That is the one you have chosen?" He eyed the sword Collier held.

"It is."

"My friend, you have simple tastes." Edmund shrugged. "But that is not all bad."

Simple tastes, Collier reflected. *That* had certainly never been said of him before. If Edmund could sample the wines he stocked in his cellar, or see the fine suits that lined his wardrobe, he would quickly reverse his opinion. But those things were lost to him now, which was not all bad.

"Come," Edmund said, "we must prepare you."

*   *   *

Hair like sable in the sun, shoulders looking broad enough to carry a world of worries on them, Gilchrist knelt before Montagu to receive the collée which would confer knighthood on him.

And Catherine was made to witness it. From the base of the steps of the keep, she had stood through Montagu's presentation of Edmund Morrow as the new lord of Strivling, followed by the oath of fealty to him—which Strivling's men had had no choice but to give. Then had come Montagu's award of coin to those knights who had proven themselves most valuable during the siege, Griffin Walther among them, and now the dubbing ceremony.

Hating Montagu for forcing her to be present, but more, Gilchrist for what he had done to her last eve, Catherine watched the king's man lift his sword.

As Gilchrist was the last of three soldiers to be knighted this morn, all fell silent as they waited to see if he would fall beneath the blow as the others before him had.

He would, Catherine told herself, for only a man truly worthy of knighthood could hold against the vicious slap of Montagu's sword. And Gilchrist was the least worthy of all.

The side of Montagu's sword struck him hard against the neck, but though he jerked sideways, he remained kneeling. Amid the enthusiastic shouts of Montagu's men, Gilchrist met Catherine's gaze—and in his eyes she saw remembrance of the night past.

Much as she wanted to look away, she stared back.

Suddenly, Gilchrist grinned.

Odious blackguard! Catherine silently cursed. He was despicable. Loathsome. Vile. Wretched—

"Arise, Sir Collier," Montagu spoke over the din.

Sir, indeed! Never would she title him such, Catherine vowed. Even were he crowned king, he would still be the ignoble knave who had tried to rape her.

And who saved your life, a small voice inside reminded her.

She swallowed. Nay, she did not wish to think about that. It was far too disturbing.

His injured arm slung against his abdomen, Gilchrist strode to where the other two stood.

Thankfully, all that remained of the ceremony was Montagu's closing words.

As he began his oration, Catherine looked to the three soldiers who had been elevated to knighthood. Whereas before their weapons had been ordinary, their boots unadorned, and their armor little more than rent mail, they now wore the knightly raiments of war—swords, gilt spurs, and plates of shining armor which had doubtless been taken from Strivling's fallen knights.

A sickening in her belly for those now dead, their knightly possessions stolen from their bodies without twinge of conscience, Catherine once again turned her gaze upon Gilchrist, and it was only then she noticed the sword at his side. Though it was not as elaborate as the ones girded on the two others, its blue-black hilt reminded her of the one she had wielded against Walther—and which Gilchrist had taken from her. Could it be the same? she wondered as shouts of approval announced the end of the ceremony. And if it were, why would Gilchrist choose it over the multitude of others?

As blessedly warm as it was this day following what must have been the coldest day of spring,

Catherine huddled deeper into the folds of her mantle. The sooner she left Strivling, the better. Of course, there was something she must do first.

"We ride within the hour," she heard Montagu's shout above the noise. His knights following, he descended the steps. Although it was usual for celebrations to follow a dubbing ceremony, he was too eager to be on his way to allow his men the indulgence.

But what of the punishment he had promised her? Catherine wondered. Surely he had not forgotten. When he had summoned her from her chamber this morn, she had been certain it was with the intention of delivering her punishment that all could bear witness to it. Why hadn't he?

As Montagu drew near, he captured her gaze. "Patience," he said with a twisted smile, then struck out across the bailey.

Nay, he had not forgotten.

As the crowd around him disbanded, Collier watched Catherine stare after Montagu. Not until the king's man had passed over the drawbridge and was out of sight did she turn back around. Then, her chin set with dangerous determination, she began her ascent to the hall.

How long would she keep out of trouble? Collier wondered. Although he had foiled whatever she had been up to last night, he felt certain she would attempt it again.

The side of his neck burning where Montagu had struck him, he probed the welt. Damn, it had hurt! But knowing Catherine was watching, doubtless hoping he would fall, he had drawn on everything within him to disappoint her. Somehow he had succeeded.

"Sir Collier!"

He shifted his gaze to where Edmund stood at the bottom of the steps. Earlier in the ceremony, it had been he who had girded on Collier's sword and fastened the gilded spurs to Collier's boots. It had all seemed so . . . surreal.

Edmund motioned for him to follow.

Collier caught up with him as he crossed over the inner drawbridge. His first look at the destruction wrought in the outer bailey nearly halted him.

Where once there had been buildings, there were only blackened remains. Where once the ground must have been clear, were links of chain mail, pieces of plate armor, broken arrows, crushed helmets, pools of dark pitch, and patches of discoloration among the dirt marking where men had fallen.

"'Tis a pity Lady Catherine did not surrender ere the outer bailey was taken," Edmund said, his eyes soured by the devastation. "It will take much labor and coin to restore it."

Still, he would do it, Collier knew, and under the Yorkist flag Strivling would rise again.

"But does the king refuse me my due, it may not be my coin that restores it," Edmund murmured.

Collier looked sideways at him. "He will not refuse you," he said, knowing he ought to say nothing, but needing to reassure this man whose loins would one day produce those from which Collier would spring.

Edmund's eyebrows rose. "You think not?"

"You are worthy, Edmund Morrow. The king would be a fool to award Highchester to any other."

With a sudden bark of laughter, Edmund slapped a hand to Collier's back. "I do think we are going to be great friends, Gilchrist."

Montagu's shouted orders ringing like a beacon to his presence, Edmund and Collier followed his voice outside the castle walls to where the first of the siege had taken its toll on Strivling. The craggy land sloping down from the high point upon which the castle was built was littered much the same as the bailey.

Amid a tumult of preparations being made for departure—the loading of wagons and carts, the downing of tents, and the dismantling of siege engines—the king's man moved.

Edmund lengthened his stride. "My lord!" he called.

Montagu glanced over his shoulder, but did not pause until he reached his destination—one of a train of carriages supporting the unmistakable bulk of cannon.

Collier frowned. Not only had he seen no evidence of the use of artillery against Strivling, but all the history books he had read on this civil war of England's had clearly stated that during the northern uprising the cannon had been used only once. Against Bamburgh Castle.

"'Tis good we made it to the winch room," Edmund said, "else there might be little left of it."

Collier looked sideways at him. "The cannon," he said.

"Aye, Lord Montagu brought them in yester morn whilst we were making good our escape from the pit. Had his tunneling efforts failed to bring down the inner wall, he would have used them."

At least his presence in the past had not affected change in this, Collier thought.

Edmund and Collier halted a short distance from where Montagu conversed with a handful of soldiers.

Shortly, the king's man turned to them. "The cannons will follow," he said, then settled his gaze on Collier. "Are you prepared to hold Strivling until Morrow returns, Gilchrist?"

Hardly, but that was not the answer this man required. Although Collier had no idea of how to "hold" a castle, he said, "I am."

Montagu nodded. "I am leaving behind a contingent of men lest Lady Catherine attempts to stir her people to revolt. They will take their orders from you."

Then Catherine would remain behind. Collier had wondered if the punishment this man planned for her would take her away from Strivling—and if so, how he was to find her again. It seemed as if all was going according to some unwritten plan. "Yes, my lord," he said.

"And Lady Catherine's place?" Edmund asked, concern in his voice. "What is it to be, my lord?"

Obviously, she did not fit with his plans of being baron of Strivling.

"'Tis that which I wish to discuss with you," Montagu said. "I can think of no greater punishment than to wed her to her enemy. A man who will keep her occupied with babes in her belly."

Collier felt Edmund's unease join his own.

"And who would this man be?" Edmund asked.

Montagu's attempt at an apologetic smile came nowhere near to reaching his eyes. "I was thinking you, Morrow. After all, 'tis Lady Catherine these people are loyal to. An alliance with her would strengthen your hold on Strivling."

Collier's thoughts rebelled. This could not be! Not only would the marriage of Edmund and Catherine twist time further out of shape—preventing his ancestor from wedding the woman by whom all the succeeding generations had descended—but it would leave him, Collier, with nothing. If not for Catherine, why would he have been brought back in time?

"'Tis not a prospect you welcome, is it?" Montagu asked.

Edmund drew a deep breath. "I must be honest, my lord. 'Tis not."

"As it cannot be said Lady Catherine is uncomely, is it that you are betrothed?"

Edmund shook his head. "'Tis just that I was thinking to marry a woman more . . . agreeable."

Understanding brightened Montagu's eyes. "A good bedding is all Lady Catherine requires. She is simply too long without a husband."

Had she never been with a man? Collier wondered again. For a brief moment, he reflected on the world he had left behind. In the twentieth century, it was considered uncommon for a woman to be a virgin past the age of eighteen. Even Aryn had had lovers before him.

"With your permission, my lord," Edmund said, "I would decline."

Annoyance flashed in Montagu's eyes. "*With* my permission," he repeated, emphasizing the power he wielded.

In deference, Edmund bowed his head.

Several moments passed, then Montagu expelled a harsh sigh. "I shall choose another."

It was his cue, Collier knew. If Catherine was to wed anyone, it ought to be him. He stepped forward. "If it pleases you, Lord Montagu, *I* will take Lady Catherine to be my wife."

Montagu's eyebrows snapped together. "You, Gilchrist?"

"Yes, my lord. Though I am lowly born, now that you have bestowed knighthood—"

"Lowly born," Montagu mused. A spark of devilment entered his eyes. "Aye, fitting punishment."

Although Collier resented being thought of as such, he realized it was more likely to gain him what he sought.

Montagu looked back at him. "Think you could tame Lady Catherine?"

Tame her? Even were he to find Aryn in Catherine, he could not imagine her turning submissive, nor would he want her to. But it was what this man wished to hear. "Yes, my lord."

Montagu smiled.

"Catherine Algernon, come forward."

Her punishment. Telling herself she was prepared for whatever this devil meted out, Catherine stepped past the castle folk and walked toward the dais where Montagu stood. Gilchrist to the left of him and Morrow to the right, the king's man held her with his gaze.

Would she be ordered to a convent to live out the remainder of her days? Or would her sentence be that of attainder, whereby she forfeited all of her civil rights? Perhaps Montagu might even act on his belief that she was better dead.

Whatever it was, no satisfaction would she give him, Catherine promised herself. She would accept her sentence without blink or startle, then she would see if there was not some way in which to thwart him.

She halted before the king's man.

From his elevated position, he peered down his nose at her. "You are accused of being a traitor to the crown, Lady Catherine. How do you answer to the charge?"

Though she knew she ought not to mock him, she

could not help herself. "Is it King Henry who charges me or that other who thinks himself the king?"

Behind her, the castle folk stirred uneasily.

Montagu's hands fisted. "You are charged in the name of King Edward the fourth."

"Then I am a traitor." *That* could not be argued with.

"You know the penalty for treason?"

"I do." Hanging, drawing, and quartering.

Montagu took a step toward her. "Then you will be pleased to know I have decided to be lenient."

She waited.

"After much consideration, I have determined that you should wed."

It was a miracle she managed to keep the vow she had made to herself to remain impassive. "That is to be my punishment?"

"Doubtless you will consider it such, but 'tis simply an alliance, Lady Catherine. To unite Lancastrian with Yorkist that these lands may know peace again."

It was an attempt to put her beneath some man's heel. To subdue her. To fill her body with child after child that she might never again rebel against the usurper. To render her naught more than chattel. "You cannot force me to speak vows I do not wish to speak," she said.

His smile was smug. "You know better than that."

What did he intend? Misgivings awakening within her, Catherine said, "The Church will not allow it."

Montagu arched an eyebrow. "And why would they not when the bride is willing?"

"Never would I willingly wed a Yorkist!"

Unexpectedly, he lunged forward and captured hold of her chin, but this time when she attempted to wrench free, he was prepared. "You will wed whomever I choose, Lady Catherine, and but to speak vows, you will do so with a closed mouth."

She had never feared him as much as she did in that moment. She glanced past him to where Gilchrist stood—and was surprised to see anger in his eyes and in the hands he clenched at his sides.

"Though that old bitch, Hildegard, raised you," Montagu said, "you forget your true family."

The shadow of defeat falling over her, Catherine looked back at him. As he had done yesterday, he would use the threat of harm to others as a means of controlling her. She was a fool not to have guessed he would do so again.

"Defy me," he said, "and I will see that every member of your family is attainted. Outlawed. Their possessions seized, titles lost, and lives reduced to less than villeins."

She hardly knew her family. Since having come to live at Strivling twelve years ago, she had seen them sporadically—and only when one or more members had come to call on Lord Somerton. But still she could not allow them to suffer for her actions.

"They will lose everything," Montagu pressed. "Have they not lost enough already?"

Her life was not her own. "Do I wed this Yorkist," she said, the words more bitter than any she had ever spoken, "would my family be allowed to remain at Toller Castle?"

Montagu's eyes lit with triumph. "In residence only. I am certain that if Sir Edmund is awarded the barony he will wish to install one loyal to him."

Of course. She looked to Morrow. Was he the one Montagu intended her to wed? It must be him. "You leave me no choice," she said.

Montagu released her. "I give you until Sir

Edmund returns from court to become used to the idea, then you shall wed Sir Collier Gilchrist."

Nothing could have prepared Catherine for the pronouncement. Nothing. Unable to hide her surprise, she stepped back from Montagu. "Surely you jest. He is a—"

"A commoner raised to the nobility," he said, pleased with himself. "Fitting, don't you think, Lady Catherine?"

She swung her gaze to the man whose sharp gray eyes awaited hers. She who had been destined to wed the Baron of Highchester was to wed this landless knight? A man who had stolen into her chamber two nights past with evil intent? Who had tried to seduce her last eve? Whose touch she detested?

"Lady Catherine?" Montagu said.

Outrage quivered through her. "I can think of no worse fate."

Montagu smiled. "Then we are in agreement." He took her arm, pulled her onto the dais, and guided her to Gilchrist. "I present your betrothed, Sir Collier. May she grace your life for many years."

The sting of humiliation upon her, Catherine stared at Gilchrist and hated the compassion in his eyes.

He lifted her hand. "Lady Catherine," he said, then pressed his mouth to the backs of her fingers.

Telling herself she was repulsed, she snatched her hand away. Before Montagu could reprove her, she swung around to face him. "I do not have to like it, do I?"

A wry smile bowed his lips. "Try, Lady Catherine." He pivoted and stepped from the dais.

Morrow followed, and then Gilchrist. He strode past Catherine without a glance in her direction.

No doubt he was angered by her response to his kiss, but that was good. Keep him angry and perhaps he would visit no more of his unwanted attentions on her. But she was deluding herself, and she knew it.

A moment later, the three men passed through the doorway and from sight.

Were it not for her audience—the castle folk who looked upon her with doleful eyes—Catherine would have sagged beneath the strain of this day. Instead, she pushed her shoulders back and said, "Return to your duties."

A short while later, she watched from the window of her chamber as Montagu and his men ascended to the saddle to begin their northward journey to subdue those who yet stood against their king.

"Where are you, King Henry?" Catherine whispered. But more importantly, where was his queen, Margaret, a woman whom Hildegard had revered and said was more worthy than any man in all of England? Was the queen still in France where she had fled nearly a year ago?

Catherine dropped her face into her hands. Unshed tears banked behind her eyes, but she would not cry them, she vowed. To do so would disgrace Hildegard's memory, and she could not do that. Even now she must be strong.

9

These men are liars. *They pledge themselves to King Edward, just as they did two years past, but still they are loyal to Henry. Do not turn your back on them.*

They were the words Montagu had left Collier with. And though Collier knew he would do well to heed them, even more he would do well to guard his back from Griffin Walther. As Montagu had accepted the mercenary's offer to head up the contingent he left at Strivling, Collier knew he would not be getting much sleep these next weeks.

With the last of Montagu's army disappearing in the distance, he turned and strode over the drawbridge. In the outer bailey, he paused to assess the damage more carefully. Although he had no idea how much coin was in the purse Edmund had given him— or its worth—it would likely take every bit of it to simply begin the rebuilding process.

But it was not as if he could pick up the phone and start calling contractors. It was going to be a good deal more complicated than that. To clear the debris from the castle and repair the walls, he would have to pull labor from among the castle folk and villagers. He would have to find a source for materials—wood, stone, mortar. . . . Then there would be the wages to deal with that took more than the stroke of a pen as he was accustomed to. On the other hand, he would not have to file paperwork and obtain permits before beginning work, nor would he have to deal with unions, building inspectors, and the headaches that went with them. Not all bad, he supposed.

"*Sir* Collier," a man called to him.

Walther—his sarcastic slur easily identifying him.

Squinting against the sun, Collier located the mercenary where he stood on the wall-walk before a section of crumbled battlement. "Sir Griffin," he said.

"The men await your orders."

Collier looked to those Montagu had left behind. The king's man had been generous, choosing only soldiers of presence and good arms to stand watch over this fallen Lancastrian stronghold. Then there were also Strivling's soldiers who had been divested of their arms until such time as they proved loyal to the Yorkists. With empty hands and little purpose, they stood upon the walls.

Collier nearly smiled. "The debris needs to be removed from this bailey," he said, "and when that is done, the inner bailey as well."

"And my men?" Walther asked.

"They will do the work—alongside Strivling's men."

Walther jerked as if physically struck. "They are soldiers, not common laborers!"

"Those are my orders, *Sir* Griffin," Collier said, knowing that if he did not assert his authority now he might lose it altogether.

Walther's face mottled red. "And who will defend King Edward's right should these people rise up?"

Collier looked to Strivling's men-at-arms and the knights amongst them. They were weary of war. It was written all over their faces—faces which reflected none of the anger Catherine's did. So long as he kept her from rousing them, they were not likely to present a threat. "Do you question my orders?" he asked Walther.

"You know I do."

He had nerve. Collier had to give him that. "If you are unable to fulfill your duties, Sir Griffin, I will relieve you of them."

The look in Walther's eyes said that were they alone, he would take great pleasure in relieving Collier of his life. Yes, Collier thought, if he wanted to stay alive in this bloody century, among other things he would have to work on his swordsmanship. "Your answer, Sir Griffin?"

Walther's silence strained the air a moment longer, then he said, "Work will begin immediately."

Knowing this was not the end of it, Collier nodded, then turned toward the keep. As the villagers had yet to be allowed to return to their villages—or what remained of their homes following Montagu's ride on Strivling—he would send them to work alongside the soldiers. Then he would see about putting a value on the coin he held.

Griffin stared at Gilchrist's retreating back and Walther stroked the handle of his dagger. God, how he burned. He had not severed his loyalty to the Lancasters and come over to the side of the Yorks only to act nursemaid to a brood of foot soldiers. He had come to be made a lord. To sit at table above others and hold the lives of many in his hands.

But his chance at Highchester had slipped through his fingers. Even if ill befell Morrow in the weeks to come, never would the opportunity come his way again. Hence, he would have to settle for one of the barony's lesser castles, but naught less than that.

For this reason, he had offered to remain at Strivling. Providing Morrow returned a baron, he intended to be first under consideration to hold a castle from him. And the fewer contenders, the better.

There was going to be a death at Strivling.

"Where did you get those?" Catherine demanded.

Collier looked up from the ledgers he had been poring over this past hour to where she stood ten feet away. She looked anxious, and perhaps he knew the reason for it.

"I had the steward retrieve them for me."

"For what reason?"

"That I might better understand Strivling's income and expenditures."

She looked taken aback. "You know numbers?"

He had forgotten that during the middle ages the average person had been unable to perform such simple tasks—especially those of lowly birth and women. Likely Catherine could not do so herself.

"Yes," he said. "I can read, write, and even compute." Of course, making sense of these numbers and this writing made him feel more than a little illiterate. He was learning, though.

Catherine dropped her gaze to the ledgers. "As happens during times of war, they have not been kept current."

He had guessed right. "You refer to the eight hundred pounds that are unaccounted for?"

"Eight hundred pounds?" she repeated, incredulous. "I did not know the old baron had ever had so much in his coffers."

"He did."

"You have looked to see how much remains?"

The steward, a muttering fellow whose fingernails were bitten to the quick, had brought Collier the coffer. It had contained five pounds. "Yes," he said, "I have looked, and there is eight hundred pounds missing."

Catherine shrugged. "It must have been spent defending against the usurper—else Montagu or Morrow took it."

He had considered both possibilities, but as the last entry had been dated the day Montagu had begun his siege, and shown there to be in excess of eight hundred pounds, it didn't hold. Too, in questioning the steward he had been told that when Montagu had ordered the coffer opened, it had contained only the five pounds. But money was not all that was missing from the barony's coffers.

"And who do you think took the rest of it?" Collier asked.

"The rest?"

"I assume that your betrothed's father had silver plate . . . gold . . . jewels." All of which might boast an even greater value than the missing coin.

Catherine looked away. "He did, but as to its whereabouts . . ." She shrugged. "'Tis likely gone the way of the coin."

"Where is it, Catherine?"

Her eyes widened. "You think 'twas *I* who took it?"

He stood. "It seems the most logical conclusion."

Indignation fired her eyes. "Then 'tis thievery you accuse me of?"

Collier strode out from behind the table. "Listen to me," he said as he advanced on her. "There is nothing you can do to change the course of this war. Edward will be king no matter how you plot against him." Which wasn't necessarily true. It was possible her life could make the difference needed to bring England back under the control of the Lancasters, but that he could not allow to happen.

"King Henry will wear his crown again," she said with determination.

True. In 1470, he would be reseated upon the throne, but for only six months. Then Edward would seize it again, and a month after that, Henry would be dead.

Collier halted before Catherine. "Where were you going last night?"

She crossed her arms over her chest. "Though I am forced to wed you, do not think I will answer to you."

That hardly surprised him. "I want you to stay out of the secret passages."

"And if I do not?"

"Then you will be corrected." How, he hadn't the faintest idea.

She laughed. "I do not fear you."

Collier caught her arm as she turned away. "It's for your own good, Catherine."

"My good! You will never convince me of that." She jerked free of him. "And though you are too lowly born to know it, I do have a title, Gilchrist. I am *Lady* Catherine Algernon."

And he was tired of being called by his surname. "As I am *Sir* Collier."

Her eyes narrowed. "Only whilst the usurper sits the throne." She turned and walked away.

Infuriating. There was no other word for her. Collier watched her disappear down the corridor leading to the kitchens. Unless he could find some way to get past her hate, being married to her was not going to be easy. In the meantime, he would have to discover where she had hidden Highchester's wealth, for undoubtedly she would attempt to smuggle it into the hands of the Lancastrians.

Expelling a harsh sigh, Collier turned back to the table and lifted the quill from its ink pot. God, what he wouldn't do for a ballpoint pen! Damned messy, this was.

At that moment, Catherine could not have said she liked herself very much. Anger had made her taunt Gilchrist about his lowly birth. Although Hildegard had often spoken such to those beneath her station, Catherine had thought it insensitive and never done so herself. But it seemed one of only a few of Gilchrist's attributes open to attack.

True, he was a treacherous Yorkist, even if he did not conduct himself as such, and had attempted to rape her, even if he had not taken advantage of the situation last eve. But other than that . . .

It was not as if he didn't deserve it, she told herself, and halted before the storeroom. She pressed a hand to the door, but only for a moment. She drew back. If she went now, not only was it likely she would be discovered missing, but more, the tide was not right. It must be done soon, though—before Gilchrist got any nearer the truth.

Holy rood, she should have burned the ledgers! Though she'd had every intention of doing so, she had never gotten around to it.

"My lady?"

Catherine turned. The young serving girl, Sara,

stood before her—a slow-witted, but sweet child whom Catherine had taken it upon herself to keep an eye out for. "Aye, Sara?"

"I'm just returned from the outer b-b-bailey. I was takin' drink to the folk, an-an-and . . ."

Although Catherine did not feel like smiling, she did. "Take your time," she urged.

Sara drew a deep breath. "They got Strivling's soldiers laborin' right alongside th-the villagers."

Further punishment. Humiliation.

"And also them that Lord M-Montagu left behind."

Had she heard right? Catherine wondered. Surely Sara did not mean . . . "Lord Montagu's soldiers are clearing the bailey?"

Sara bobbed her head up and down.

"You are certain?"

"Aye, my lady."

Catherine was shocked. It had to be Gilchrist who had ordered it, for she couldn't imagine Griffin Walther would have done so. And certainly the soldiers would not have taken it upon themselves. But why? Didn't Gilchrist understand the differences between the classes—men who fight, men who work, and men who pray?

"Thank you, Sara," she said.

"My lady." The girl hurried toward the kitchens.

Nay, Gilchrist did not behave like a Yorkist—nor a Lancastrian, Catherine acknowledged. He was unlike anyone she had ever met. Again, the question of who he was rose to mind. Who was this man she would be forced to wed to protect her family? What was his secret? And why had he set men trained in arms to do the work of laborers? She returned to the hall.

Gilchrist had resumed his seat. His dark head bent over a ledger, he flipped from one page to the next, then returned to the previous page. He studied the entries a long moment, turned the page again, and dipped his quill. He scratched something on a sheet of parchment.

"Why?" Catherine asked without preamble.

Annoyance grooving the corners of his mouth, he looked up. "Why what?"

She stepped up to the dais. "Why have you set soldiers to do menial work?"

"It needs to be done. The sooner the castle is cleared of rubble, the sooner it can be rebuilt. You object?"

Did she? Only in that he was overstepping bounds that had been set hundreds and hundreds of years ago. "It is not usual to have soldiers perform such duties when it can be done by laborers," she said.

Gilchrist returned the quill to the ink pot, leaned back in the chair Hildegard had once filled, and clasped his good arm over the injured one. "As they had nothing better to do, I saw no reason they should stand idle while others worked."

Catherine pressed her palms to the tabletop and leaned forward. "If you do not know it, Gilchrist, a soldier's lot is to guard and protect, not—"

"As they are responsible for the state of Strivling, they can clean it up."

Where did such thinking come from? "You make no sense," Catherine said.

He lowered his gaze to the ledgers, considered them a long moment, then looked back at her. "No, I don't imagine I do, but that is how it is going to be."

Catherine straightened. "'Tis as Morrow says: You do not fit."

He raised a thick, black eyebrow. "I was wondering how much of that conversation you listened in on."

"I assure you, 'twas not intentional."

His smile was wry. "Of course not." He pushed his chair back.

As he rose, Catherine glimpsed a brief expression of pain. "Why did you refuse the physician his use of medicines?" she asked.

"Trying to make sense of me, Lady Catherine?"

"Someone must."

"And who better than the woman who is to be my wife, hmm?"

His wife. "Why?" she asked again.

"Would you believe . . . religious convictions?"

Now he made even less sense, but before Catherine could question him further, he strode out from behind the table and started toward the stairs.

"Where are you going?" she called to him.

He looked around. "The rest room."

She had never heard the word before. "Rest room?"

Frustration flashed across his face. "Bathroom . . . indoor outhouse . . . whatever it is you people call it."

Was he, perhaps, a bit mad? "You speak of the garderobe?"

"Garderobe," he repeated. Then, with a shake of his head, he ascended the stairs.

No, he did not fit at all.

Once he was gone from sight, Catherine reached across the table and retrieved the parchment he had written upon.

"Write, indeed!" she spoke aloud. Not only was his handwriting appalling, but he could hardly spell. Among his numerous mistakes was "seed" for what she surmised to be "sed," "meat" for "meate," and "wood" for "wud." And if that were not bad enough, his control of the quill was poor. In three different places he had left large blotches of ink.

Guessing that he was attempting to project the cost of supplies, she summed his numbers and arrived at the total he had written. He was a learned man, she grudgingly conceded. Lowly born, yet versed in numbers.

She returned the parchment to the table. Collier Gilchrist had much explaining to do.

10

London, May 1997

　　"God, man, open up!" James shouted, pounding his fist on the door.

Silence.

"Do you hear me, Collier?"

Still no answer—as if the room beyond lay empty.

Growing more uneasy with each passing moment, James looked to the housekeeper. "How long did you say he's been in there?"

She wrung her hands. "Since early yesterday evening, sir."

Almost twenty-four hours. "You're certain he didn't leave?"

"I am."

James tried the doorknob again.

"I'm worried about him, sir," the housekeeper said. "He was raging something mighty last eve—throwing things and cursing."

She had called James this afternoon, begging him to come to his brother's aid. As James's relationship with Collier had been strictly adversarial these past years, he had nearly refused her. But she had sounded so desperate.

So what had gotten into Collier? What had enraged him so that he had let his infuriatingly controlled emotions loose? Strivling Castle? James remembered the phone call he had made to Collier nearly three months past—it being the last time they had spoken.

"Should I call the police, sir?"

James sized up the door. It was not going to give easily. "No," he said, and motioned for the woman to stand back.

Time and again he slammed his shoulder against the door, and finally it burst inward. His arm throbbing, he stepped inside. The sharp splintering beneath his shoes drew his gaze to the carpet where shards of porcelain and glass were strewn. The former was part of a lamp that lay nearby, the latter a framed picture of a woman. A very pretty woman.

A prickling sensation ran up James's spine. On the floor before the hearth was a sword, and all around it pieces of colored . . . paper? Something was very wrong. "Collier?" he called.

No answer.

He swept his gaze from a fragmented vase to books that had been flung from a shelf, then to the chair that lay on its side. What had happened here? Fear boring through him, James glanced at the bathroom door. It stood open a crack. Was Collier in there?

The housekeeper gasped.

Not knowing what he would find, but knowing it best if he discovered it alone, James turned to her. "Return downstairs," he said. "I'll join you shortly."

With a jerky nod, the woman turned away.

Steeling himself, James strode to the bathroom. "Collier, it's James," he called out. Receiving no response, he pushed the door inward.

The bathroom was empty.

He closed his eyes. God, what he had imagined! Drawing a long breath, he turned back into the room. So where was Collier? Though the housekeeper was adamant that he had not left his room, he obviously had.

Was it some game he played? No, that wasn't Collier at all. He was not given to playing games—unlike himself, James grudgingly admitted. He rarely missed an opportunity to mess with a person's head.

Once more, he looked around the room. It was then he noticed the portrait. Could it be? "I'll be damned," he muttered. Collier had succeeded in having it restored as had been his obsession for years. Although the mystery of the Algernon woman had always bored James to tears—someone who was dead long enough to be nothing but dust—he was drawn to the portrait.

He traced the lovely woman with his eyes, from her auburn hair to the unfinished hands she clasped a red rose between. There was something familiar about her, he thought. Something—

His foot struck the sword that lay before the hearth. Halting, he looked down and saw that in two places the blade was discolored with what looked like dried blood. He swallowed, then knelt and touched the darkness. It flaked away to reveal the shining silver beneath. Foul play?

With deepening disquiet, James looked more closely at the paper scattered around him. He picked up a piece. Not paper, he realized as it disintegrated between his fingers. Old paint.

But where had it come from? What did it mean?

As if beckoning to him, the portrait drew his gaze back to it. He stared at it a long moment, then looked down. Farther out was a larger piece of paint with small flowers dotting its surface. The landscape.

No, he thought. Ridiculous. The finest restorers in all of England had been unable to remove the top layer of paint. Surely Collier could not have done so himself. But what other explanation was there?

He sat back on his heels. He shouldn't worry about Collier. Shouldn't care. Far too much had happened between them for him to feel anything other than contempt for his younger brother.

As James rose, a wadded piece of paper standing white against the dark of the fireplace caught his eye. He retrieved it and smoothed it open.

The letter was short, but to the point. Aryn was dead.

Aryn? James pondered the vaguely familiar name, then remembered the grainy photograph that had made the tabloids six months ago. It had shown Collier and a dark-haired woman emerging from a New York theater. The caption had read: Collier Morrow with latest love, Aryn . . . —something or other.

Realization struck James like a blow to the belly. The breath rushing from him, he jerked his gaze to the portrait, then to the framed photograph that lay several feet away. The hairs along his arms standing, he retrieved it from the carpet. Smiling up at him through the cracked glass was the woman from the theatre. Aryn. Now he understood the reason Catherine Algernon looked so familiar.

What the bloody hell was going on?

11

Northern England, May 1464

Collier glanced at Catherine where she sat silently beside him. She had hardly touched her food.

He hadn't an appetite either, though more because of the meal. The meat had been edible, having come from a deer hunted down this morning, but the rest would be better put down a garbage disposal. In a carved out piece of stale bread, the crust of which was dappled with mold, floated withered vegetables in an unappealing yellow-brown broth.

Collier grimaced. Until the food supplies arrived, this would have to do. He only prayed he would not find himself stricken with food poisoning.

"It does not find favor with you?" Catherine asked.

As it was the first time she had initiated conversation with him since confronting him on the use of soldiers for menial work three days past, he was surprised.

He followed her gaze to his trencher, then looked to hers. Although he had learned that in the Middle Ages trenchers were typically shared between two, he had said nothing each time Catherine was served one separate from his. "Does it find favor with *you*?" he asked.

Her gaze cool, she pushed the spoon away and clasped her hands in her lap. "I am simply without appetite."

From the look in her eyes, it was not the food that was responsible for her loss of appetite. It was him. But he understood—or at least was trying to. Though he had felt her begin to thaw the one time he had kissed her, she continued to hate him. But he would convince her otherwise. Time and patience was all he needed.

Collier leaned back in his chair and waited for the others to finish eating. With Catherine returned to silence beside him, it seemed a long time he sat there, but at last, most of the trenchers and tankards bottomed out. He stood.

In the ensuing commotion, Catherine rose and headed toward the kitchens.

Knowing she would be occupied there for some time, Collier took the stairs two at a time, then traversed the corridor to her chamber. He stepped inside. With the waning of day shining gray through the windows, he paused to remember the night he had first entered Catherine's bedroom. He had been so certain it was a dream and that he would soon awaken from it, but no longer. It was far too real.

Reminding himself of the reason he had come, he crossed to the chest at the foot of the bed. It took only a few moments to determine that the contents were nothing more than clothing, and that the chest was without a false bottom.

So where else might Catherine have hidden the coin? He patted down the mattress and peered beneath the bed, but found nothing. What of the hidden passages? Might she have stowed Strivling's wealth somewhere within them? As he turned toward the tapestry, something to the left of the windows caught his regard. Large and draped with a cloth, it stood propped against the wall.

Though Collier doubted Catherine would have left the coin in so conspicuous a place, curiosity drew him to the object. He lowered himself to his haunches before it. He had only lifted a corner of the cloth when his heart sped. He knew what it was.

It might have been a minute he knelt there. It might have been thirty. Finally, he pushed the cloth away.

The portrait was the same as when he had looked up through the flakes of paint drifting down around him—unfinished, and without trace of the landscape that would later be painted over it. The only noticeable difference was the vividness of the colors. Even in the dim of the room, the blue of Catherine's eyes was deeper, the auburn of her hair richer, and the red of the rose that proclaimed her a Lancastrian more intense. It was Catherine Algernon as she had appeared just before her death in 1464.

A death Collier had reversed when he had come through this same portrait more than five hundred years from now. He lightly traced the face of the woman who would be Aryn, then her lips. How strange to think the one he had fallen in love with would not be born for half a millennium, and yet in that distant future she was already lost to him.

Longingly, Collier grazed his fingers over her unfinished hands, then the rose between them—and in that instant, the future opened up to him. Like a magnet to iron, he was pulled toward the portrait, though with nowhere near the force that had propelled him through it the first time.

He wrenched back.

The unseen force released him.

Collier stood. "Damn!" he muttered. It seemed there *was* a way back—providing he wished to return to the twentieth century. Did he? Although he had wanted to, he was no longer certain.

He met Catherine Algernon's level gaze. No, he couldn't leave. To walk away from the second chance he had been granted might mean walking away from the woman he loved. "I will find you, Aryn," he vowed. "Somehow."

From where she stood outside the door, Catherine pondered what she had just witnessed. Upon discovering Gilchrist within her chamber, she had nearly burst in on him, but his curse and the way he stood looking at her portrait had calmed her anger. Now, appearing to address the painting, he spoke that woman's name again.

Though she hated herself for the fear stealing up her spine, Catherine could not deny it. Was Gilchrist of the devil? she wondered as she peered at him through the narrow space between door and frame. Was he an evil invoked by the ungodly Edward to assure his wrongful claim to the throne of England? He was certainly dark enough—especially with his new growth of beard.

Her superstitions aroused by the teachings of the Church, Catherine took a step back from the doorway. Beneath her feet, the floor creaked alarmingly. Praying Gilchrist had not heard, she stilled.

A moment later he flung open the door and pinned her with his gaze. "Catherine," he said.

Drawing on her anger in hopes he would not see her fear, she demanded, "What do you in my chamber?"

He made no attempt to mask his suspicion. "I was looking for something."

And she knew what it was. "I have told you, the coin is not in my possession."

"I think it is, and I intend to find it."

She crossed her arms over her chest. "Then you will be searching a very long time."

"If that is what it takes."

So sure of himself. She glanced beyond him. "Are you quite finished trespassing?"

"For now."

"Then good eve."

He stared at her a moment longer, then stepped past her and strode down the corridor.

Feeling a bit breathless, Catherine shouldered the door closed and turned into her chamber. She looked to the chest Gilchrist had undoubtedly delved, then to her bed which he would have searched, and lastly the portrait. With the cloth pushed aside, the canvas reflected her image like a mirror—or nearly so, for the portrait was still several sittings from being completed. But now it never would be. Her betrothed was dead, and where he lay he had little need for such possessions as this which his father had commissioned as a wedding present for him. Poor Lambert . . .

Though older than her, he had always seemed more of a younger brother than a man whose children she would one day bear. Like his father, who had looked to Hildegard for approval and guidance, Lambert had looked to Catherine. He had been weak, but she had cared for him. And she missed him. If not for the murdering Yorkists, he would be here with her now.

Her heart grown heavy, Catherine traversed the room. As she lifted the cloth to drape it over the portrait, her gaze fell to the Lancastrian rose standing red against her unpainted hands.

She smiled with remembrance of how the artist had objected when she had directed him to paint the rose before all else. Had the canvas been any color other than white, she would not have insisted, but the offensive color had to go. In the end, it was the rose the man painted—transforming it from Yorkist white to Lancastrian red.

Catherine touched the unfolding petals, and in doing so, drew strength from it. She was a Lancastrian, and not even the devil could turn her from her purpose. She drew the cloth over the portrait and straightened.

She did not need the passages, she assured herself. She would do what needed to be done by daylight. But she must do it soon.

What had she seen? Collier wondered as he stared at the wall the masons would begin work on tomorrow. Had Catherine come upon him during his search of her bedroom? Afterward? Had she seen the portrait pull him toward it? Had she heard the vow he had made Aryn?

When he had found her standing in the corridor, he had felt her wariness, but then she had hidden her reaction behind anger. Whatever she had seen or heard, it had caused her to be more fearful of him than she already was. He could well imagine how her fifteenth-century mind would construe what she had witnessed. If he wasn't more careful, he was going to find himself the target of a witch hunt organized by Catherine herself.

Weary from too little sleep, too many worries, and the burden of responsibilities he had taken on himself, Collier rubbed a hand over his stubbled jaw. He needed a shave, but as there were no electric shavers or twin blade razors to be had in this century, it could probably wait a while.

With the sound of the sea breaking on the rocks below, he descended the wall-walk and returned to the keep.

Retaliation did not come in the form of a dagger in the back as Collier expected. Rather, it came in the guise of a load of stone being raised up a scaffold. Fortunately, some sixth sense warned him and he'd gotten out from beneath the falling stone in time. But though he'd escaped with only a few minor bruises and scrapes, the girl who'd been ladling water for the workers had not.

If only he had seen her, Collier wished past the terrible anger gnawing through him. Perhaps . . . he shook his head. He couldn't have reached her in time. She had been alive when they'd carried her to the keep, but if she lived much past the hour it would be a miracle.

He brushed a thumb over the frayed end of the rope. It had not been worn through, of that he was certain. Just as he was certain he knew who had cut it.

He raised his gaze to the mercenary on the wall. From the tense set of Walther's shoulders, he was as angered by what had happened as Collier—though only because it was the girl who had fallen victim to the "accident."

Collier's ire boiled. More than anything, he wanted to set upon the bastard—to beat him to a bloody pulp, then beat him again—but his arm . . .

Damn his arm! He took the steps two at a time to the wall-walk.

Walther turned as he approached, but though his eyes narrowed warily, he did not react in any outward way to the anger seething from Collier. "A pity," he drawled. "The girl was quite good with that pitcher of hers."

Collier swung, but it was Walther who landed the first blow. Sidestepping, he punched the hilt of his dagger into Collier's belly.

Adrenaline surging through Collier, he quickly recovered.

The mercenary waved the blade before him. "Come on, Gilchrist."

Though one arm was slung at his side, Collier hardly noticed as he lunged forward.

Walther braced his feet apart and swept the dagger toward his opponent.

Had Collier not seen it coming and moved to avoid it, the blade would have drawn blood. Instead, it drew air. Capturing the mercenary's wrist, Collier twisted the man's arm behind his back and forced him to release the dagger. It clattered to the walk between them.

"You killed her," Collier growled.

Walther strained forward. "What speak you of?"

Around the walls and in the bailey, the people stilled to witness their clash.

"You cut the rope," Collier said.

"You're mad, Gilchrist."

"And *you* are a murderer."

"I am a knight—of noble birth," Walter reminded Collier of his own lowliness. "I kill only in service to my king and God."

Collier pushed the man's arm higher. "And yourself," he said.

Walther grunted. Then, suddenly, he wrenched sideways.

Having the use of only one arm was what lost Collier the advantage, but before the mercenary could pull his sword from its scabbard, Collier was upon him. He found only minor satisfaction in the crack of Walther's nose beneath his fist, but he was not finished with him.

Spewing curses, Walther retaliated with a punch that was meant for Collier's jaw, but landed to his shoulder.

Then it was Collier's turn again. Without regard to the ground below, he fought Walther along the wall-walk. As a knight's training emphasized the use of arms and horsemanship, rather than hand-to-hand combat, the mercenary's blows were mostly ineffective. Thus, Collier endeavored to stay near enough to Walther so he would be unable to draw his sword as he tried to time and again.

It was just such an attempt which proved Walther's undoing. Stumbling back, he seized his sword hilt, but in the next instant lost his balance.

Reflexively, Collier caught hold of Walther's belt, preventing him from plunging to the bailey below.

His mouth gaping and eyes large with disbelief, Walther teetered on the edge of the wall-walk. The fall would not likely mean his death, but surely grave injury.

"I want you gone from Strivling," Collier said.

Walther looked to the ground below, swallowed, then turned his gaze on Collier. "And if I refuse?"

"My hand might just slip."

Walther searched for the truth in Collier's eyes. Then, enmity darkening his face, he said, "I will leave."

"Immediately."

"Aye."

Collier yanked him back onto the wall-walk.

Walther was quick to put distance between himself and the fall he had nearly taken. "'Twas by Lord Montagu's hand that I was put here to watch over his men," he said.

Collier motioned two soldiers forward. "I know, and I will answer to him if he questions your absence. But I do not think he will."

Walther glanced to the advancing soldiers. "It does not end here, Gilchrist," he warned.

No, it didn't. "Accompany Sir Griffin to the stables to retrieve his horse," Collier instructed the soldiers. "He is leaving." He turned and strode to the steps.

Having observed Montagu's soldiers these past days, Collier knew which man would best do the job Walther had thought beneath him—a lean, sparsely-bearded soldier named Peter Duby.

Collier called to him, and in the time it took to apprise Duby of his new duties, Walther was mounted. A moment later, the mercenary spurred his horse over the drawbridge.

"You have made the right decision, Sir Collier," Duby said.

Collier looked sideways at him. "How is that?"

"A Yorkist Walther may call himself, but he still stinks of the Lancastrians."

Had he heard right? "He was on the side of the Lancasters?" Collier asked.

"You did not know?"

"No."

"Ere he pledged himself to King Edward, it was Henry he stood beside."

"Then he turned."

"Aye, once he realized there was no advantage to remaining a Lancastrian. 'Tis the way of many who were once loyal to Henry. But you know that."

Collier did, though he'd never considered Walther's roots might go back to the Lancastrians. Still, it made sense.

Duby squinted at the horse and rider in the distance. "I would not be surprised if next we see him across a battlefield," he muttered.

Catherine felt as if she were breaking into a thousand pieces. After all the deaths she had witnessed with dry eyes and stubborn resolve, this one proved too much. Sitting back on her heels, she stared through tears as Tilly pulled the blanket over Sara's bruised and cut face.

They had been unable to do anything for the girl. For what had seemed hours, Sara had gripped Catherine's hand and cried out her suffering. Then, suddenly, she had collapsed back onto the straw pallet and expelled her last breath.

"She is at peace, my lady," the old woman said.

Catherine shook her head. "There is no peace, Tilly."

Tilly laid a hand to her shoulder. "But of course there is. God's hands are gentle. In them, Sara knows no pain. She is as free as a bird."

"She is dead!" Catherine shoved herself to her feet. "If not for Edward and the ungodly men who bloodied a path for him to the throne, she would be alive."

"'Twas an accident, my lady."

Catherine's laughter was forced. "'Twas by no accident that hole was put in the wall that it would need repair. Montagu did that. For Edward."

Tilly sighed. "Ah, my lady, such is life—"

"Life has naught to do with it!" Catherine cried. Then she lowered her voice. "I am sorry, Tilly. I do not mean to be harsh with you."

The old woman inclined her head, causing the odd lock of dark hair amongst the silver to spring onto her brow. Hurriedly, she tucked it beneath her head covering. "Perhaps you should lie down, my lady."

"Nay. There is too much to—"

The doors opened, and Catherine swung around.

As Gilchrist strode across the hall, he said naught, nor did he look anywhere but at the prone figure before the hearth.

As if he cared, Catherine silently scorned. He who raised walls against her people for his usurping king. Who cared not if it was one who died or a thousand. Her animosity burgeoning, it was not until he was nearly upon her that she noticed the cuts and bruises marring his face, neck, and hands. Although the men who had carried Sara to the keep had said something about Gilchrist having been near when the stone had fallen, they had not mentioned he'd sustained injuries himself.

He halted before Sara and stood there a long time looking at the forlorn figure beneath the blanket. When finally he turned, there was regret on his face. "I am sorry," he said.

Trying to hate him even though some part of her rebelled, Catherine stared at him. "It should have been you."

She did not know how true the words she spoke, Collier thought. However, his next thought was like a slap in the face. Or did she know? He remembered Duby's revelation regarding Walther. Although in history the mercenary had killed Catherine, was it possible that in this past they had united to oust the Yorkists from Strivling—starting with Collier? Many were the times he had caught Walther watching Catherine, but never had he seen the two talking. But that did not mean they hadn't.

"Griffin Walther is gone," he said. "I have sent him from Strivling."

The anger in her eyes leapt higher. Anger. Not dismay. Either she acted well, or knew nothing of what Walther had planned.

"Think you I care what you do with your men?" she demanded.

"Don't you?"

"What are you asking, Gilchrist?"

He glanced to where the old maid stood with a worried brow and knit hands, then back to Catherine. "It was Walther who cut the rope that loosed the stone."

Her eyes widened. "Then it was no accident?"

"No accident. As you said, it should have been me, not Sara."

Catherine stared blankly at him, then realization struck. "You think I . . ." Color surged into her cheeks. "I am not like you, Collier Gilchrist! I have no deaths upon my conscience. I—"

Just as suddenly, her words fell into nothingness and the fire in her eyes extinguished. As if gone to some other place in her mind, she stared through Collier. Then, her shoulders sagging, she turned and slowly walked to the stairs.

Feeling her pain, Collier started to follow, but the old woman's hand upon his arm stayed him.

"Sara was a favorite of hers," she said. "She needs to be alone, sire."

It went beyond the girl's death, Collier knew—just

as he knew Catherine would not welcome him anywhere near her at this time. If ever. "Could you bring
me some hot water and a towel?" he asked. "And
salve?"

"At once, sire."

Collier rubbed a weary hand over his eyes. God, he
hoped he was wrong about Catherine. He prayed she
did not hate him that much.

No deaths upon her conscience.

Aching from the hours she had spent on her knees
in the chapel, Catherine rolled onto her back and
stared at the darkened ceiling of her chamber.

Nay, her conscience was not clear. More than
Montagu, she was responsible for those who had died
during the siege. Too many to number. Even had
Strivling stood with the giving of their lives, their
deaths were still too great a price to pay.

She squeezed her eyes closed. What had she done?
What had driven her to such madness?

Your woman's heart is showing, Hildegard's
reproving words drifted to her from the past. *Be
strong, Catherine. For God, King Henry, and me.*

Catherine tried not to hear the voice, but it kept
playing louder in her head until she had no choice but
to attend to it. Clenching her hands on the coverlet,
she slid back into the woman Hildegard had groomed
her to become.

She would be strong, and soon—very soon—she
would fulfill the vow she had made.

12

Soon did not arrive soon enough for Catherine. Every opportunity that came her way was hindered in some way or another—be it Gilchrist's presence or the needs of the castle folk. But now, more than a fortnight since the end of the siege, she had her chance.

As Gilchrist had left the hall to check on the progress of the work on Strivling's walls, she would have at least an hour to do what needed to be done, and likely more.

She pulled on boots that had belonged to her betrothed, the toes of which she had stuffed to make them fit, then snatched up her gown and drew it on over her tunic and breeches. As she fastened it closed, her gaze was drawn to the bed.

She had dreamed again last eve. Though the dream had been frightening enough to awaken her, she could not remember any of it. But surely it was a portent of ill.

Most of her dreams began the same way—indistinct, but with each passing night growing more detailed and memorable. Then there were also those dreams that never fully took shape, but were soon followed by misfortune.

She wished she could remember last night's dream. But even if she could, there was naught she could do to change it. Gilchrist could, though . . .

Not wanting to think about it anymore, Catherine left her chamber and descended to the hall. Upon entering the corridor that led to the kitchens, she saw that the door to the storeroom stood open.

Disquiet settled over her. The last barrel of ale and sacks of grain had been carried to the kitchens yesterday. What business had anyone in there when there were no more stores to be had? Had her secret been found out?

Holding her breath, Catherine stepped into the doorway. The upper level of the storeroom was empty but for the trapdoor flung open in the middle of the room, and the rope pulley dangling above it. Could it be—

"There will be fine," the cook's voice drifted up to her. "Stack it neatly."

Catherine sighed. Her secret was safe. The stores Gilchrist had purchased must have arrived. Unfortunately, the timing was poor—at least, for Catherine. As she could not do what needed to be done in the presence of others, once again she was thwarted. Of course, if the stores were quickly put away, she might still make it. She descended to the lower room of the storeroom.

The cook spotted her immediately. "My lady," he said, his face lit with excitement, "the supplies have arrived just as Sir Collier said they would." He was tired of trying to make substance of water, pathetic vegetables, and grains.

"So they have," Catherine said, her gaze drawn to the two villagers who were stacking sacks of milled grain in a shadowed corner. "Nay," she said, stepping forward, "stack it against that wall." She pointed opposite.

Their breathing labored, both men looked around. "But my lady," one huffed, beads of perspiration standing out on his brow, "there must be fifty or more sacks here."

At least a dozen of which she would have to move if they did not. "'Tis too dark there," she attempted an explanation. Feeble. "I wish you to move them."

"Leave them," Gilchrist's voice filled the room.

Catherine spun around.

He stood on the stairs, the sling which had heretofore held his injured arm absent.

"They would be better against the other wall," she said. These were her first words to him since Sara's death, when he had accused her of seeking his demise.

His gaze was hard on her. "And how is that?"

"It . . ." Though she wanted to argue the matter, she could think of no excuse, and to do so would likely rouse his suspicions further. "As you would have it." Avoiding Gilchrist's gaze, she brushed past him.

On the upper floor of the storeroom, two men knelt alongside the trapdoor. They secured the rope around the barrel between them, then began working the pulley to lower the stores to the floor below.

Catherine slipped into the kitchens. As the kitchen maids were abuzz with excitement over the prospect of preparing a meal worthy of their attention, they paid her little heed, and when the cook returned a long half hour later, Catherine slipped out.

No light shone from beneath the door of the storeroom.

There was time, she assured herself. There had to be, for this could be the last chance she had. Taking a torch with her, she entered the storeroom and pulled the door closed.

Damned northern weather, Collier thought as he shifted his shoulders beneath the short mantle. He looked from the merchant's wagons rumbling over the drawbridge to the darkening skies. It wouldn't be the first time work in the bailey had to be suspended to allow a storm to pass over, and, doubtless, it wouldn't be the last.

Wondering how long before it rained, he absently thumbed a silver groat—the coin being all that was left of the purse he had paid the merchant from. Though he had expected repairs on the southern section of the wall to be completed before day's end, it was not going to happen now. He heaved a sigh and tossed the coin high into the air.

As he watched it turn head over tail, a vision of Catherine standing in the storeroom flashed before him. Why had she wanted the grain moved across the room? She had seemed so desperate.

Losing momentum, the coin began its descent.

What did it matter whether the grain was stacked in the corner, or—

The coin.

In the dust of Collier's flight, the groat fell to the ground.

Over the inner drawbridge he ran, past the surprised

stares of the castle folk, and up the steps to the keep. With his entrance, the servants within the hall looked up from their work. "Where is Lady Catherine?" he demanded.

"'Tis some time since I have seen her, sir," a woman said.

The man servant shook his head. "Neither have I seen her."

Cursing, Collier ran to the storeroom.

Although the upper floor was darkened, light flickered up the stairway. Relief washed over him. She was still down there. And so was Strivling's wealth. Hurriedly, he descended the stairs, but it was only to be faced with a storeroom empty but for the supplies stacked against its walls. No Catherine—unless she had heard him coming and hidden.

"Catherine," he called to her.

Silence.

Collier settled his gaze to the grain she had protested the placement of. Standing in shadows, they appeared untouched.

Had he guessed wrong? Or had he simply come too late? Though he questioned whether Catherine was strong enough to move the grain, one thing was certain—she was determined enough to try. Of course, with so many loyal to her, she would not have to look far for assistance.

Collier retrieved the torch and strode across the room. Even with light upon it, the stacked grain looked the same as it had when the workers had laid the last atop the pile—until he stood directly before it. Only then did he notice that the torchlight fell deeper against the back corner of the wall. As if—

"Holy rood!" he swore, unaware he had substituted

a curse of the Middle Ages for his twentieth-century profanity. Taking the torch with him, he climbed atop the grain.

From the ground up, the back corner of the wall had been cleared to a width of three feet—enough for Catherine to fit down into to retrieve the coin and household valuables she intended to deliver to the Lancastrians.

Guessing it to have been hidden beneath one of the stones in the floor, Collier directed the light down into the space. But it was not a loosened stone that came to light. It was a wadded gown, and from the color of it, it was the same one Catherine had worn earlier.

Collier groaned. It seemed the castle's secret passages did not end at the hall. There was another, and though he had never heard tell of it, he had little doubt it led outside the walls. Meaning Catherine was leaving—and taking Strivling's wealth with her.

Wondering how much of a start she had on him, Collier dropped down into the space. As the torchlight revealed nothing out of the ordinary, he pounded a fist against the stone wall. A moment later, he heard it—a hollow sound. At least he knew where the door was.

He peered at the surrounding mortar. It seemed intact. He pushed against the stones, but they were as ungiving as the rest of the wall. A catch, then—a release of some sort. He searched a hand over the stones, but found nothing.

Think! he ordered himself, aware that with each passing moment Catherine grew more distant.

The catch would be separate, though nearby. Obvious, yet disguised as something other than its true purpose. He swept his gaze upward. To the left was a wall sconce. It certainly belonged in this darkened corner, but that might just be the beauty of it.

Hoping he was right, Collier stood. He pushed on it. Nothing. He pushed harder. Still nothing. He pulled.

The door swung inward.

Wasting no time, Collier shoved the torch through the opening and crawled in after it. He straightened. Cut from the rock Strivling had been erected on, the landing was five feet wide, and like a funnel, narrowed toward what appeared to be a shaft.

It *was* a shaft, Collier soon discovered, complete with crudely-fashioned steps that wound an inordinately steep path downward. It was a good thing he wasn't claustrophobic.

He descended the stairs as fast as his footing would allow. He turned sharply left, right, then left again. With portions of the stone steps having broken away, it was treacherous going, and worsened the deeper he went.

Catherine had obviously prepared for this arduous trek, Collier thought, remembering the gown she'd left behind.

So how much farther? And what was her destination? He had his answer a short while later when the muffled roar of what could only be the sea reached him. Did a boat await her? Was she aboard and heading into waters that would soon be tossed by the storm stirring overhead?

God, let him reach her first, he prayed. Recklessly, he quickened his pace. The steps turned twice more. Then, suddenly, the landing appeared below—and surging over it was the incoming tide.

It could not get any worse.

Emerging from the shaft into chilly, ankle-deep

water, Collier had to stoop to accommodate the low ceiling of the cavern. He paused only a moment to survey his surroundings.

No, it could definitely get worse, he corrected himself. Much worse. The floor of the cavern sloped up from the shaft, meaning that very soon the entrance to the passageway would be flooded. Sealed off.

"Catherine!" Collier shouted. It was useless. Even if she heard him, she would not answer.

In the flickering light cast by the torch, he ran up the incline to where the floor of the cavern leveled off. Here, the ceiling rose allowing him to straighten. He glanced at the moist walls. They reflected the light of his torch, but not of day, meaning the entrance to the cavern lay distant.

Using the sound of the sea to guide him, Collier negotiated the twists and bends of the cavern as the deepening tide crept up his legs. Finally, daylight appeared ahead.

With the water swirling around his calves, Collier searched the expanse before him. It cut a gently curving path to the entrance of the cavern beyond which the sea lay. But very soon the sea was going to fill this place, and then retreat would be impossible. If it was not already. . . .

Ahead, against the left wall of the cavern, a light suddenly appeared. Collier peered at the silhouetted figure laboriously wading through the water. It had to be Catherine. Under the circumstances, he almost wished she had made it to the boat. To be on the water in such weather would be dangerous, but to be in the cavern might prove more so.

"Catherine!" he shouted.

The light jerked, then it extinguished. Even with the tide rising steadily around her, she had no intention of abandoning her objective.

Did she believe the boat would still be waiting for her? Collier wondered. Had she not earlier been thwarted by the delivery of the food supplies, she would have made it, but now . . . no, the boat was surely gone.

Berating himself for having alerted her to his presence, Collier threw down the torch and thrust through the water. It hindered him, but at least he was not also burdened by that which Catherine sought to put into the hands of the Lancasters. Not until the water had risen to the middle of his thighs did he catch sight of her again.

Moving among the shadows near the entrance of the cavern, she struggled against the tide and the weight of the chest she dragged behind her.

Collier corrected his course, and a moment later heard her labored breathing above the waves breaking on the rocks outside.

She was within arm's reach when she jerked her head around. With a cry of distress that echoed around the cavern, she relinquished her burden and lurched away.

Collier grabbed her, but the sleeve of her tunic slipped through his fingers. In the next instant, she lost her footing and disappeared beneath the water. He plunged his arms into the cold tide, caught hold of her, and pulled her upright.

Although drenched and shaking with cold, Catherine struck at him, twisted side to side, kicked, and tried to slam her knee into his groin.

Collier dragged her against him. "Stop this, Catherine! We haven't much time."

Her teeth grazed his hand, but before she could sink them into him, he jerked his arm away and wrapped it around her waist.

"Let me go!" she shouted.

"Listen to me. The passageway is going to be flooded if we do not—"

"'Tis already flooded!"

He wasn't surprised. "With that storm in the making, your boat is long gone, Catherine."

She stilled. "My boat?"

Her deliberate obtuseness angered him. "You are telling me you were not leaving—taking the money with you to give to your beloved Lancasters?"

She turned her head.

Even caught red-handed, she was not going to admit it. But they were wasting precious time. "We have to get to higher ground," Collier said.

"There is only th-the sea." Catherine's teeth chattered. "Swim, if you think y-you can make it."

If the entrance to this cavern was the outcropping of rock below Strivling that jutted out into the water, then swimming was going to prove difficult. In fact, Collier doubted it was an option. But what else was there?

He tipped Catherine's chin up. "And you," he said, "can you make it?"

"If I were going with you, but I am not."

Meaning there had to be another way out, and she was not going to tell him where it was. But he was not about to argue the matter. He began pulling her toward the cavern opening.

"What do you intend?" she cried, struggling against him.

"We are going out there, Catherine, and we are going to swim." And if a higher being truly existed, perhaps they would make it to the shore. If not, they would drown as surely as if they remained here. There was nothing to lose.

"I cannot swim," Catherine said.

No other words could have stopped him as surely as those. "Another lie, Catherine?"

Her fear was tangible. "You go. I c-cannot."

Collier shook his head. "Not without you."

"What do you care what becomes of me—a woman whom you believe tried to murder you?"

Had she? Collier wondered. Though her face was shadowed, he picked out the familiar planes of the one who had welcomed his touch in another time and place. "As I told you, I came a very long way to find you. I am not leaving you now." Explanation enough. It was time to go.

"There is another way," Catherine blurted.

Collier looked over his shoulder. "Where?"

She pointed toward the cavern opening. "A ledge lies above. We can wait out the tide there."

That or fight her fear of the water which might see both of them drowned. "Show me," Collier said.

She resisted his pull. "What of the chest?"

He had forgotten about it. What had been its fate in that other past? he wondered again. Wherever Catherine had hidden the chest before she had died, it would have remained there until discovered by someone else. As its contents were likely valuable enough to have an impact on this civil war, it was imperative that it be put back in its original hiding place.

"I will carry it," Collier said. He released Catherine and bent to search for the chest beneath the water. He found it easily enough, but the damned thing proved far heavier than expected—and not just from the water seeping into it, he warranted. No wonder Catherine had dragged it. Gritting his teeth, he hefted it. "Lead the way," he said.

To the left of the cavern opening, they climbed

steps cut from rock. Though not as steep as those in the shaft, they proved nearly as treacherous. Somehow, they made it to the ledge without mishap.

It was dark here, but the sound of Catherine's breathing guided Collier to her. Gratefully, he set the chest down, then lowered himself beside her.

For a long moment neither spoke, then Catherine asked, "How did you know?"

"About?"

"The passageway."

"You are considerate toward the servants," Collier said. "I could not help but wonder why you were suddenly eager to commit them to more work than was necessary."

Water breaking hard against the cavern opening rained droplets on them.

"So you c-came looking for me." Catherine's teeth chattered again.

Collier reached for her, but she snatched her arm away. "Do not!"

"You're chilled, Catherine," he tried to reason with her. "I am also wet, but I can warm you."

She scooted farther down the wall. "I am sure you would like to, b-but I do not need, nor want, your *warmth*."

He could force the issue, but Catherine, not unlike most twentieth-century women, would not appreciate being manhandled. He looked to the floor of the cavern. The darkening day reflected its light upon the surface, showing it to be alive with the incoming tide. A tide that was steadily rising. How safe were they? he wondered. Was it possible the tide would rise to this ledge that was all the refuge to be had in this cavern? He would have to watch it closely.

Catherine huddled deeper into herself—clasping

her knees to her chest and burying her face against them in an attempt to prevent the chills from shaking her apart. It was useless, though. Each chill came harder than the last, jarring her from wet scalp to toes that had lost nearly all sensation. She'd been cold before, but never like this. Only in her dreams had she ever known such pain. But she would not turn to Gilchrist.

He touched her shoulder. "Catherine."

I will not, she reminded herself as a wave hit outside the cavern and sprayed water on her.

"Let me help you."

His breath was so warm in her ear—like the sun breaking through a clouded winter day. She was weak. God, how she hated herself for being weak. Hildegard would have let herself die of the cold before she would ever have allowed her enemy so near her.

"Catherine," he said again.

She lifted her head, but rather than turn him away as she should have, said, "'Tis so"—she gasped—"cold."

A moment later, she was on Collier's lap and his arms were around her. "You are a stubborn woman, Catherine Algernon," he whispered against her wet hair.

She melted into his warmth. Though his clothes were damp, he exuded a heat that made her want to bury herself in him forever. She pressed her face against his chest and slid her arms around him.

He pulled his mantle over her.

The chills began to recede, but when Catherine's body finally calmed, she still could not bring herself to heed the warnings whispering through her. Just for this moment, she vowed, then never again. Tomorrow Gilchrist would be her enemy the same as before.

He stroked a hand down her back, as if she were a child in need of comforting.

It soothed her—deafened her to even the loudest inner voices which spoke against her being in this man's arms.

Lightly, he trailed his fingers up her neck, then down again.

A strange tremble skipped through her. She had never been touched as Gilchrist touched her, but she could not find it in her to stop him—not even when he lifted her chin and found her mouth in the dark.

Wine. That was how he tasted. Heady. A slow trickle that kindled her senses and warmed places she had not known were cold.

"I won't lose you again," he spoke against her lips.

How strange the things he said.

He urged her mouth open and touched his tongue to hers.

Although the contact had shocked Catherine when he had kissed her in her chamber, this time it roused her. Clasping his softly-bearded face between her hands, she tentatively drew her tongue over his, then pressed it into his mouth and tasted the smooth flesh of his inner lips.

A fine mist fell coolly to her upturned face.

What was this? she wondered, her breasts beginning to ache and her woman's place beginning to stir. Was it that thing she had heard servants speak of in hushed tones? That which put smiles on faces, light in eyes, and songs on lips? Which Hildegard had said was beneath noblewomen? Which only whores felt?

Always there was Hildegard to answer to.

The light within Catherine sputtered and died. It was not anger she felt, but remorse—and a certain sadness. Her life was not her own, and never would it be. She pulled back and searched out the light of Gilchrist's eyes. "You cannot lose what you have never had," she said, his words returning to her as if he had just spoken them.

He was slow to respond, but when he did, it was with another of his riddles. "But I did have you . . . once."

What did he mean? Was he of the devil as she feared—or simply mad?

He laid a hand to her cheek. "You are not leaving Strivling, Catherine. Not without me."

Sweet mother of Jesus, how she wanted to turn her mouth to his palm. The admission pained her nearly as much as that which she had allowed him to do to her. She swallowed, then said, "There was no boat."

"No boat?"

She shook her head, and in doing so brushed her lower lip across his thumb. Her breath caught.

"Then what did you intend?" he asked. "To swim with that chest on your back when you profess not to know how to?"

"'Tis true, I cannot."

"Then?"

It hardly mattered if he knew now. As he had discovered the passageway, the cavern would be of no more use to the Lancastrian cause. "I was going to leave the chest on this ledge."

"And?"

"Get word to the Lancasters that they might send a boat for it."

"Then you were not leaving?"

"To do so would endanger my family," she said, reminding him of Montagu's threat. "I would not have them punished for my actions."

"It is not as if you know them," he pointed out.

True. Hildegard had become mother, father, brother, and sister to her, making those of her own blood strangers. "Nay, but I remember them," she said, "and I remember having loved them." Sorrow rising from the vague memories of her early childhood, she tried to turn back the unwanted emotions. "Do you not have family yourself, Gilchrist?"

His silence spoke louder than any words he might have uttered. He answered to no one. His life was his own.

Beginning to feel the cold again, Catherine shivered. "I am resigned to marriage to you, Gilchrist," she said, then added, "until King Henry takes his throne again." She had to believe he would.

Gilchrist sighed harshly. "His reign is over, Catherine. You will see." He pulled her down against his chest and closed his arms around her.

She thought about resisting him, but his warmth was too welcome. "You are wrong," she said.

Gilchrist did not argue the matter.

13

They could not stay.

Having turned to the wall to shield Catherine from the spray, Collier stared over his shoulder at the dark waters churning less than four feet below. Hardly had the tide begun to ebb when a wave crashed against the cavern opening, sending water streaming down Collier's face.

They had to leave. And now.

He shook Catherine's shoulder.

She stirred, muttered something, and nestled deeper against him.

"Catherine," he said sharply, "you must awaken."

She lifted her head. "Collier?"

Obviously, she was too drowsy to realize she called him by his first name. "We have to leave. The water is nearing the top of the entrance."

Her silence stretched as if she struggled for her bearings, then she rose from his lap and looked out over the ledge. "Surely it will not rise anymore," she said, hopeful.

Collier stood beside her. "Perhaps, but if it does, we will be trapped."

"But we needn't leave." Desperation crept into her voice. "We can stay here until the water recedes."

"It could reach this ledge—and even higher. By that time, it will be too late to get out."

She turned to him. "'Twill not rise this high." There was pleading in her voice for him to agree with her.

"You don't know that, Catherine. We have to leave."

"I cannot swim!"

Collier pulled her toward him. "Perhaps we won't have to."

"What?"

"All you have to do is hold tight to me. Understand? Hold on to me, Catherine."

She was trembling again.

"Catherine?"

"I am afraid, Collier."

She had every reason to be. Even he, a strong swimmer, might not be able to resist the currents of this storm. But they had no other choice. "I won't fail you," he said. "I swear." God, let him not fail her as he had Aryn.

A breath shuddered from her. "I will hold to you."

He slid his hand down her arm and intertwined his fingers with hers. "Let's go."

Choosing his footing carefully over the slick rock, Collier guided Catherine across the ledge. The first three steps down were above water, but beyond that lay the surging tide. As Collier pulled Catherine after him into the stingingly cold water, she gasped and strained backward.

"It's the only way," he said.

He felt her indecision. Her fear. Then she yielded.

The water welcomed them to its depths, rising around their thighs, hips, and chests as if to swallow them. Given the chance, it would.

With one hand, Collier secured a firm grip on the step above, and with the other, turned Catherine to face him.

She shuddered.

"Put your arms around my neck," he ordered.

She complied.

The water supporting most of her weight, Collier searched along the cavern wall and found his first handhold, and a moment later, a foothold beneath the tide. It was something he had done hundreds of times before, his passion for rock climbing having driven him to challenge mountain after mountain, cliff after cliff, and even a glacier or two, but never had he done it submerged in water with a current dragging at him. Nor with an arm hindered by its recent injury.

He slowly worked his way toward the cavern opening, stopping only to press himself and Catherine to the wall when the larger waves hit. Twice he lost a handhold, and three times a foothold, but he quickly regained them. Fortunately, the water was more forgiving than the heights he was accustomed to. Far more forgiving, he thought as memories of his accident rolled out of the recesses of his mind. He forced them back.

Throughout, Catherine was silent, the only evidence of her presence being bouts of shivering which were coming closer and closer together.

She was in the beginning stages of hypothermia, Collier realized. He'd seen it before, and even experienced it himself. Though he was warmed by the effort of traversing the wall and maintaining his holds, there was nothing to warm Catherine. He had to get her out of here.

The currents became more treacherous near the cavern opening. They thrust Collier side to side and bloodied his fingers where he clung to the rock. Although years of free climbing had toughened his hands to the point where he hadn't had to tape them for his climbs, since the accident, his fingers and palms had softened. And now he was feeling the pain.

Focus, he commanded himself. *Concentrate.*

With every chance, he maneuvered nearer the opening, and finally they were on the other side. An instant later, an incoming wave slammed into him. It forced him against Catherine, and her against the rock.

She cried out.

"We're nearly there," he assured her. "Keep holding on."

How near were they? he wondered. He lifted his face into the slashing rain. As he had guessed, the cavern was located at the tip of the rock that jutted out into the sea. High atop that cliff Strivling Castle perched unaware. Even were it a clear day, Collier knew it was not likely any on the walls would notice them clinging to the rock below. They were on their own.

He braced himself for the next wave, and after it battered his body, looked to where the shore should have been. It was not. The sea had claimed it as well. That left only this rain-swept outcropping. But he could not scale it. Alone he could, but not with Catherine. He would have to work his way around to the side of the rock and pray there was a way up from there.

"Ready, Catherine?"

She shivered hard against him.

"Look at me."

Not surprisingly, she was slow to respond—sluggish—and when she raised her face from his shoulder there was such confusion there, it could only mean she was worsening.

Another wave hit.

Fiercely setting his mind to what he must do to keep his vow to her, Collier blocked out the pain of his bloodied fingers, his strained arms, and his burning injury. He would not fail her.

The sea was cruel. It pounded at him, drenched him repeatedly, and time and again tore his fingers from the rock, but for Catherine he kept going. Finally, they made it around to the side of the out-cropping.

Collier's searching gaze settled on a shelf of rock that lay thirty feet ahead. In that moment, he could almost have said he believed in God. He turned his mouth to Catherine's ear. "Not much farther," he assured her, and reached for a crack in the rock.

It was easier going along the side, but still the forces of nature tested him. In the end, he proved himself. "We're there, Catherine."

She lifted her head. "There?" Her face was cast gray and lips tinged blue. Time was running out.

Fear gripping him, Collier maneuvered her around. "I'll help you up."

"Up?" she echoed. Then, realizing he meant for her to climb onto the shelf of rock, she shook her head. "Nay, I c-cannot."

"Of course you can."

"Nay."

If not for the handhold he must maintain, he would

have shaken her. "You are Catherine Algernon," he said. "Catherine Algernon can do it."

As if she had forgotten, she blinked, and a moment later, nodded.

Collier shielded her against the next wave. When it withdrew, he released a handhold and began boosting her upward. It proved more difficult than expected. Having only the one arm to assist her, his leverage was poor. Worse, she was so stiff with cold her grasping hands were unable to find the purchase needed to pull her onto the shelf. He could not help her anymore, though, for if he let go of the rock, the sea would too eagerly welcome him to its depths.

"That's it, Catherine," he urged her.

She struggled to raise herself, and just when it looked hopeless, finally pulled her torso onto the shelf.

But not soon enough. Another swell was coming. Collier did not need to look around to know its size, for it was there in the roar preceding it.

"Damn!" he cursed. Knowing Catherine would be swept away, he tightened his hold on her and started to pull her down. Too late.

The water crashed around them.

He heard Catherine's scream the moment before she was torn from him.

The brutal sea proved itself a thousand times over.

With terror closing around his heart, Collier shouted, "Catherine!"

The rent wave lurched backward, laying a path for the others rising up in the distance. But there was no sign of Catherine.

"NO!" Collier bellowed. He was not going to lose her again.

He had only just loosened his hold on the rock

when she surfaced ten feet out. Her frantic gaze found his a moment before she went under again.

Although Collier's first instinct was to jump in after her, he struggled to think rationally. The only way to bring her to safety was to stay where he was. Otherwise, they would both be hurled against the rocks.

A moment later, she appeared again—five feet away. The water rushing ahead of the swells had carried her nearer as Collier had prayed they would, but it also meant he had only seconds to reach her before she was caught up in the force of the wave. It was the only chance he would have.

God, he silently entreated, *give me this and never again will I question your existence.* Gripping the rock, he threw out an arm.

Catherine called his name. Then, reaching for him, she sank beneath the surface. Her hand—fingers splayed wide—brushed Collier's.

"God!" he pleaded from the depths of his soul. Although he had thought himself stretched out as far as he could go, he stretched farther. And then he had her.

His fingers clenched around Catherine's, he dragged her through the water. "Hold on to me," he ordered as he sandwiched her between the wall and himself.

Coughing and sputtering, she wrapped her arms around his waist.

The wave struck just as he found his handhold again. When it drew back, there was no time to comfort or reassure Catherine. "We have to try again," he said.

He caught a glimpse of her face as he turned her toward the shelf. Though fear was etched there, she tried again. This time she made it onto the shelf, and Collier after her.

Wasting no time, he grabbed her arm and pulled her over the rough terrain. Catherine stumbled after him, but knowing she needed to move to ward off hypothermia, Collier gave her only enough support to prevent her falling.

Once they were clear of the threat of the sea, Collier stopped. The wind blowing stinging rain across them, he looked at Catherine.

She raised her gaze to his, and in her eyes he saw the tumult of emotions she had never cried out: Fear. Sorrow. Regret. Even anger. Then she took an uncertain step forward and fell into his arms.

He held her as warm tears soaked through his wet tunic. She sobbed, spoke things he could make no sense of, and clung to him as if he were life itself.

He let her cry, and when finally she calmed, pulled back. "We made it, Catherine."

She tried to smile, but the cold quivered the expression from her mouth.

"And now we need to find shelter. Can you go a bit farther?"

"Aye."

Although his mantle was soaked, Collier removed it and draped it over her shoulders. If nothing else, it would keep the wind off her.

As they picked their way over the rocks toward the cliff, Collier searched for some place that might shield them for the duration of the storm. There was none. But they couldn't last out here much longer—especially Catherine. He halted and looked up the face of the cliff. Right of center, the rock was rougher and heavily veined with cracks. Hand and footholds aplenty. But no harness. No rope. Nothing to catch him if he fell.

"Y-you are bleeding," Catherine stammered against the cold.

He followed her gaze to his hands. His fingers were raw from the handholds he had fought to keep. And they were going to bleed a lot more before he got them out of this mess. Odd how dull the pain was. "They will heal," he said, and turned his attention back to the cliff.

He was going up.

This time he could not turn the memories away. Reaching for the lip of rock overhead. Curling his fingers around it. Pulling himself up. The rock breaking away. Losing one foothold, then the other. Lurching downward. The harness tightening around him and the rope pulling taut. Then the link snapping . . .

When he had lain broken on a hospital bed, he had vowed his climbing days were over. That even if, by some miracle, his body was put back together, he would never face another rock.

Aryn had told him he would.

Pained by the memory, Collier opened and closed the hand of his injured arm. Would it hold him? It had to.

"Wh-what is it?" Catherine asked.

She was shivering again, and her color was poor.

Collier urged her to the base of the cliff and turned her to face him. "I have to leave. The only way—"

"Leave?" she repeated, disbelievingly.

"There is no adequate shelter, and it's only going to get colder."

"I don't un-understand."

He looked up the cliff. "I am going up there, and then I'll be back for you."

She shook her head. "How?"

"I am going to climb it, Catherine."

Eyes widening, she slid her gaze up the sheer rock wall. "You c-cannot climb that."

"I can."

Her teeth clicked together. "D-do not leave me, Collier. P-please."

He pulled the mantle closed around her. "I will return. I promise you."

Moisture gathering in her eyes, she lowered her head.

Collier tilted her face up. "Trust me, Catherine," he said, then covered her cold mouth with his. Something to warm both of them until he returned.

Although she did not respond as before, she leaned into him.

It was time to go. Collier drew back. "Soon you will be safe again," he promised.

She stared at him a moment, then started to lower herself to the rock.

Collier pulled her back up. "You have to keep moving. Walk, run in place, whatever you can do. Just keep moving. It will keep you warm. All right?"

Though her confusion was returning, she nodded.

Would she do it? Collier wondered. She looked too tired, but the sooner he got up the cliff, the sooner he could get her to safety. He swung away, but in the next instant turned back around. "And Catherine," he said, "even if you start to feel warm, do not remove any of your clothing." It wasn't uncommon for a person with hypothermia to develop a sensation of extreme warmth once they began to lose consciousness. "Understand?"

She nodded.

Feeling the cold, but knowing the climb would warm him, Collier walked to the cliff. He chose his first handholds, tested their strength, then found his footholds. At least there was one good thing about the thin-soled boots he had previously found so uncomfortable—they were flexible enough to allow him to feel the rock and bend to it. Providing he could stand against the elements, he could make it. God, he prayed he could make it.

Images of his last climb assailing him again, he squeezed his eyes closed. *Focus. Let nothing come between you and the rock. Just you and the rock.*

As Collier began his ascent, Catherine clutched the edges of the mantle together. So cold. What had Collier said? That if she kept moving she would stay warm? Her thoughts thick and muddled, she took a step forward, then another, but she was simply too stiff. And it hurt. Nay, he must have said she should not move. Of course.

She slid down the rock onto her haunches and peered up at Collier. He clung to the face of the rock fifteen feet above. Huddling there, Catherine watched this man who had changed her life more than once do the impossible. Of course, what he had done in bringing them out of the cavern had also seemed impossible. Now, without rope to gird him, he climbed steadily upward.

Was it magic? she wondered. Witchery? Of the devil? It didn't matter. All she wanted was for him to return—and to be warm again.

The wind whipped a strand of hair into her eyes. She lifted a hand to push it aside, but her fingers ached unbearably. Shivering, she began rocking herself back and forth.

A short while later, she watched as Collier attempted to make it over a ledge of rock. He leaned out with an outstretched arm, gripped the ledge, grabbed it with the other hand, then brought a foot up and began pulling himself over it. A moment later, he disappeared from sight.

Never before in her life had Catherine felt as alone as she did at that moment. But at least she had stopped shivering, and was finally beginning to warm. Much better.

Fatigue dragged at her lids. Perhaps she would sleep the time away until Collier returned. Aye, that's what she would do, and when next she opened her eyes, he would be here. Just as he had promised.

Her lids fluttered closed. *Ah, sweet mother of Jesus*, she was tired. So very tired.

It was nothing short of a miracle that Collier was sighted three-quarters of the way up the cliff—just as he had summoned the last of his strength. Sending profuse thanks heavenward, he watched the coil of rope plummet toward him.

It landed well out of reach.

He could climb to it, Collier told himself. He had come this far, so what was ten feet more? He looked to where the soldier, Peter Duby, leaned out over the battlements, nodded, then began traversing the wall.

His hands throbbing painfully, he jammed his fingers into a crack, secured them in the tight space, and changed footholds. Still, he was several feet from the rope, and the next available handhold was a long reach away. He stood up on his toes and pulled his body close in to the rock to attain maximum extension, but it was not enough.

His heart pounding harder, he acknowledged there was only one way he could make it to the handhold. A dynamic move. For an accomplished climber, it was a common enough move and carried little risk—providing your equipment was good and the one controlling your rope was alert. But he had neither. If he didn't make it, he was going to take a fall that no amount of medical expertise could save him from.

Catherine was waiting for him.

Collier forced his thoughts to a singular focus, then lunged. At the "dead point," the apex of his movement when his body was weightless for a split second before falling, he grabbed the handhold. It held. Heaving a sigh of relief, he jammed the thumb and index finger of his other hand into a thin crack and "smeared" both his feet against the rock. Once stable, he reached for the rope and quickly secured it around his waist.

"Only a few more minutes, Catherine," he said, and looked up the cliff face to the wall where Peter Duby awaited his signal. Collier made eye contact. Then, knowing he would not be heard above the wind and rain, he pointed down.

The soldier cocked his head questioningly.

Collier nodded and pointed again. Time was too precious to waste on being pulled up to offer an explanation. Duby and the others would understand soon enough.

Slowly, the rope began to feed out.

Now came the easy part. Pushing off, Collier rappelled downward, landed his booted feet to the rock, then pushed off again. And so it went, all the way down the cliff face. As he neared the bottom, he picked out Catherine's huddled figure. All through the climb he had refused to look down, knowing that to do so would break his concentration, but he had known he would find her like this.

Reaching the ground, he quickly removed the rope

and ran toward her. He called her name, but she didn't respond. Head bent to her knees, she sat propped against the rock.

His heart constricted. She was all right, he assured himself. Just cold and tired. He crouched beside her and lifted her chin. "Catherine?"

Her head lolled on her neck, and though her skin was icy, she did not shiver. Her body had given up trying to warm itself.

Pain opened up within Collier—the same which had overcome him when he had learned Aryn was dead.

Not Catherine. No.

He bent his ear to her mouth, and in the time it took to detect her breathing, did not draw breath himself. There it was. Thready, but present. Time had not run out.

Collier fashioned a seat harness from the rope—loops for his legs, a sling beneath his buttocks, and secured around his waist. Gently cradling Catherine against his chest, he gave the rope a jerk.

The slack was drawn up immediately and their journey upward began. Knowing that, in Catherine's state, her heart might snap at the slightest jolt, Collier carefully walked his legs up the rock.

One more miracle, he prayed. One more.

14

He was done waiting.

Thrusting the door open, Collier stepped into the warm chamber.

The three women looked up from where they bent over the tub.

"You should not be in here, Sir Collier," Tilly said, rising.

He looked past her to where Catherine was supported in the bath by the two other women. Still she had not regained consciousness. "Anything?" he asked.

Tilly folded her hands over her abdomen. "She has warmed, and her breathing is deeper."

He walked farther into the room.

The old woman stepped into his path. "Our lady is not presentable. You ought to leave, sire."

Collier looked down at her. "She is to be my wife."

"Aye, to be, but is not yet."

Did she think him a rapist the same as Catherine? "I assure you, your lady's virtue is in no danger."

Tilly pressed a hand to his arm. "There will be talk."

"Let there be." He strode to the tub and, ignoring the nervous stirrings of the maids, knelt beside it. At least color had returned to Catherine's face. He lifted a hand to touch her, but remembering his fingers were bandaged, laid his cheek to her brow instead. She was warm. Now if only she would awaken.

"You will not be needed anymore," he addressed the two women.

They looked to where Tilly had come to stand behind Collier. A moment later, they relinquished their lady and withdrew from the chamber.

Supporting Catherine beneath the arms, Collier felt the water seep through his bandages. It was hot, just as he had ordered it should be. The buckets alongside the tub attested to the heated water that had been added periodically to sustain the temperature. "Prepare her a place before the fire," he told the old woman, and nodded to a nearby chair.

"But 'tis in bed my lady ought to be."

"She has hypothermia, Tilly. Now that she is warmed, her temperature must be kept constant."

The old woman's eyebrows arched. "Hypo . . . thermia?"

Of course she wouldn't understand twentieth-century terminology. Collier shook his head. "Never mind. Just do as I ask."

She turned to the bed and began removing the covers.

Collier looked back at Catherine. Would she awaken? He had to believe she would.

"'Tis ready, sire."

Collier lifted Catherine from the tub and lowered her into the chair.

Hurriedly, Tilly pulled the covers around her lady. "I will send for you when she awakens," she said.

He shook his head. "I am staying with her, but you may leave."

She straightened. "I should leave her alone with you?"

Collier met her kind eyes. "After all that has happened, do you really believe I would do her harm?"

She considered him a long moment, then said, "I have been watching you."

As well he knew. Many were the times he had looked up and discovered the old woman's gaze upon him.

"You are not what you claim to be," she said.

"No, I am not, and neither am I your lady's enemy." He laid a hand to her shoulder. "I would give my life for her, Tilly."

She glanced at his bandaged fingers. "I believe that has already been proven, Sir Collier."

Was she a possible ally? he wondered.

"However," she continued, "you must consider appearances. Already you bring talk upon yourself and our lady just by being in her chamber. To leave you alone . . ."

"I will deal with it."

She sighed. "Very well." She stepped around him, paused to fuss over Catherine's covers, then started for the door. She had not gone far when she turned back around. "How are your dreams, Sir Collier?"

An odd question. "They are dreams." What more was there to say about them?

Tilly clasped her hands before her. "Have you ever . . ." She looked down a moment, then pinned him with her gaze. "Have you ever dreamed something that later came true?"

Where was this leading? "No, I can't say I have."

She slid her gaze to Catherine. "She has just such dreams, though she will not admit it. I have wondered if, perhaps, she dreamed of you—of your coming."

Catherine a soothsayer? Able to foresee events not yet occurred? Another thing Collier had never believed in. But what of the night he had apprehended Catherine when she had stolen through the darkened hall? When he had later told her that Walther would have killed her, he had seen in her eyes that she had known it as well. Was it through these dreams Tilly spoke of?

"Ah, but such are the ramblings of an old woman," Tilly said, as if realizing she had spoken of things she should not. "Pay me no heed, Sir Collier." She drew up her skirts, walked to the door, and pulled it open.

Although Collier wanted to call her back and press her for an explanation, he did not. Later would be soon enough. He dropped into the chair beside Catherine, and it was only then he allowed fatigue its due.

She felt warmed through—as if by a summer's day. She sighed. And to think she had believed she would never be warm again.

Remembering, Catherine opened her eyes and looked from the covers tucked around her to the glowing fireplace. It had not been a dream. It had truly happened.

She flexed her fingers and toes. They ached, but she could feel them.

Why hadn't she awakened when Collier had returned for her? More, where was he? As she sat forward, her gaze was drawn to the chair opposite.

He filled it. Legs stretched out before him and hands draped over the arms of the chair, he slept.

Trust me, he had said, and here she was warm again just as he had promised.

As she stared at him, something tugged at Catherine's heart. Something that had never touched it before. Was it that which Hildegard had warned her of? Which made slaves of women? Which ground their spirit beneath a man's heel? Which Hildegard had claimed her own son was unworthy of?

Catherine waged a battle between the past and the present. Between what she felt and what she should not. Then, her woman's heart showing, she pushed back the covers—only to discover she was naked beneath.

The thought of Collier having seen her thus warming her further, she quickly pulled a sheet over herself. Nay, Tilly would never have allowed him to see her unclothed, she assured herself. Collier must have come into her chamber afterwards. But then, why had Tilly allowed him to remain alone with her? Unless the old woman was also within . . .

Grasping the ends of the sheet together, Catherine rose. In the next instant, she gripped the arm of the chair to steady herself. She felt weak. Drained. Drawing a deep breath, she looked around her chamber that was quickly gathering dark. But for her and Collier, it was empty.

What did it mean? That Tilly trusted this man? Was it possible? The old woman having been with her since her birth, Catherine knew Tilly to be cautious in the extreme. Why, even Hildegard, who only had

Catherine's best interests at heart, had never gained Tilly's trust.

But she had trusted this man alone in Catherine's chamber with her—that or Collier had resorted to force to remove the old woman. Nay, in spite of all the terrible things Catherine tried to believe him capable of, she could not imagine him doing such.

She walked on uncertain legs to where Collier reclined. She had never before looked so closely at him—knowing that to do so would only invite his gaze upon her. Now, though, she was free to do so. Standing over him, she gazed from the bearded planes of his face to the cheekbones jutting above them, then up from his strong nose to dark lashes and brows.

Collier Gilchrist was not unbecoming, she admitted. In fact, it could be said he had been most kindly looked upon. Though tempted to touch the black hair that sprang back from his forehead, Catherine curled her fingers into her palms. His shoulders were broad, his chest full, his hips tapering, and his legs muscled. A good-sized man, taller than most, and with presence not even Montagu could command by the sword.

Noticing the bandages on Collier's fingers, Catherine was reminded that he had risked his life for her, been her shield against the force of the waves, pulled her from the sea, scaled the cliff face that surely should have seen him dead, and through it all had bled for her.

Too weak to stand any longer, Catherine sank to her knees. Who was he? she wondered. Who was this man who spoke in riddles? Who was as certain as she that Walther would have killed her? Who said he would not lose her again as if he had once lost her? Who kissed her as if she were dear to him?

Suddenly, he opened his gray eyes.

Although Catherine's mouth felt as weary as the rest of her, she tried to smile.

Collier's brow furrowed, as if he did not believe what he saw, then he sat forward. "I had feared you might not awaken."

Catherine knew she ought not to be kneeling at his feet, most especially in her state of undress, but she did not retreat. "I have you to thank for that," she said. "Once again you have saved my life."

"Again?"

Realizing she had spoken without thinking, she glanced down. Disturbing as it was, it was true that twice now he had been her champion. She looked back at him. "How do you know Walther would have killed me?"

Could he trust her? Collier wondered as he stared at her. Her lips softly parted and damp auburn hair falling over her shoulders, she looked ready to take a lover to her. No, he firmly told himself. Though he wanted to trust her, he could not—yet.

"He is the kind of man who wields his sword for the blood of it," he said, "not for the right."

The look in Catherine's eyes said she believed there was more to it.

"But tell me," Collier said, "how did *you* know Walther would have killed you?"

She averted her gaze. "I did not."

Although she might be grateful to him for having saved her life, she trusted him no more than he did her. Not exactly the stuff good relationships were made of, Collier thought wryly. But he did not question her about the dreams Tilly had told him of.

"How are you feeling?" he asked.

"Sore and tired, but otherwise well. And you?"

Weary. An occasional yearning for painkillers. "Nothing a good night's sleep won't make right."

She nodded. "What did you tell the castle folk?"

"I saw no reason to tell them anything, but they seem to have reached the conclusion you were trying to escape—and would have had the storm not descended so rapidly."

Catherine was silent a long moment, then reached forward and lifted one on his bandaged hands. Though the movement caused the sheet to slip off a shoulder, she seemed not to notice. "You have given much blood for me. Why do you care so?"

"I just do."

She searched his face. "Who is Aryn?"

An image of Aryn Viscott as she had appeared the last time he had seen her flashed through Collier's mind. Angry. Hurt. Defeated. He had failed her terribly. "Someone I once loved."

"Once?"

His fingers began to throb and his joints to ache. Yes, once—when he had been untouchable Collier Morrow who had not believed he could lose Aryn. How wrong he had been. But he should be past that by now. He had been given a second chance, and as painful as this day had been, it seemed he had finally broken through some of Catherine's defenses. Still, his guilt over Aryn's death persisted, and the pain that carved a craving through him.

He should leave, he decided. Tomorrow or the next day he and Catherine could talk more, but he was in no state to do so now. He stood.

Struggling with the sheet, Catherine rose beside him. It was too much for her. She swayed toward Collier.

He steadied her, but it was a mistake to touch her.

The skin of her bared shoulder felt as silken as he remembered it. Suddenly it was Aryn before him.

It was and was not her, he told himself, but still he bent his head and put his mouth to the ivory skin of her shoulder.

Her breath came out in a rush, then she slackened against him.

Collier gathered her nearer. Tasting her, licking and nipping from her shoulder up to her neck, he spun forward through time.

"Collier," she gasped.

He pushed aside the sheet and curved a hand around her breast. Damned bandages. He could hardly—

"Collier."

She sounded breathless, but with desire? He lifted his head.

Cheeks pale and eyes half-hooded, she stared at him. Catherine, not Aryn, and she looked ready to collapse. In fact, were he not supporting most of her weight, she would have.

Silently, he cursed himself. She had yet to recover from the effects of hypothermia and here he was ravishing her. He swung her up in his arms, carried her to her chair, and lowered her into it. As he arranged the covers over her, she captured his gaze.

"You loved her once," she said, her voice hardly more than a whisper, "but no more?"

There was only the truth. "I will always love her," he said.

Something flickered in Catherine's eyes.

Hurt? Did it really matter to her if he cared for someone else? Was it possible he had broken through more than *some* of her defenses? If only he could explain it all to her.

Looking wan and fragile, Catherine asked, "She waits for you?"

He shook his head. "She is dead." He pulled the covers around her and straightened.

"Why do you call me by her name?"

Collier had known she would eventually ask. "You . . . bear a marked resemblance to her."

She stared at him a long moment, then shifted her gaze to the fire. "You must have loved her very much."

Unfortunately, he hadn't realized it soon enough. Collier picked up the goblet of watered wine from a nearby table and handed it to Catherine. "Drink this. You need to replenish your fluids."

She took it from him.

He waited for her to drain the goblet, then refilled it. "I will send Tilly to you," he said, and turned away.

As he pulled the door open, Catherine called to him. He looked over his shoulder.

"I had naught to do with Walther's attempt to murder you," she said. "I . . . I pray you will believe me."

Although he had doubted her before, he no longer did. "I do," he said, and pulled the door closed.

Catherine sank back into the chair. Why had she called to him? Why was it so important he knew she'd not been a part of Walther's plans? She ought to be fighting him, and yet here she was trying to make peace with him. Why?

Because, her heart spoke to her, *you feel something for him. Something you have never felt before.* It went beyond gratitude and the kisses he had burnt into her memory. Just the thought of him having loved this Aryn made her hurt, and hurt even more when she remembered the look that had come into his eyes when he had spoken of his love for the

woman—and when he had told her she was dead.
Would he ever love again? Would he love as deeply?
Or did this Aryn possess him heart and soul—even in
death?

"My lady?"

Catherine had not heard Tilly enter. She looked up
at where the old woman stood beside her chair. "I
was surprised to find you were not here when I awakened," she said.

Tilly pressed her fingers to Catherine's brow. "Sir
Collier assured me you would be safe with him." She
straightened.

"And you trusted him?"

The old woman's eyebrows rose. "Twice now he
has saved your life. But you know that, don't you?"

What she was asking was whether or not Catherine
accepted it and saw in it what she herself did. "Aye.
Had he not pulled me from the sea, I would now be
dead."

Tilly nodded, then asked, "Was it the coin, my
lady?"

Catherine felt as if struck. Collier had said he'd
told the castle folk naught. Had he, perhaps, told the
old woman of Catherine's real purpose in leaving the
castle? "What do you know of it?" she asked.

Tilly shrugged. "'Tis only a guess, my lady. You
see, though the others believe you were trying to
escape Sir Collier, I know different. To do so would
endanger your family, and that you would not do."

Still, how did she know Catherine had possessed
the money? The only other person to know of it had
been Sir Severn—though he had not known where
Catherine had hidden it—and he was dead. Catherine
simply could not imagine him telling the old woman.
He would not have.

"Tell me how you know of the coin," she said.

The old woman smoothed back the dark lock of hair that had worked free of the surrounding silver. "I know naught of it, my lady. As I told you, 'twas only a guess."

It was far more than that, Catherine knew, but from experience she also knew there was nothing that would move Tilly to reveal what she did not wish to. Thankfully, the old woman was trustworthy.

"Sir Collier cares for you, my lady," Tilly turned the conversation.

Aye, he was no rapist as she had first believed him to be. "I should hate him," Catherine said.

"And you do not?"

"I find I no longer can." She sighed. "What would Hildegard say were she here now?"

Tilly walked to the front of Catherine's chair. "She is not here, my lady, and 'tis time you stopped living as if she were. If ever you are to find happiness, you must forget Hildegard, and cease trying to be her."

Had Tilly spoken such to her yesterday, Catherine would have been angry and resentful, but now she found herself listening. And questioning. "She is all I have ever known."

"And what of your mother, my lady?"

What of her? She was little more than a memory. A face Catherine had not seen since the age of seven. "I hardly remember her."

"Ah, but still she is inside you. When Lord Morrow awards Toller Castle to Sir Collier—"

"You think he will?" Catherine had not considered the possibility.

"But of course. Gilchrist is much favored, my lady. Did Morrow not entrust Strivling to him?"

Indeed.

"You will be going home," Tilly said, "and when you arrive, your mother will surely welcome you back."

Home. Was Strivling not home? Nay, no more, but that did not mean Toller was home. Although she might be returning to the place of her birth, it would be foreign to her.

"Methinks you will finally find happiness there," Tilly said, "and that Sir Collier will make you a fine husband."

He would be dutiful, but when he took her in his arms, would it be only because she resembled the woman he had loved and lost? Would he imagine it was Aryn he was kissing? Aryn he lay with?

"Is it love you feel for him, my lady?"

Catherine nearly choked. "Love? Certainly not! He is a Yorkist and I—"

"Nay, my lady, you are not. Not if you speak with your own voice and feel with your own heart."

Catherine stared at Tilly, wondering who this woman was, and whence came these words she spoke.

With a small smile, Tilly tucked the covers more snugly around Catherine. "Sweet dreams, my lady."

She *was* tired, Catherine admitted, which would explain these feelings. Aye, perhaps on the morrow she would awaken to find she could, indeed, hate Collier. Perhaps.

15

The light reflected off the cavern walls and ceiling to reveal how high the water had risen—well above the ledge.

Collier lowered the lantern. Had he not surmounted his pain to bring Catherine and himself out of this place, they would have been trapped. Drowned. And had his prayers not been answered when he could reach no more for Catherine, he would have lost her to the sea.

Remembering the moment his fingers had clenched around hers, he closed his eyes. He had failed Aryn, but not Catherine. Surely there must be some redemption in that. He could go on now. He could love Catherine as he had loved Aryn, but this time better. This time with feeling. Couldn't he?

He sighed. Not until he told her the truth and she trusted him enough to confide in him. Only then, when no more lies stood between them could they be together as they should have been five hundred years from now.

But at least he had finally reached Catherine. This morning, when he had carried her down to meal, the hate was not returned to her eyes, and she had even smiled. It was a beginning.

Collier looked to the chest at his feet. He had thought it might have been washed away, but other than being waterlogged, it was untouched. He had to get it back.

He lowered himself to his haunches and set the lamp beside him. As he had no key with which to open the chest, he tipped it onto its side to let the water out through the seam of the lid. Then he retrieved the lantern, hefted the chest, and began his descent from the ledge.

A quarter hour later, he reached the storeroom. It was empty. Leaving the chest behind the sacks of grain, he went into the hall.

Catherine sat in a chair before the hearth. The needlework Tilly had brought her lying untouched in her lap, she stared into the fire.

He knew what occupied her mind. Ever since word had come this morning that Alnwick Castle, followed by Dunstanburgh and Norham, had capitulated to King Edward's army, she had hardly spoken a word. She knew all was lost.

"It was there?" she asked as he approached.

She had guessed where he had gone. "Yes."

She looked at him. "You will give it to Morrow?"

He couldn't, but should he tell her that? "When he returns."

She nodded. "It will not be long now, will it?"

Although word of the defeat of the Lancaster's last remaining power base in the north—Bamburgh—had yet to reach Strivling, Collier knew it had also fallen. By cannon. "No, it will not be long." He halted before her.

Absently, she plucked at her needlework. "Will we be married then?"

Was she simply accepting her fate? "I would think so."

"And then?"

What *did* the future hold for them? "I do not know, Catherine."

She looked up. "Tilly believes Morrow will award you charge of Toller."

She named the estate which had been held by her family, and which, in that other past, had been given to Walther. It was a strong possibility, but what effect might it have on time? Collier wondered. In the next instant, he reminded himself that Walther had faded into obscurity. A significant figure only in that he had killed Catherine. The same as the sword. "I suppose he might confer Toller on me," he said. "Do you wish to go home, Catherine?"

She shrugged. "My family is there."

"But you do not know them."

"I do not."

Glimpsing vulnerability in her eyes, Collier touched her cheek. "I will be with you."

She sighed. "And yet I hardly know you either."

Collier straightened. "You will come to know me better. I promise you that."

She searched his face a long moment, then lifted the needlework and bent her head to it.

As Collier turned away, he remembered the reason he had sought her out. "Where was the coin hidden?" he asked.

She looked back at him. "What does it matter? You have it now."

"Humor me, hmm?"

Her eyebrows drew sharply together. "Do what?"

"Where was it hidden?"

She pursed her lips, as if weighing the advantage of keeping the place secret against what might be lost in telling him. Finally, she said, "In the lower store-room."

"Where?"

"At the back. In the far right-hand corner there is a stone in the floor which lifts out. But why do you need to know? There is naught there anymore."

But would soon be again. "Curiosity," Collier said, and strode from the hall.

King Henry yet lives. Do not forget with whom your loyalty lies.

The scrawled words glared at Catherine, reminding her that the pleasure of this day was not hers to feel. They were the same words Hildegard would have spoken, and *had* in Catherine's mind, but the handwriting was unfamiliar.

She looked at the retreating back of the gangly lad who had delivered the missive to her. He had said that the man who had sent him had been cloaked and hooded. Then, having earned his coin, the lad departed.

Catherine drew a finger over the curving line at the bottom of the missive. At first glance, she had thought it merely a flourish, but it might also be the initial "S."

Could it be . . . ? Nay, he was dead. Even so, there was someone out there who was concerned with where her loyalties lay.

Although it was a relatively warm day, a shiver

went through Catherine. Had she lost sight of
something she should not have? Had her woman's
heart blinded her to the duty she owed the Lancasters? Memories swirling around her, she closed her
eyes.

These past days with Collier had been strangely
lovely. Not only was he attentive and gentle, but
throughout her struggle to reconcile her hate for the
Yorkists with the feelings blossoming for him, he had
shown more patience than any man she had ever
known. At times she felt almost happy—as if that
emotion lay within reach.

"Ready?" Collier called.

Catherine folded the missive and tucked it inside
her bodice. Pulling the edges of her mantle together,
she turned to face him.

He led a bay stallion and a mottled black mare out
of the stables.

The sight of him, dark hair gleaming in the sun and
his fresh, clean-shaven complexion, eased some of
Catherine's foreboding. But it was not enough. The
words of the missive were still too fresh.

"Mayhap we ought to save the ride for another
day," she suggested, searching the sky for clouds.
Unfortunately, there were none.

Collier looped the stallion's reins over a fence post
and glanced overhead. "You know something I do not?"

He did not realize how near the truth he was—that
she had been sent a missive, nor that the one who had
sent it might be nearby, but she could not tell him
that. "'Tis just that I am suddenly tired," she said.

Collier guided the mare alongside her. "You could
ride in front of me." He nodded to the stallion.

The thought of his thighs trapping hers warmed
Catherine's cheeks. "'Twould not be proper."

His lips tugged with regret. "No, but it would certainly make for an enjoyable ride."

Feeling a bit breathless, Catherine mounted the mare. "Shall we ride?"

Collier grinned.

Such beautiful teeth, she fleetingly thought. A rarity, especially for a man.

He handed her the reins, then mounted the stallion and led the way over the drawbridge.

Catherine was halfway across it when she halted. For fear of what she would see, in all this time she had not looked upon the land outside the castle walls. She swallowed. Here lay the greatest evidence of Montagu's siege. The ground was torn, in places burned, and everywhere was strewn the fragments of broken weapons. An atrocity.

"It's in the past, Catherine. Leave it there."

She looked up to discover Collier watching her from the opposite end of the drawbridge.

Was it in the past? Not according to the missive pressed against her bosom. The Lancasters would not rest until they took back what had been stolen from them, and they expected her to continue to support them.

She felt torn. Although it had been a lie when she'd told Collier she was tired, it was no longer.

"Catherine," he called again.

Telling herself she could ride away these misgivings, she put heels to the mare and sped past Collier. The wind freed her hair from beneath her head covering, lifted the mantle back from her shoulders, and rushed through her blood like the strongest of wines. And for those few moments, her life *was* her own.

Then Collier overtook her.

As her horse was no match for his, she expected him to surge ahead to demonstrate his male superiority. Instead, he gentled the stallion's pace to that of the mare's.

How different he was from other men, Catherine thought as they raced side by side, and how unlike any enemy Hildegard had ever warned her of.

Catherine stole a sidelong glance at Collier, and in the next instant stole another. He was not just sitting on the stallion. Rather, he moved as if one with the great animal, his body bent low and held close in. Never would she have expected such expert horsemanship, especially as Collier could hardly wield a sword. Another curiosity that had yet to be explained.

They rode until the castle lay far behind and there was naught but the open land on three sides and the sea on the other. Collier veered his mount toward the latter.

A short while later, they reined in atop a bluff overlooking the tranquil sea. Like diamonds cast upon its waters, it reflected the sunlight.

Catherine looked out at the calm which had three days past been violent and deadly. The memories rolled in like the waves that had pounded her and Collier against the rocks. She blinked away the terrible images. "Your horsemanship is splendid," she said. "I would not have expected it."

Collier's smile was half-hitched. "*That* I have had training in."

"And yet you can hardly wield a sword."

The other corner of his mouth rose. "No, I cannot."

"A fighting man who knows horses, yet not the sword. A knight who knows letters and numbers, yet not the difference between the classes. 'Tis very strange, Collier Gilchrist."

His smile fading, he looked to the sea. "The life I have lived is far different from this. Where I come from is a world away from here."

Something told her that beneath the somber words lay the answer to the mystery of him. She wanted to know more. "Is it beautiful there?"

"Not really," he said without hesitation. "We have our classes just as you have yours, and those who murder and steal without conscience. It is all just more carefully disguised—for the most part."

She was confused. "Where is this place?"

His profile to her, eyes fixed straight ahead, Collier sat unmoving.

He was not going to answer her, Catherine realized. Why couldn't he just tell her? Was it something to be ashamed of?

Suddenly, he pinned her with his gaze. "Do you believe in God?" he asked.

What a strange question. "Of course I do!"

"Why? Because you have been told you should? Or do you truly believe in a higher being?"

The automatic response died on Catherine's lips. It was a day for remembering. She saw Hildegard's death. The death of the old baron and his son. The men whose lives she had spent upon the defense of Strivling. Then herself falling to her knees in the bailey and praying for a miracle—only to be defeated shortly thereafter. *Did* she believe in He who had not answered any of the prayers she had poured out of her heart? She wanted to, but where was He? "Do *you* believe in Him, Collier?"

He lifted her hand in his. "Until three days ago . . . not really."

The caress of his thumb across her fingers fluttered feeling through Catherine. "But you do now?"

"I do."

He seemed so certain of it. Aye, that they had lived through their confrontation with the sea was evidence enough. Wasn't it? "I suppose I believe only because I have been told I should," Catherine admitted. "Ever I find myself questioning Him—why He allows such horrible things to happen."

Collier stared at her a long moment, then said, "One day you will understand."

"Perhaps." She looked at her hand in his. "But will I be able to forgive myself?"

"What is there to forgive?"

She drew a deep breath. "I should have let Montagu in. 'Twas wrong of me to defend Strivling as I did."

"We all make mistakes, Catherine. Some for the better, some for the worse. You could not have known—"

"But I did." She touched her breast. "In here. Yet still I sent men to die for a hopeless cause."

"Are you sure it was you who did it? Or was it Hildegard?"

Catherine stared at Collier. What did he know of the woman who was to have been her mother-in-law?

"What did she want from you?" he asked. "For you to be unyielding? Hard? Just like her?"

Had he heard the talk of the servants, or was it Tilly who had told him of Hildegard?

"You feared failing her, didn't you?" Collier pressed. "So much that even after she was gone you did what you knew she would have done."

Defend Strivling to the death—just as Catherine had done in her dream. Had Collier not stepped between her and Walther, she would have died. "Aye," she said.

He nodded. "It wasn't you who sent those men to their deaths, Catherine. It was Hildegard."

Had she heard correctly? "You are saying I am not responsible for what happened?"

"No, I am saying you are human. We all answer to someone. Unfortunately, the one we answer to is not always right. Nor are they looking out for our best interests. They mislead us and manipulate us to their way of thinking. In short, they do their utmost to make us over in their image. That's what happened when you came to Strivling. You were an impressionable child and Hildegard took advantage of that."

It was true, but still . . .

Collier turned his hand more tightly around hers. "What matters is where you go from here, Catherine. That is what you will be held accountable for. Learn from your mistakes and go on."

Was it possible? "How easy you make it sound."

He shook his head. "It's not. In fact, it's the hardest thing you'll ever do, but if you don't, you will never truly live."

He obviously spoke from experience. "What in your past have you had to let go of?" Catherine asked.

He stared at her a long moment, then released her hand and dismounted. "One day I will tell you."

"Will you?"

"I will." He reached up to her.

Catherine hesitated a moment before going into his arms. They did not tremble as Lambert's had whenever he had assisted her down from a horse. Collier's arms were strong. Solid. As if they might hold her forever.

He set her on her feet.

Knowing it could prove dangerous to stand so near him, Catherine walked to the edge of the bluff. A breeze feathered her brow, and she drew a breath of the salty air. Although it had proven itself a terrible foe, she would miss the sea, she realized. As Toller lay far inland, its access to the sea was several hours ride away.

Of course, Tilly might be wrong, she reminded herself. Morrow might award Collier Harden Castle instead. Or none at all. In which case, would Collier make his place at Strivling as a household knight, with her, his wife, to wait upon the lady whom Morrow would eventually wed?

She sighed. Either way, her life was changed—even if the Lancasters gained back their throne. She pressed a hand to her bosom. What was she to do? Could it be God's will that England be ruled by the Yorks? Was this the reason He had not answered her prayers?

Collier's hands closed over her shoulders and his chest pressed warmly against her back.

Although Catherine's instinct was to pull away, she did not. It was weak of her, but more than anything she wanted to feel what Collier made her feel. To find peace in his arms.

She sighed. It was that woman's heart of hers again. She turned.

The hard line of Collier's mouth had gentled, and the gray of his eyes was softer than she remembered it.

Could he love again? Did that which he felt for her go beyond desire? She laid a hand alongside his jaw.

He stared at her.

Catherine swallowed. She shouldn't. She really shouldn't. She leaned forward. Quivering at the brush of her breasts against his chest, she tilted her head up and pressed her mouth to his.

He let her kiss him, but only a moment before drawing her nearer.

Although the sea was calm, a storm rose. In Collier's arms, Catherine felt as if she were drowning again—yet this time she did not fear.

His mouth and hands expert on her, he pulled her under . . . consumed her . . . filled her senses with him . . . caressed those places never before known to a man. It was like breathing after having never breathed. Living after having never lived. But it was soon over with. Hardly had the rustle of parchment reached Catherine's ears when Collier extricated himself.

Realization rushed through her, then fear. She slapped a hand to her bodice. It was too late. He had the missive.

"What is this?" he demanded.

She met his gaze. Suspicious. Accusing. "I beseech you, give it back." She reached for it, but he evaded her grasp.

"What is it, Catherine?" he asked again.

She moistened her lips. "It is . . . personal. Naught you need concern yourself with."

He glanced at the folded missive. "We are going to be married," he reminded her.

"Please, Collier."

His stare was hard. "I want to trust you."

"Then do."

The minutes creaked by, and just when Catherine was sure he was not going to respect her privacy, he handed her the missive.

Lest he change his mind, she snatched it from him and turned away. Although she had every intention of returning it to her bodice, something prevented her from doing so. She unfolded the missive and read it again.

Which path to take? The way of the heart? Or the way of hate?

She swung back around and saw that Collier no longer stood there, but was stalking to where he had left the horses to graze.

Catherine had to run to catch up with him. "Collier," she called as she neared.

He looked over his shoulder.

She drew alongside and handed the missive to him. "I also wish for you to trust me."

Collier searched her face a long moment. "You are certain?"

She nodded.

He read it. "Who wrote this?"

"I do not know."

"Where did you get it?"

"'Twas delivered by a village lad ere we left Strivling. I questioned him, but he said the man who gave him coin to bring it to me was hooded."

Collier's eyes grew distant. "Walther," he murmured.

"You think he would send me such a missive?"

Obviously, Collier had not realized he'd spoken aloud. He quickly recovered. "Very possible."

"But why?"

"He was first a Lancastrian."

She was shaken. "What?"

"He is a mercenary, Catherine. For the promise of greater gain he joined with the Yorkists. It is my guess he has gone back over to the side of the Lancasters."

And Catherine had thought Walther a model of vile Yorkism. "He tried to kill you," she said.

"And will no doubt try again."

"Why?"

Collier tucked the missive into the pouch on his belt. "Because he wanted Toller, and believed I stood in his way."

"Didn't you?"

He cocked an eyebrow. "We shall see, won't we?" He took her hand in his. "Come, it is time we returned." A few moments later he handed her up onto the mare.

"Will it ever be over with?" she asked as he mounted the stallion.

"One day."

"You truly believe Edward will keep the throne of England?"

He met her gaze. "I know he will, which is as it should be."

"But it belongs to—"

"No, Catherine. Edward is not the usurper. He is simply taking back that which the Lancasters stole from his family sixty years ago. He is the rightful heir to England."

Catherine had heard the argument before, and knew that Edward's claim to the throne had been upheld by the Lords in Parliament as being superior to Henry's. Still—

"Let's go," Collier said.

As before, they raced side by side across the land, and slowed only when Strivling came into sight. There, crossing the drawbridge into the bailey, was a retinue numbering a full score or more.

It could mean only one thing.

16

Edmund Morrow was returned. A baron.

Catherine stood silently beside Collier as the triumphant Yorkist took his place at the table. Would a Lancastrian ever again sit the high seat of this barony? she wondered amid the still of the castle folk who had just been told that the hated Montagu had been made Earl of Northumberland. Would the Lancasters never again rule England as Collier said?

"Sir Collier," Morrow called.

Collier glanced at Catherine, then stepped forward. "My lord."

Morrow looked around the hall. "You have done well in my absence, and for that I wish to reward you."

Toller Castle, Catherine thought. Soon she would be going home, but how would she be received?

"What think you of keeping Harden Castle for me?" Morrow asked.

From the stiffening of Collier's shoulders, Catherine could see he was as surprised as she. "Harden Castle, my lord?"

"Aye. You have certainly proven yourself worthy."

"My lord, I am flattered, but what of Toller?"

Morrow's eyebrows arched. "I paused at both castles on my journey here, and I assure you, Harden is the finer of the two."

It was true, Catherine thought with sinking heart. And as with all men, Collier would surely wish the best.

"I understand, my lord," he said, "but if you are to bestow such a gift upon me, I would ask that it be Toller."

Catherine started. He would choose Toller over Harden?

"For what reason?" Morrow asked.

Collier was silent for a long moment. "It is where Lady Catherine's family resides," he finally said.

Catherine warmed.

Looking past Collier, Morrow briefly settled his gaze on her. Obviously, he was not keen on the idea. However, in the next instant he smiled. "Have you tamed her, Gilchrist?"

Tamed her? Catherine could not have been more offended.

Collier's shoulders stiffened further. "Lady Catherine and I have come to a kind of . . . understanding," he said.

The sparkle in Morrow's eyes said he could well guess at the nature of that understanding. "Very well, Sir Collier. It shall be Toller Castle."

"I thank you, my lord."

"We shall see. Now, there is the issue of your marriage to address. Ere supper this eve, you and Lady Catherine will be wed."

"This eve?" Catherine exclaimed.

"You object, Lady Catherine?" Morrow asked.

Collier looked over his shoulder at her, but she avoided his gaze. "'Tis so sudden," she said.

"The banns have been read," Morrow reminded her. "What more must needs be done?"

True, thrice now the priest had publicly announced that she and Collier were to wed, but still she had expected to have a few days past Morrow's return to ready herself. "There are preparations to be made."

Morrow leaned forward in his chair. "All that is needed is a willing bride and groom, and do we not have both?"

"But—"

"Lady Catherine, did you or did you not agree to wed Sir Collier?"

She met Collier's gaze. "I did."

"Then it shall be as Lord Montagu instructed—you will speak vows this day."

Montagu was taking no chances. Wed and beneath a man's heel was how he wanted her. Tamed.

"When you go forth from Strivling on the morrow, it shall be as Lady Catherine Gilchrist."

Tomorrow they would leave for Toller? Catherine felt as if caught in a gale.

Morrow waved a dismissing hand. "I give you an hour to prepare yourself, Lady Catherine."

What should have been the most important day of her life reduced to insignificance. . . .

Tilly appeared at Catherine's side. "Come, my lady, we've not much time."

Catherine considered Collier once more, then turned away.

*   *   *

"Lady Catherine Algernon, do you freely give yourself in marriage to Sir Collier Gilchrist?"

Catherine looked from the priest to the man beside her, and in his eyes saw something that made her heart stagger. But was it she, Catherine Algernon, he gazed upon, or his beloved Aryn? Aryn who warmed his eyes and curved his mouth into a gentle smile?

The late afternoon breeze lifted a tendril of Catherine's hair and swept it across her face. Absently, she tucked it behind her ear.

"Lady Catherine?" the priest asked.

Collier arched an eyebrow, prompting her to respond as he had moments earlier.

Did she freely give herself to this Yorkist? She who had agreed to marriage only that she might save her family from Montagu's wrath? Who had been thoroughly repulsed by the idea, but now found herself drawn to this man who had risked his life to save hers?

Loudly, Edmund Morrow cleared his throat.

Freely or not, he intended to carry out his overlord's order that she wed. She swallowed. "I will."

The priest heaved a long breath, as if he had been holding it, then proceeded to enumerate the duties Collier would be bound to perform as her husband. He must love her, comfort her, honor her, keep her in sickness and health, and be faithful to her.

Considering what Catherine had learned of him these past weeks, the last four were not entirely out of the question, but love?

Her duties were to be the same, but with one glaring difference: she must also obey and serve Collier. Although Hildegard had served her husband well, she had not obeyed him, and neither had the old baron expected her to. Catherine clenched her hands in her skirt. She, who was to have wed and ruled a future baron, was now to wed and be ruled by a Yorkist.

The priest leaned toward her. "Your answer, Lady Catherine?"

She started. "I will," she replied, though whether or not she would obey Collier was to be seen.

"And who gives this woman to be married to this man?"

Morrow, presiding as her guardian, stepped forward. "I do." He took Catherine's right hand and put it in the minister's who, in turn, passed her to Collier.

Her hand seemed so small in his, Collier thought. So fragile. And yet she was hardly petite. Feeling her tremble, he looked up and found her watching him. Beautiful, especially with her eyes drawn wide as a deer's, lips softly parted, and hair—heavily crimped from the braid it had been loosened from—flowing nearly to her knees.

"And now you will pledge your troth," the priest said.

Troth? Confused, Collier looked around.

Annoyance sparked the priest's eyes. "Your vows, Sir Collier."

Of course. "I am ready," Collier said.

The priest inclined his head. "Then speak them."

The clergyman was not going to recite them first? Though Collier had attended weddings in the past— rather, the future—he had never paid enough attention to the vows to commit them to memory. But even if he could muddle through them, would they be appropriate for this time?

"I must ask that you lead me," Collier said.

The priest raised his eyebrows, then sighed heavily. "Repeat after me: I, Collier Gilchrist, take thee, Catherine Algernon, to be my wedded wife."

Collier met Catherine's gaze and recited the familiar words.

"To have and to hold," the priest continued, "for fairer for fouler, for richer for poorer . . ."

So, the traditional wedding vows of the twentieth century had roots that went deeper than he would have guessed. Collier repeated them.

"In sickness and in health, for this time forward, till death us do part . . ."

This time forward. Till death us do part. An unearthly sensation rocked Collier. For a long moment, everything and everyone but Catherine faded away. Feeling as if caught in the vortex that had transported him here, Collier stared at the woman he had hoped to have spoken vows with had her death not parted them. Aryn—with the love of five hundred years in her soul.

Emotion nearly choking him, he squeezed his eyes closed.

"Collier?" Catherine asked, concern raising her voice.

He swallowed hard, then again. When he looked back at her, he saw it was not love that shone from her eyes, but fear. For that brief moment, it had been Aryn before him—shoulder length hair and all.

"Are you well, Sir Collier?" the priest asked.

Without answering, Collier repeated the vows and those that followed.

Then it was Catherine's turn.

Though she needed no assistance from the priest, the vows seemed awkward on her tongue. Forced.

He mustn't forget she did not wed him willingly, Collier reminded himself. That she had no choice.

". . . and thereto I plight thee my troth," Catherine finished.

"The ring, Sir Collier." The priest held out his hand for it.

From the pouch on his belt, Collier retrieved the simple band Edmund had provided him with and laid it in the priest's palm.

The priest bowed his head. "Let us pray."

As Collier bent his head, he felt Catherine's gaze upon him. The priest's mutterings fading into the distance, he met blue eyes that peeked at him from beneath sweeping lashes.

Sensing the emotions that churned within her, he squeezed her hand, and when that failed to ease her uncertainty, grinned.

Surprised, she blinked, but a moment later the corners of her mouth turned up ever so slightly.

It would work out, Collier assured himself. Everything was going to be fine.

The presentation of the ring followed, and a blessing. Afterwards, the wedding party filed into the chapel and Collier and Catherine knelt before the altar. Then came the nuptial mass, a long recitation spoken entirely in Latin.

Collier couldn't remember the last time he had been on his knees, but for some reason it felt right.

"I suspected Walther was not to be trusted," Edmund said after a long silence.

Collier had to drag his thoughts from Catherine, who was being readied in her chamber.

"Where do you think he has gone?" Edmund asked.

Collier met his questioning gaze. "You are aware he was a Lancastrian turned Yorkist, my lord?"

Edmund's eyebrows shot up. "I am not."

"It is what I was told. Thus, I would not be surprised if he has gone back to the side of the Lancastrians."

Edmund considered Collier's words a long moment, then said, "Even so, they are crushed."

"You do not think they will rise up again?"

"Not likely. What do you think?"

Collier knew he had to be careful. "Henry and his queen are still out there, my lord."

Edmund thought on it over a long swallow of ale. "Aye, but what can they hope for when their coffers run empty and their followers have fallen under the rule of King Edward?"

Even though Catherine was also under Yorkist rule, she had intended to replenish those coffers, as Collier knew too well. Remembering, he ran his thumbs over tender fingertips.

Edmund shook his head. "Methinks the House of Lancaster has seen its last days."

It had, but still Henry would hold the throne again, though only for a short time. "Perhaps," Collier said.

Edmund stared at Collier, then, with a shrug, set his tankard down. "I have heard tale of your extraordinary feat of climbing. Is it true you scaled the cliff without rope?"

Collier had hoped the furor over what had happened would have died that none would mention it to Edmund. He had been fooling himself. "It's true."

Edmund shook his head. "I have never heard of such a thing. It sounds most remarkable." He leaned forward in his chair. "How is it done?"

"Usually with ropes," Collier said, wondering how he was going to get Edmund off the subject. "But as I had none, I had to . . . improvise."

"Is it difficult?"

"It takes years of training."

Edmund rubbed a hand over his jaw. "And why would one train to climb rocks?"

He was wondering how it fit in with warfare, Collier realized. "For the pleasure of it. The challenge."

Edmund sighed. "You are like no man I have ever met, Gilchrist—noble or otherwise. Still, methinks your time would have been better spent learning the sword."

In which case, Collier thought, he and Catherine would have perished.

"How did Lady Catherine escape?"

Collier had hoped Edmund would not ask, for he could not tell him of the underground passage. It was something he would have to discover for himself—if ever. "She went out through the postern gate." He hoped there was none who could dispute the lie.

"There was a boat waiting for her?"

"No, but I am sure there would have been if not for the storm."

"You were trapped by the incoming tide?"

Collier nodded. "We sought higher ground on the outcropping of rock, but as we were wet and there was no shelter, the only way out was to climb the cliff."

"I hope you punished Catherine for attempting to escape."

Collier met his ancestor's gaze. "I saw no reason to. It was enough that she nearly died."

Edmund's brow furrowed. "You risked your life trying to save her, and not for the first time. Is she worth it, Gilchrist?"

Worth losing his life over? Without her, he had no life. "Yes. She is worth it."

Edmund was silent a long moment, then he grinned. "No doubt, you are anxious."

"Anxious, my lord?"

"To bed your bride, of course."

Collier's thoughts veered to Catherine. During the banquet that had followed the wedding ceremony, she had said no more than a half-dozen words to him. Then, accompanied by Tilly and the priest, she had gone upstairs for the blessing of the marriage bed. It would not be long before Collier was summoned to exercise his "husbandly rights" over her.

What a strange time to be living, he mused. He was accustomed to twentieth-century women who would never stand for being treated as possessions. But then, neither would Catherine stand for it.

"Well?" Edmund prompted.

"What can I say? She is a beautiful woman."

"Aye, that she is, and were she not Catherine Algernon, I would envy you. But that brings me to the reason I wished to speak with you." Edmund settled back in his chair and clasped his hands over his chest. "She has two brothers—one, a wicked fellow who can't be more than ten, and who twice tried to bite me, and the other of seven and ten who stood before me and vowed that did I show him my back he would put a knife in it. Then he spat on my boots."

Lovely. "Obviously they still harbor Lancastrian sympathies," Collier said.

"Aye. The younger served as a page at Dunstanburgh, and the older was squire to the lord of Bamburgh. Both were sent home following the fall of those castles."

Interesting. "What of their father?"

"Lewis Algernon is harmless, though only because of the apoplexy he suffered when Montagu brought

his army on Toller. Otherwise, methinks he would
have attempted to hold the castle rather than yield."

Perhaps he should have accepted Harden Castle,
Collier thought wryly. Now that Catherine was finally
softening, he was going to take her into an environment strong with Lancastrian sentiment, and
strengthened further by the fact these people were her
family. Not a winning combination.

"It is not too late to change your mind about
Harden," Edmund said, as if reading Collier's
thoughts.

No, Toller it was. Difficult as it might prove, it was
where Catherine needed to be. Also, he was taking
enough chances with time by filling Walther's shoes.
Harden belonged to whomever Edmund had chosen
in that other past. "You are most generous, my lord,"
he said, "but I would prefer Toller."

Edmund sighed. "Let it not be said I didn't warn
you, my friend." Something catching his eye, he
glanced toward the stairs. "'Tis time."

Collier followed his gaze to the old woman. "Good
eve, my lord," he said, and stood.

Tilly led the way up the stairs. "Have patience,
sire," she said as they stepped onto the landing above.

"Patience?"

She offered an apologetic smile. "My lady would
not allow me to undress her that she might be put to
bed. It has been a difficult day for her."

Of course. "I understand."

The old woman nodded, and continued on to
Catherine's chamber. She opened the door.

Collier stepped inside. As Tilly eased the door
closed behind him, he settled his gaze on Catherine
where she stood before the window with her back to
him. "Catherine," he said.

She slowly turned.

Although that chin of hers was high, Collier picked out the fear in her eyes.

Was she a virgin? he wondered again. Either way, he was not going to force himself on her. He wanted her, but only if she came to him willingly.

"Do you want me to stay, Catherine?"

She could not hide her surprise. "You are my husband."

Which, according to these times, gave him every right over her regardless of her own wishes. "I am," he said, "but if you are not ready, I will leave."

Confusion marring her brow, she glanced at the bed. The covers were drawn back in silent invitation. "You would not take me if I did not wish you to?"

"No."

Her shoulders relaxed and an uncertain smile tugged at her lips. "You are most strange, husband."

"This is not the first time you have accused me of that."

"Indeed, nor do I think 'twill be the last."

For certain. "Should I leave?"

Catherine's lashes fluttered down. "You should, but I do not wish you to."

It was the invitation Collier had been waiting for. His body stirring, he walked forward.

Although Catherine had said she wanted him to stay, there was wariness in her eyes when he came to stand before her—suggesting again that this would be her first time. He had to know. "Have you ever been with a man, Catherine?"

She needn't have said a word, for the disclaimer flew off her face. "Of course not!" She took a step back.

Then it was going to be new for both of them, for

Collier had never been with a woman who had not previously been with a man. "Forgive me," he said, "I thought perhaps you and your betrothed—"

"Never."

At least the fear was gone from her eyes. He sighed. "As I told you, where I come from is very different."

"Women of gentle birth freely give themselves without first speaking vows?"

Collier laid his hands to her shoulders. "More often than not." Beneath his fingers, he felt the tension begin to flow out of her.

"I do not think I would like living in this place you speak of," she said.

He smiled. "No, you would not." Just as he did not think *he* would wish to live in the twentieth-century again. Strange how content he had become these past weeks. Especially now that there was the promise of Aryn in Catherine. He pulled her into his arms.

"Collier," she whispered against his lips. Then she let him in.

Breathing her breath, he swept her silken mouth.

She whimpered.

Coaxing her uncertain tongue to join with his, he took from her the small, throaty sounds she made.

She pressed nearer to him.

He felt her nipples erect beneath the material of her gown. Then his own body answered, hardening him against the cradle of her thighs.

"Touch me, Catherine," he groaned.

She opened her eyes, stared dazedly at him a moment, then began to give back. Tentative at first, but growing more confident with each passing moment, she pressed her mouth to his, caressed her tongue over his, nipped at his lips, and trailed kisses across his jaw.

Her breath in Collier's ear caused sensation to spiral through him. Then she began to touch him. Her hands pressed and stroked, withdrew, and returned to seek him again. Over his shoulders. Down his back. Across his buttocks. Around his hips.

It was a time of gentle learning, of finding and seeking, of giving and taking. Ingenuous. Sweet.

Something Collier had not felt before awakened within him. Something that went beyond the needs of his body. Was this what it was like to not only desire a woman, but also acknowledge that he loved her? *Did* he love Catherine?

Suddenly, her hand was upon him, but only for the briefest of moments before she snatched it away.

It took every bit of Collier's restraint not to push her against the wall, drag her gown up, and answer the need she had brought him to. But he wouldn't, he vowed. He wouldn't hurt her.

"I want you, Catherine," he said, hardly recognizing his voice.

Her color was high, her eyes wide. "I . . . I do not think I can."

He smoothed a hand down her cheek. "There is nothing to be frightened of. I will not hurt you." God, he hoped he didn't hurt her.

She looked away, swallowed, then nodded.

Collier drew her to him again and kissed her. He must go slowly he reminded himself. Unfortunately, his body fought him every inch of the way.

Catherine did not immediately respond, but patience rekindled her passion. When Collier's breathlessness became hers, all that stood between them were their clothes.

Aching with want, he pulled back. "Soon," he said, then turned her around and unfastened her gown. He removed it, then her chemise, leaving only her undergarment and stockings.

Holding onto his control, Collier pushed aside Catherine's hair and put his mouth to her neck.

With a sigh, she bent her head back against his shoulder.

He traveled his lips up to her ear, flicked his tongue over it, then started back down. As he went, he slid her undergarment down and released it to the floor. Shortly, her stockings followed.

Straightening, Collier noticed the fine hairs risen across Catherine's skin. "You'll be warm soon," he promised.

Her voice was husky when she spoke. "I am not cold."

And neither was he. He lifted her in his arms, carried her to the bed, and laid her down.

She was beautiful—from her long, shapely legs to the soft place between her thighs, from her high-peaked breasts to eyes which were now more black than blue. She was a woman ready for love.

Standing alongside the bed, Collier began to remove his clothes.

Catherine watched him. Her gaze upon him palpable—as if it were her fingers she trailed across his chest and over his abdomen—Collier tossed his tunic aside. Soon he was naked.

Catherine dipped her gaze to the evidence of his manhood, and once again, fear replaced passion.

"Trust me," he said.

She reached out a hand.

Collier came to her as he had never come to a woman before. Not even Aryn. He took her beckoning hand in his, kissed the inside of her wrist, trailed his lips up her arm. Then, joining his mouth with hers, he laid down beside her.

The sweetness of Catherine was like a flower unfolding. Petal by petal she opened to him, touch by touch she explored his body as he did hers, and sigh by sigh she came nearer the moment when they would become one.

His maleness pressed against the outside of her thigh, Collier slid his fingers through the mound of softly curling hair below her belly. Lower, he found the bud of her femininity. She gasped at his touch, and when he began to circle his finger over her, pushed against his hand.

First her pleasure, Collier reminded himself. First Catherine.

Her breath coming in sharp, short gasps, she turned her face into his shoulder and began seeking the rhythm he set her body. Though awkward at first, she found it and began to move as if he were inside her.

It was almost too much for Collier, but still he held back. Beginning to perspire beneath the strain of his body, he clenched his jaws and slid his finger inside her. Moist.

With a cry, Catherine arched upward, causing the barrier of her innocence to yield.

"Collier," she gasped.

He stilled. "Have I hurt you?"

"Ah, nay, I . . . I feel . . ." She drove herself against his hand. "Pray, do not stop."

He thought he might explode. As he stroked her, he felt her teeth scrape his shoulder, her nails rake his skin, and her body tighten around him.

With a moan and a murmur, she thrust harder. She was near. Very near.

He positioned himself between her legs, and at the moment her breath caught, pushed into her.

She cried out—not a cry of pain, but of pleasure.

Collier had thought he would know her body but, once inside her, realized he did not. It was Catherine he felt around him, not Aryn. Catherine clinging to him as she spasmed. Catherine he sought his release in.

Moments later, he found it. Collapsing to the side, he pulled her with him.

They lay there a long time, neither one speaking. Holding on to one another. Each warming the other with the heat of their afterglow.

Catherine gloried in it. This night she was made Collier's wife, and all the nights hereafter she might know him again. She smiled against his neck. Was this the lust of her body the Church preached against, or love? Love. As soon as the thought entered her mind, she shied away from it. Lust, she decided. Collier had given her great pleasure. Thus, it was only natural for her to feel kindly toward him.

"Did I hurt you?" he asked.

She tilted her head back. "Never have I known such pleasure. Never did I know I could." Though Hildegard had spoken briefly of the duties a woman owed her husband in bed, it had been enough for Catherine to believe it would be an entirely unpleasant experience. How wrong the older woman had been.

Collier glided a hand down her arm. "You're beautiful," he said.

As beautiful as Aryn? the question crept to her mind. When he had made love to her, had he imagined that was who he held beneath him? No, she shouldn't do this to herself. The moment was too perfect to ruin with such thoughts.

Collier's thumb warmed the pulse on the inside of her wrist. "The next time it will be even better."

Catherine turned her hand into his. "How could it be?"

"I will show you."

And he did. Twice more that night he set her afire, each time drawing the flame higher than the last. Finally, with the light of dawn filtering through the window, Collier's breathing deepened into sleep.

But there was no sleep for Catherine. Cradled in his arms, she stared at the opposite wall. There was tenderness between her legs, but she hardly felt it as her thoughts returned time and again to the woman Collier loved.

Was this jealousy? Wanting something that belonged to another which she could not hope to attain for herself? She ought to let it go. She ought to be content with what she had, but the ache inside her would not leave her alone.

Did she love Collier? she allowed the thought to creep in once more. Had Catherine Algernon, Yorkist hater and defender of Strivling, finally learned to love? She squeezed her eyes closed.

Impossible. Utterly impossible.

17

It was not as large, nor as grand as she remembered it from her childhood, Catherine thought as she looked at Toller Castle against a darkening sky. Still, it was impressive, and would soon be her home again.

Collier's hand touched hers.

She looked to where he sat atop the destrier Morrow had given him—a horse which had belonged to her betrothed. For most of the ride she and Collier had hardly spoken, due to his refusal to allow her to bring along her portrait. He had given no explanation, saying only that it should stay. Her plans of having it completed to present to him as a gift thoroughly ruined, she had done her best to ignore him these past hours, but she no longer could.

He pressed her hand. "You are not alone, Catherine."

The last of her anger dissolved. Nay, she was not,

but still she wondered at the reception that awaited her. Seeking Tilly, she glanced past Collier and the men-at-arms who had accompanied them from Strivling. The old woman sat wearily in the saddle, but it was as if she had been waiting for Catherine to look her way. She nodded.

"Are you ready?" Collier asked.

"Aye," Catherine said, "And you?" After all, he was less likely to be welcome at Toller than she. Though they were wed, he was still a Yorkist. Still the enemy.

"It will be a challenge, I am sure." He urged his destrier forward.

By the time they reached the drawbridge, darkness had cast its mantle over the land. In the light of torches set about the castle, they passed beneath the portcullis.

At once, Catherine felt the restless stirring of their escort. Not only did the men distrust what they could not see, but also what they could. She did not have to look around to know their hands were on their weapons.

Although Collier had sent a man ahead to announce their arrival, it was not Catherine's father who received them as he should have, but the castle garrison—soldiers who stood silently brooding as the new lord of Toller came among them.

Their hostility was tangible, something Catherine recognized only too well. As Collier had worked so hard to win the respect of Strivling's people, he would have to do so at Toller.

Reining in before the keep, he looked at the looming structure. "Some welcome," he muttered.

Catherine pulled her mantle more closely around her. At the very least, her family should have received them before the keep, but the landing stood barren. Obviously, her father no more welcomed Yorkists at Toller than she had at Strivling—even if his *daughter* was among them.

"Catherine."

She looked down at where Collier stood alongside her horse, his arms raised.

Knowing she was watched by those who had served her father for years, and that she would be judged by how she responded, she nearly declined Collier's offer to hand her down. However, the reminder that they were married prevented her from doing so. She went into Collier's arms.

It felt so right. If only this day had not so soon followed the wondrous night they had shared. If only they could have remained at Strivling a bit longer.

Gripping her elbow, Collier led her up the steps to the keep.

The two men-at-arms who had preceded them pushed the doors open.

Seated across the hall at the lord's table were the four who, in blood, were Catherine's family. Although they watched Collier and Catherine advance, they did not stand. Worse, her father occupied the high seat which now belonged to Collier. An outright gesture of defiance.

As Catherine walked beside Collier, she glanced sideways at him. If he was angered, he did not show it.

She looked back at her family. It was more than a year since she had seen her father, but she recognized him, haggard though he appeared from a distance. In contrast, her brothers were only vaguely familiar. Neither had she seen for three or more years, but from their expressions, they did not like Collier's hand upon her, and most especially that she allowed it—even though Morrow must have told them she was to wed this Yorkist.

As for the woman whose gaze was intent on her, Catherine did not think she would recognize Lavinia Algernon, even up close. After all, twelve years stood between them. Not once since the day Catherine had been sent to live with Hildegard had she seen her mother.

Long-buried resentment and hurt surfacing, she watched Lavinia clasp and unclasp her hands. She looked nervous. Agitated.

Was Lavinia eager to be reunited with her, as Tilly had said she would be? Catherine wondered. If so, why, in all these years, had she not corresponded with her daughter?

Collier guided Catherine up to the dais. "I am Collier Gilchrist. The lord of Toller by grant of Baron Edmund Morrow."

Lewis Algernon stared at him, but said naught.

There was something strange about her father, Catherine thought. He did not look well, but it went beyond that. His mouth—

Lavinia surged up out of her chair. Barely had she taken a step from it when her husband slapped his palm to the tabletop.

Catherine heard the sound of Strivling's men-at-arms readying themselves for trouble. Simultaneously, the two household knights who stood right and left of her father tensed. It would take very little provocation for blood to be shed this day.

Lavinia looked at her husband. For a long minute their eyes clashed, then she said, "Our daughter has come home." Her bearing erect, she turned from him.

Again, he slapped his hand to the table.

Why did he not speak? Catherine wondered.

He slapped the table twice more.

Lavinia ignored him. A few moments later, she stood before Catherine. As she looked at her daughter, her eyes filled with tears.

What was she to do? Catherine wondered. Embrace this woman as if she knew her? As if she loved her?

Lavinia lifted a hand, hesitated, then swept the hair back from her daughter's brow. "We were told it was Harden Castle you would be going to with your husband."

Catherine was surprised that her mother's voice sounded familiar, that the brush of her fingers should be so comforting. She swallowed. "It *was* to have been Harden, but my lord husband asked to be given charge of Toller instead."

"Lord husband!" one of Catherine's brothers said with disgust—the eldest, Antony.

Lavinia glanced sharply over her shoulder, but whatever look she sent her son, he was not intimidated by it.

Was that how she had looked when she'd stood before Montagu? Catherine wondered as she gazed at Antony. Had she as much hate in her as he? Nay, more. It was truly an ugly thing.

Lavinia returned her gaze to Catherine. "I am pleased," she said, a tightness in her voice. "So pleased." She clasped Catherine's face between her trembling hands, stared long and searching at her, then kissed her cheeks and embraced her.

Something awakened within Catherine. She *had* loved her mother. And Lavinia had loved her. Though it felt awkward, she put an arm around the woman, and over her mother's shoulder, met Antony's gaze.

He was not pleased.

Lavinia drew back. "Now that you are returned, we have much to talk about."

Catherine looked from Antony to her younger brother, Eustace, then to her father. They thought her a traitor. Her smile was forced. "I thank you for your welcome ... Mother." She turned to Collier. Although she appreciated that he had not interfered in her reunion with her mother, she also knew it would be seen as a sign that he was far less noble than the title conveyed upon him. He should have received recognition before she. Should have demanded it.

"My husband, Mother. Sir Collier Gilchrist."

Though disquiet transformed Lavinia's face, she acknowledged him. "Lord Gilchrist—"

From the table came a strangled grunt, followed by the slamming of a tankard.

Lavinia turned to her husband.

Although Catherine hardly knew her father, his occasional visits to Strivling having been spent almost entirely with Hildegard, there was one thing she *did* know: if he could have spoken aloud the emotions reflected on his face, he would have.

Her heart lurched with realization. Try as Lewis Algernon did to look the lord of Toller, his body betrayed him terribly. He must have had an attack of apoplexy.

"'Tis time to step aside," Lavinia said to him. "The new lord of Toller has arrived."

He glared at her.

What had become of these people under the lordship of Griffin Walther? Collier wondered. It could not have been good. Once again he was dabbling with time, but it was not as if there were any other path he could take now that he had set his feet on this one.

Antony stood. "I accept no mercenary as my lord," he said, "nor Yorkist. And neither does my father."

"Antony!" Lavinia reproved.

He seemed not to hear. "Play the lord of Toller, Gilchrist, but know your days here are few." He strode from the hall.

Eustace watched him go, then also rose from the table. "Neither do I accept any Yorkist," he said in a voice he tried hard to project with maturity. Still, he sounded like a ten-year-old trying to be a man. He swept Collier and Catherine with a look of warning and descended the dais.

Collier reminded himself that he had known to expect this, but there was not much consolation in discovering how right he had been. He looked at each of Lewis's knights. The younger of the two stared back without flinch or waver. In contrast, the older man, his silver hair and beard proclaiming him near the end of his prime, swept an assessing eye over Collier.

Inwardly, Collier groaned. Until he proved himself capable of ruling Toller, it was not going to be pleasant. If ever. But at least he was no longer up against Catherine—providing he could hold on to her in the face of such opposition.

"I pray you will forgive my sons, Lord Gilchrist," Lavinia said. "They are too young to know better."

She was shorter than her daughter, but her auburn hair, blue eyes, and generous mouth, evidenced that she was, indeed, Catherine's mother. "I understand," Collier said.

"Mabel, Sibyl"—Lavinia called to the servants—" bring food and drink for your lord and lady, and their men."

The women scurried away.

"I will send maids to clear the lord's solar that you might have it for yourselves," Lavinia said.

Collier glanced at Lewis Algernon. He looked as if he might blow another gasket. "It will not be necessary. You and your husband may remain in the solar."

He felt all gazes on him.

"As you are now the lord of Toller, 'tis rightfully yours," Lavinia reminded him, as if in being lowly born he did not understand his new station.

"One of the other rooms will do just as well."

"There are only Antony's and Eustace's chambers," Lavinia said, looking more than a little flustered.

The boys could share one. "Then we will take Antony's."

Lavinia inclined her head. "As you would have it, Lord Gilchrist." As she turned away, one of the serving women returned to the hall bearing a pitcher. Lavinia glanced back at her husband who occupied the seat that was also Collier's by right of rule—where he ought to take his drink and food.

Lewis Algernon was not going to give it up without whatever fight he had left in the half of his body that still functioned, Collier saw. But as easy as it would be to dispossess him, it was unnecessary.

"It is cold in here," Collier said. "We will sit before the fire."

"You are certain?" Lavinia asked.

"Aye."

Relief smoothed the older woman's face.

Catherine stepped toward the table. "I would speak with my father," she said.

Lavinia caught her arm. "'Tis not the time."

Catherine opened her mouth to object, but in the next instant heeded her mother's warning. "Very well."

Lavinia released her. "I shall see that your chamber is made ready." As she stepped down from the dais, Tilly caught her eye. "Tilly," she said.

Her gait stiff from the long day's ride, the old woman stepped forward.

The two women embraced.

Collier looked at Catherine. Though she offered him a smile, she was clearly uneasy. Putting a hand beneath her elbow, he guided her down from the dais.

From his place at the high table, Lewis watched his daughter seat herself beside the Yorkist. Did he not know her face, he would have said she was not of his seed. But it was her. Catherine Algernon—now Gilchrist—who, a year ago, would have died rather than wed her enemy. Catherine who had held against Montagu's army even in the face of defeat.

What had happened to change the young woman Hildegard had made in her own image? Where was the daughter who had made his own hate for the Yorkists seem like that of a child?

Weariness settling deeper in his bones, Lewis closed his eyes. Many were the nights since he had sent Catherine to Strivling that he had lain awake with regret—ruing that he had ever proposed marriage between her and Hildegard's son. But at the time he had thought it the best thing for Catherine, believing that if ever she was to surmount the curse upon her, she would need much discipline. There had seemed none better suited to it than Hildegard. However, never had he expected to lose his daughter so completely.

Lewis opened his eyes and settled them on Gilchrist. A stranger Yorkist he had never come across. Not quite as easy to hate as the others. Was he the reason for the change in Catherine? Could it be she loved him—providing she was even capable of love? Or did Gilchrist simply bed her well?

He sighed. Was Catherine still dreaming those dreams of hers?

Antony came for him just as Lewis knew he would. In the wake of the others who had bedded down for the night, the boy strode the shadows. It was how Lewis wished it, that none might see the indignity he suffered at being carried to bed as if he were a child. Ere first rising, Antony would carry him down again.

Lewis wiped the saliva from the sagging corner of his mouth. Antony was a tall boy. Nearly a man, but though he was beginning to thicken, it would be yet some years before he reached his full physique.

And then what? Lewis's resentment welled. As long as Edward was on the throne, there would be naught for his son. Toller was Gilchrist's now, and unless King Henry miraculously returned with an army capable of burying the usurper's, it would remain that way. Much as Lewis despised Yorkist rule, there seemed no hope for the Lancasters. Or his son.

Antony knelt beside his father. "I have had word," he spoke low.

"Wor . . . ?" Lewis asked. Just as he allowed none to witness the extent of the infirmity that caused him to be carried to bed, only with Antony did he use his grossly deformed speech.

His son leaned near him. "An army is being assembled. We are to await instruction."

Hope? Or a useless cause that might see Antony dead?

"Father?"

Lewis looked into his son's face. The anger that had been there an hour past was gone, and in its place was the light of confidence, he believed in the Lancastrian cause. Foolishly.

"Father?" Antony prompted again.

Lewis nodded.

Antony lifted him and carried him to bed.

"I should have told you about your father."

Catherine met Collier's gaze in the mirror. "You knew?"

"Edmund told me."

She lowered the brush she had been pulling through her hair. "Why did you not tell me?"

"I meant to, but the time was not right."

Because she had refused to talk to him on the ride here. "What happened?"

He laid his belt over the back of a chair. "I know only that your father had a stroke—an attack of apoplexy—when Montagu brought his army against Toller."

Catherine looked down. War. So many lives it had taken. Hildegard, the old baron, her betrothed, and now her father was near death. Of course, she ought to be dead as well, shouldn't she? She turned. "Tell me about the winch room, Collier. Why did I not die there?"

A guardedness entered his eyes. "Because . . . I could not allow it."

There was more to it. Would he never tell her? Frustrated, Catherine stood. "You speak in riddles, Collier Gilchrist."

A wry smile turned his lips. "Ah, but we both have our secrets."

"*I* have no secrets."

His smile faded. "Don't you?"

Did he think she meant to betray him? That her Lancastrian sympathies went deeper than the night she had spent in his arms? Strange how it hurt. "Nay, I do not." She swung away.

"Then tell me about your dreams."

Catherine's breath caught. He knew? But how? Had he dreams as well? Was this the means by which he knew Walther would have killed her? She turned back around. "How do you know about my dreams?"

"Tilly told me."

"Tilly? I have never spoken to her of them."

"She knows."

From time to time, the old woman inquired as to her dreams, but Catherine always told herself it was only idle chat.

"She thought, perhaps, you had dreamed of my coming," Collier said.

How had Tilly known?

"Did you?"

Catherine dragged herself from her musing. What was she to tell him? The truth? If she did, would he think her a witch as her father had warned her all those years ago? "'Tis true," she said, "I did dream of your coming, but not until the night you came to me."

He stepped toward her. "What did you see in your dream, Catherine?"

She moistened her lips. "'Twas a dream I'd had many times, but this time it ended differently."

"Tell me."

"I was in the winch room. There were Yorkists there, and one who raised his sword to mine. I swung, and would have cut him had you not appeared. It was you who took the blow, Collier. Then I saw the blood upon my gown and thought myself dead."

"My blood."

"Aye, but in all the other dreams it had been *my* blood, and the one I had cut . . ."

"Walther?"

She nodded. "I saw my death, Collier. No matter how I have tried to change my dreams, always they have come to pass. Until you. How can it be? Do you have such dreams?"

He shook his head. "Only if you are a dream, Catherine, and I pray you are not."

"Do you think me a witch?"

"A witch?"

"Before my father sent me from Toller, I told him of a dream I'd had. He made me promise to never speak of it or any others, and said that if I did I might be thought a witch."

"Then you have never told anyone else of them?"

She shook her head.

"Not even Hildegard?"

"Nay."

Collier pulled her into his arms. "Some things simply cannot be explained," he said against her hair.

She reveled in the strength of his arms around her.

"You will tell me if you have such dreams again?" he asked.

That he could change them as he had changed the dream of her death? She nodded. If he was capable of doing that, then she would gladly tell him. Which brought her back to the question she had earlier posed, and which he had not answered. Reluctantly, she drew back. "What of *your* secret? Will you trust me as I have trusted you?"

Guardedness returned to his eyes. "I will," he said. "I promise."

"But?"

"I need more time."

"Then you do not trust me."

Collier saw the hurt in her eyes. *Did* he trust her? He wanted to, but he could not forget the Catherine he had first come to know. It was true she had shown him the missive, but now there were her father and brothers to consider. For certain, they would try to influence her against the Yorkists. The question was what she wanted more: him, or the Lancasters returned to the throne of England. "Do you love me, Catherine?"

Her eyes widened.

If she did love him, she was yet unwilling to admit it—just as he had been unable to admit it to Aryn. "Time," he said, "that is all I ask for."

She slipped out of his arms.

Collier closed his eyes. Though he risked losing whatever he had of her, he needed to be certain she would not betray him. He had to know that what she felt for him was not just gratitude for his having saved her life. That it went beyond the pleasures they had found in one another's arms. That she loved him as he loved her.

He opened his eyes. He *did* love her. Catherine Algernon. He ought to tell her. Perhaps she needed to hear it as much as he did, but . . .

He needed time.

18

"What do you know of my dreams?"

Tilly looked up from her needlework, but showed no dismay as Catherine expected.

"Dreams, Catherine?" Lavinia asked from where she sat beside the old woman. "What do you speak of?"

Although Catherine had wanted to confront Tilly in private, the day had waned without an opportunity to do so. Unable to wait any longer, she had come to the lord's solar. "I speak of the dreams my father told me I should never speak to anyone of. Those that show me the morrow."

The confusion that rose on Lavinia's face could not have been acted.

"Sit down, child," Tilly said, nodding to the chair opposite.

Catherine complied.

Tilly turned her needlework over, fingered the

back stitches, then laid the piece in her lap. "You have the gift of your grandmother, Lady Catherine."

"My grandmother?"

"Aye, your father's mother. When I had fewer years about me, I served as her maid."

Tilly had never mentioned it. "And the gift?"

"'Tis of sight, as you surely know."

She would never have called it a gift. Rather, a curse.

"As in your grandmother's dreams, into your dreams come the future," Tilly continued. "That which will be and cannot be changed."

But Collier had changed it—

"What is all this nonsense about dreams?" Lavinia demanded. "Foretelling the future? It sounds most unholy."

"Lord Algernon could not tell you, my lady," Tilly said. "He feared that if he did, he would lose you."

Lavinia raised her chin. "Though my husband tried to hide it, I am aware that his mother did not have all of her wits about her. I have ears that I can hear the things people say behind their hands."

"But she was not mad, my lady," Tilly protested. "'Twas the sight she had, not a sickness of the head."

"I think we ought to leave this subject be." Lavinia set her needlework aside. "'Tis time we begin preparations for the evening meal."

"Nay," Catherine said. "I wish to know of my grandmother." She turned from her mother's wide-eyed countenance to Tilly. "Tell me."

It was a long moment before the old woman spoke. "She was a fine lady," she finally said. "Giving . . . good . . ." She sighed. "But she tried to change what she could not."

As Catherine had too soon learned she could not change those things shown her in her dreams.

"Her great misfortune was that, in hopes of effecting change, she began speaking of her dreams. It was then—"

Lavinia surged to her feet. "You will cease speaking such drivel!"

Catherine caught her mother's hand. "I have these dreams, too. I need to know."

Lavinia opened her mouth to protest, but closed it in the next instant. She searched her daughter's face, her eyes desperate to be told otherwise. "It cannot be true."

"It is."

Lavinia closed a trembling hand over the cross hung around her neck, then looked to Tilly. "Never did you tell me of this," she said, the pain of betrayal in her voice.

"I could not, my lady. 'Twas not my place."

"God have mercy on us." Lavinia walked to the window.

Feeling her mother's anguish, but needing to know the rest of it, Catherine leaned toward the old woman. "What happened to my grandmother?"

Sadly, Tilly shook her head. "Though she never more than cared for your grandfather, he loved her very much. But no matter how he pleaded with her to cease speaking of her dreams, she would not. For fear she would be accused of sorcery, he committed her to a convent and compelled her to a vow of silence."

"And my father?"

"It broke his heart to lose his mother. He was still a boy, you see. He did not understand."

"He never saw her again?"

"Never."

This had to be the reason her father had made her promise not to speak of her dreams. Could it be he loved her after all? That he had only feared for her? "Did my grandmother keep her vow of silence?"

"It is said she did not speak once during her ten years at the convent. That she died with not even a murmur."

Catherine's heart swelled for this woman she had never known, but who had passed to her granddaughter the sight of things to come, and had had to live with the consequences of trying to change them. Such unspeakable sadness. Torn from her son, her husband, her home—

A thought struck Catherine. Would Collier send her away? If she bore him children, would he tear them from her arms and commit her to a convent? She laid her hand to her belly. Even now she might carry his child.

"What is it, my lady?"

Catherine clasped her hands in her lap. "I told Collier of my dreams. It was he who told me you knew of them."

Tilly nodded. "As I thought."

"I should never have told him. I should have denied it when he asked."

"You need not fear he will send you away, my lady."

Catherine shook her head. "You do not know that."

"I know he loves you."

Collier loved her? No, it was the image of her he loved. Looking at her with eyes that beheld this Aryn he spoke of. "Nay," Catherine said, "and even if he did, so did my grandfather love my grandmother. You said so yourself."

"'Tis true, but your husband is different from your grandfather—as you are different from your grandmother."

Aye, Collier was different. There was no disputing that. "Tell me how *I* am different," she said.

"You have self-control, something your grand-mother had so little of."

In that she had not spoken of her dreams to any-one.

"Your father did not easily send you to live with Lady Hildegard," Tilly continued. "'Twas only after much thought he did so."

Out of the corner of her eye, Catherine saw her mother turn from the window.

"He knew your mother loved you too much to give you the discipline needed to contend with your gift. For this reason, he sent you to Strivling—that Hildegard would take you in hand and strengthen you."

Then it had been more than an alliance. Her family's silence all these years had been for a purpose. To harden her. "Did Hildegard know of my dreams?"

"Certainly not. Had she, she never would she have accepted you. She was very superstitious. All she knew was that you were in need of a strong hand. And that, with her guidance, you might make a suit-able wife for her inept son."

Tilly clasped Catherine's hands in hers. "I was sent with you to Strivling that I might watch over you. To alert your father did you begin speaking of your dreams. Just as he knew what he might gain in send-ing you to Hildegard, he also knew what he risked if she learned of your dreams."

Then Lewis Algernon was not the detached father he had seemed all these years. "What of my grand-mother's mother? Had she also the sight, Tilly?"

"Nay, your grandmother was the first girl child born to the family in more than two hundred years."

Two hundred years? "And before that?"

Tilly inclined her head. "The last girl child born before your grandmother was said to also have the sight."

"Then it is passed through the female line?"

Tilly shrugged. "It would seem so, and 'tis what your grandmother believed. For this reason she refused to take her husband into her bed after your father was born. She had given Toller its heir, and that was enough."

Might it happen again? Catherine wondered. It was something to be feared.

There were tears in Lavinia's eyes.

"If you knew naught of this," Catherine said, "why did you never visit, or write?"

Lavinia stepped forward. "Your father forbade me. He said it was how Hildegard wished it."

It made sense Hildegard would not want any interference with raising her son's future wife, and Lewis Algernon had enforced it with the belief it would strengthen Catherine.

"I never forgave him for sending you away— especially to that woman," Lavinia said. She halted before Catherine. "If only he would have told me. If he would have trusted me."

But he had not, Catherine thought, just as Collier did not trust her. Would her destiny be that of her mother's? Or worse, her grandmother's? "I am sorry if my coming has brought you pain," she said.

A tear fell to Lavinia's cheek. "Aye, pain, but so much more happiness." She touched Catherine's face, then put her arms around her.

Over her mother's shoulder, Catherine met Tilly's gaze.

The old woman smiled sadly and pushed the dark lock of hair out of her eyes.

*   *   *

"I have heard tale you cannot even swing a sword," Antony said.

Collier looked at the battered blade the boy had been practicing with when he had come upon him. "Never mistake a man's facility with weapons with his ability to defend himself."

"Then 'tis true you fight with your fists like a man of the soil." Antony smiled. "Ah, but then, that is what you are—a commoner who wears the boots of a dead noble."

"You are challenging me?"

With mock disbelief, Antony glanced at his brother who watched from the fence, then to those on the walls. "Challenge the new lord of Toller? Dare I?"

"Aye, you dare."

Antony smiled wider, and lifted his sword. "Would you like to sport, *my lord*?"

He could certainly use the practice. Collier drew his sword and mirrored his opponent's stance.

Beneath the gaze of the castle guard, they parried for the first minute or so, then Antony lunged forward.

Collier thought himself prepared, but the boy was quick—and even more surprised than Collier when he scored the flesh of his opponent's arm.

A scratch, but it was enough to turn Antony reckless. Issuing a triumphant shout, he leapt forward and slashed at Collier without regard to himself.

Thus, Collier caught the edge of Antony's sword with his own and sent the boy's weapon flying.

Antony froze.

"Retrieve your sword." Collier nodded to where it lay.

His eyes never leaving Collier, Antony scrambled for his weapon.

Shortly, they were trading blows again. Around the training yard they moved, Collier on the defensive, Antony on the offensive. Not exactly matched, but what the boy had in skill, Collier had in strength.

A moment later, that skill spun Collier's sword from his grasp and into Antony's.

It was magical. Sleight-of-hand. Had it been a movie, Collier would have rewound it and watched the sequence frame by frame. "Well done," he said. "You will have to show me how you did that."

Antony smirked. "You are at my mercy, *Lord* Gilchrist."

Collier opened his arms wide. "That I am. So what do you intend?"

Antony glanced at those who watched from the walls.

Collier did the same. It was the older knight, Sir Mathis, who caught and held his attention. Unlike the others, he was not smiling. Rather, his bearded face reflected intense thought.

"I ought to kill you," Antony said.

Collier looked back at him. "I am sure you would like to, but you won't."

Antony's eyes narrowed. "You think I fear that pig, Edward?"

"No, for certain you do not."

Questioning creased Antony's face. "Then?"

"You have not yet learned to kill," Collier said— just as he, himself, had not. "And until you do, you will not kill me."

"You could be the first." Antony waved his sword.

Collier wiped his forearm across his moist brow. "Could be, but not today, nor tomorrow."

Antony knew it himself. It was there in his eyes.

Sneering, he tossed Collier's sword to him.

"Same time tomorrow?" Collier asked as he slid the blade into its scabbard.

Antony's laughter was dry. "If you dare."

A few minutes later, Collier crossed into the inner bailey and started up the steps to the keep.

"You are dropping your shoulder," someone said.

Collier looked around.

It was the older knight. From the bottom of the steps he stared at Collier.

"My shoulder?" Collier asked.

Sir Mathis inclined his head.

What did he care how his Yorkist lord wielded the sword? "I will keep that in mind." Collier started back around.

"And you put too much weight on your front leg."

Collier eyed the man. "Why are you telling me this?"

"Toller deserves a lord capable of defending it— and defending it well."

"Which I will do."

From the knight's silvered jaw, a smile arose. "Then you had best learn how to use that sword of yours, hadn't you?" He pivoted and strode across the bailey.

Collier followed the man's progress until he was gone from sight. Was Sir Mathis more concerned with the welfare of the castle than whether or not it was a Lancastrian who governed it? Or did the knight have an ulterior motive? Time would tell.

Collier entered the hall. It was empty but for the old man where he sat in his chair and Catherine beside him. With every intention of announcing his presence, he stepped forward, but then Catherine spoke.

"I know about grandmother," she said. "About her dreams."

Collier stilled.

In her father's eyes, Catherine saw the alarm he could not contain—the words he was incapable of speaking. She pressed her hand over his clenched fist. "I know why you did not tell me."

He opened his mouth, but all that came out was a strangled sound.

She shook her head. "No words are necessary. I understand 'twas out of love you kept the truth from me—that you sent me to Strivling."

Lewis Algernon stared at her a long moment, then tears welled up in his eyes.

Catherine's heart swelled for this man she had never known. For his pain. His sacrifice. "I dream too, Father, but I am not my grandmother. What you did *was* for the best."

He closed his eyes and shuddered a long breath. Then he turned his hand and clasped her fingers in his gnarled ones.

Catherine put an arm around him. "I love you, Father," she whispered. How strange the words. Other than the childish declarations she had spoken before being sent to Strivling, she had told no one she loved them. Hildegard had not believed in love.

Her father dropped his chin to his chest.

Catherine held him until the tremors of his silent weeping subsided. When, finally, she drew back, he tried to smile, but the half of his mouth that refused to obey his mind remained turned down.

She kissed his cheek. "We have much to—"

Looking past her, her father's eyes widened.

Catherine followed his gaze. There stood Collier. The front of his tunic was darker than the rest, as if he had been exerting himself. How long had he been there? How much of her reunion with her father had he witnessed? She sighed. Though she ought to resent his intrusion, she could not.

Lewis Algernon grunted his displeasure.

Catherine turned back to him. "I have told my husband," she said.

His eyes reflected alarm.

"He is trustworthy," she assured him, though she feared Collier might send her away as her grandmother had been sent away. He wanted her now, but later? What if she lost the self-control Hildegard had taught her and began telling others of her visions?

Trust me, Collier had said, and she had. But should she?

Catherine straightened. "You wish something, husband?"

Collier shook his head. "I did not mean to intrude." He strode across the hall and ascended the stairs.

Lewis made a low, guttural sound.

"Father?"

He jerked his chin toward the stairs, then raised questioning eyebrows.

Words were not needed. He wished to know her feelings for her Yorkist husband. "I do not know," she said. "Truly I do not. But I do know he is good."

Lewis's eyes asked what his lips could not.

"Twice he has saved my life, and in doing so nearly given his own. He is not like other Yorkists. He is . . . different."

In silent acknowledgment, Lewis Algernon lowered and raised his lids.

He had grown weary these past minutes, Catherine saw. "Do you wish to lie down?" she asked.

He shook his head.

Did he sleep here? When she had come belowstairs to break her fast this morn, it had looked as if he had not moved since the night past. Did he think it all the dignity left to him—a lord's seat he was no longer the lord of? Catherine's thoughts turned to Collier. Why had he not demanded her father's removal? Had Griffin Walther been awarded Toller, he certainly would have had him removed.

She sighed. It always came back to the one thing she knew for certain about Collier: he did not belong. Meeting her father's gaze, she found him watching her. "I will leave you now," she said, "but we will talk again."

His wry smile fit his crooked lips well.

She touched his cheek. "You may not be able to talk, but I know your heart. It speaks most loudly to me."

As it did in that moment.

Leaving him to his rest, Catherine walked to the stairs and began her ascent. As she neared the landing, her mother appeared.

"How did he receive you?" Lavinia asked.

Catherine smiled. "Methinks it is time you spoke with him. Time to forgive."

Lavinia sighed. "'Tis what I wish to do. I just do not know how."

Catherine's eyes stung with sudden tears. "I am sure you will find a way."

With a nod, Lavinia stepped around her daughter.

Catherine found Collier in their chamber. Bared from the waist up, he stood before the chest that contained her clothes and the few that were his. Remembering the feel of him, his masculine scent, and how he tasted, she averted her gaze. "I am grateful," she said.

"For?"

"That you allowed my father to keep the high seat. Methinks he is going to die soon."

Collier turned. "You have dreamed it?"

"Nay, 'tis just a feeling. He is not well." And could rest in peace now that the burden of these years was finally lifted from him.

"What happened to your grandmother?" Collier asked.

How much could she say? What would he think? Although she was tempted to refuse to tell him as he would not tell her of his secret, she said, "My grandmother spoke of her dreams as she should not have. Fearing for her, my grandfather . . . sent her away."

Collier searched her face, then strode forward and gripped her arms. "Do you think I would send you away, Catherine?"

"Will you not?"

As if her question pained him, he said fiercely, "I could not. Wherever you are is where I will be."

"I wish to believe you."

"Then do."

Catherine lowered her gaze to his chest. "I will try," she said, her breath suddenly tight, her fingertips aching to touch him.

Collier tipped her chin up, searched her face a long moment, then bent his head.

The mere brush of his mouth caused her defenses to weaken alarmingly. Catherine pulled free and turned away. She knew where such caresses would lead, wanting it herself, and that if she was not pregnant now, to lie with him again might result in a child. Perhaps a girl child with the curse of the sight. Nay, she needed to think on this.

Collier stared at her back. What could he say to

convince her he would not abandon her? That he loved her? God, he wasn't ready for that declaration. Would he ever be?

It was happening again, he realized. Although he had finally acknowledged what he felt for Catherine, by refusing to tell her, he risked losing her the same as Aryn. Regardless of her feelings for him—be it only gratitude, or love—and regardless of his foolish Morrow pride, he had to tell her. Not since having admitted himself to drug rehabilitation had he faced so great an obstacle.

He searched for the right words, for the best way to phrase his feelings, but in the end there were only three words that mattered. "I love you," he said.

She swung around. "What?"

"I love you, Catherine." He strode forward, lifted her hand, and touched the ring he had placed there. "With my whole heart. My soul."

She did not throw herself in his arms, nor declare her feelings for him. Instead, tears flooded her eyes. "Are you sure 'tis not Aryn you love? Aryn you see when you look at me? When you touch me?"

Of course she would think so, and weeks ago she would have been right. Collier shook his head. "No, Catherine. It's true that in the beginning I did see her when I looked at you, but no longer. It's you I love. Aryn is . . . but a memory."

Uncertain, she searched his face.

"Do you return my feelings?" Collier asked, daring to believe.

She swallowed hard. "I . . . do not know."

God, he ached. This must be how Aryn had felt when she'd confessed her love and not had it returned. Wrenching. So what more would it take to convince her of his feelings? What more to win her heart? He knew the answer even before the questions formed. It came back to the secret he kept from her—asking for her trust and withholding his. But was she ready to hear his unbelievable tale? Was she ready to believe?

Catherine pulled her hand from his. "I am sorry, Collier. 'Tis just that I, too, need time."

No, she was not ready to believe. Later. Always later. "Of course," Collier said. He crossed to the chest, drew on a fresh tunic, and without further word withdrew from the chamber.

Feeling pulled in a dozen different directions, Catherine stared at the empty doorway. As Tilly had said, Collier loved her. Though his declaration had swelled her heart with new emotion, it had just as quickly emptied with the reminder he did not trust her. Of course, if she returned his feelings—

Did she? Was that what she felt for him? She agonized over her emotions a moment, then thrust them aside. Impossible.

"I've a message for you, *Sister*."

Catherine had not seen Antony lurking in the shadows. Disquieted, she turned from her chamber which she had been about to enter.

Antony stepped into the light.

"Message?" Catherine repeated, hoping Collier would not soon be retiring for the night.

"Aye."

"And that is?"

Antony leaned a shoulder against the wall. "King Henry lives."

She was not surprised. It was the same as the missive sent to her two days past. For certain, it was dispatched by the same person. But was it Walther as Collier believed?

"Who do you stand with?" Antony asked.

Catherine lifted her chin. She had been through more pain and suffering, more bloodshed, and more death than he could even imagine. She was not now going to be intimidated by this whelp who only thought himself a man. "Who wishes to know?" she asked.

"Someone who is concerned about you."

She arched an eyebrow. "About me? Or about a cause that can never be again?" She had finally spoken it aloud.

Antony's eyes turned hateful. "What has happened to you? You held Strivling against Montagu—took up a sword against the enemy when they tried to take the winch room. And now—"

"Morrow told you that?"

"One of his men. The bastard thought it amusing, but I . . ." Antony jerked his gaze down.

"What?"

He straightened from the wall. "I looked up to you for what you did. Imagine that, a man revering a woman. His *sister*."

That he admitted it surprised Catherine. "I did all I could, and now there is no more to be done. After all the bloodshed, Edward is still king and stronger than before. It is over, Antony." Just as Collier had said it was.

Color suffused his face. "You are wrong. 'Twill not be over until all the Yorkists lay dead—including that one you take between your legs like a—"

Catherine slapped him. "Hate me if you must, but you will show me the respect due my station. I *am* your lady."

The imprint of her fingers rising on his cheek, Antony glared at her. "Toller is mine. Stand by Gilchrist and die by him." He swung away. A moment later, the door of the chamber he shared with Eustace slammed closed.

Catherine dropped her head back and stared sightlessly at the ceiling. She should have tried to be more understanding. After all, she had also known such anger when Montagu had set himself upon Strivling. If only Antony had not been so cruel. . . .

At least she had her mother and father back, she consoled herself. And though Antony might be a hopeless cause, Eustace was still young enough that perhaps she could befriend him.

Feeling burdened, Catherine stepped into her chamber, and a short while later slid beneath the bedclothes. As she stared into the dark, a faint masculine scent stirred her senses. Longingly, she touched the place where Collier would lie this night. If only . . .

She sighed. He did not trust her, and until he did, it was best she put such thoughts from her head. If only she could.

19

Collier looked over his shoulder.

Catherine slept. With her auburn tresses tousled over the pillow, lashes dark against her cheeks, and lips softly parted, she roused in him an ache so fierce it was all he could do not to seek its relief.

He clenched his hands. It was three weeks since they had made love—on their wedding night—and nearly as long since he had tore himself open declaring his love for her. A love that was not returned. They shared a bed, but that was all. As Catherine's relationship with her father, mother, and Eustace strengthened, the tentative bonds forged between her and Collier weakened. Just as he had feared they might. So would she betray him? Would the Lancastrian sentiment that ran high at Toller seep back into her veins?

Collier's thoughts turned to Antony. He had hoped to win the boy over, but the likelihood of that diminished with each passing day. And neither would Antony have anything to do with his sister. Still, Collier supposed he ought to be grateful. Otherwise, Antony's influence on Catherine might prove her undoing—might turn her back into the hard-hearted woman who had yielded up her life, and the lives of others, in the name of King Henry.

Collier looked one last time at her, then took up his sword, which had become as essential a part of his daily wear as a tie had once been. He belted it on without much thought, then retrieved his mantle and strode to the door.

Dawn was radiating fingers of light through the windows when he entered the hall. Most of the people who slept here had already arisen, and those still upon their benches and pallets were beginning to awaken.

The old man sat in his chair. Each morning when Collier came down from his chamber, Lewis Algernon was there, and his gaze followed Collier wherever he went. But though it was clear he did not like the man his daughter had been forced to wed, the hate Collier had felt the night of their arrival seemed to have lessened. Or, perhaps he had simply adjusted to it.

This morning, however, Lewis slept. He must have had a rough night.

Collier stepped outside. The air was crisp, but soon his mantle would not be needed. It was going to be another warm day—perfect for visiting the outlying villages. Thinking of the report he would prepare for Edmund this afternoon, he crossed the drawbridge into the outer bailey.

His horse was saddled and waiting when he reached the stables. Quentin, the young man who had previously been Lewis's squire, stood alongside it. He was a good lad, though not of the sharpest wit as Collier had soon discovered.

"'Tis a fine day, my lord," Quentin said, handing him the reins.

"Indeed." Collier looked around. "Are you ready?"

Puzzlement pleated the boy's brow. "Sire?"

Suddenly, out of the stables came Antony astride a horse that looked more than a handful for him.

Now Collier understood. Antony had dismissed Quentin. He must have told the squire he had gained Collier's consent to do so. Interesting. "Never mind," he said to Quentin, then to his brother-in-law, "Are you ready?"

Antony's mount fought the pull of reins as he drew alongside Collier. The color of embarrassment tinging the boy's cheeks, he wrenched hard and brought the animal to a halt.

Much as Collier wanted to suggest he try a horse a bit tamer, he knew it would only make the boy more determined to ride this one.

"I am ready," Antony said.

"Then you will show me where the village of Tipping lies." Collier mounted and urged his horse toward the drawbridge. A short time later he and Antony rode over the gently swelling land.

What was Antony up to? Collier wondered. Although every day since coming to Toller he and the boy had engaged in swordplay, that was the extent of their relationship. It met Antony's need to defeat the man who had taken his birthright from him, and Collier's to better his swordsmanship. So why Antony's sudden show of interest?

It was just like dealing with James, Collier thought wryly, and turned his thoughts to what his brother might be doing now. If the days in the future paralleled

those in the past, by now James would know of
Collier's absence. Though he surely wondered what
had become of his rival, did he care? Did he know the
regret Collier felt that things could not have been better
between them? Unless something happened to bring
Collier back through time—and he would certainly
fight it—they would not see each other again, would
never have the opportunity to heal what their father
had wrought.

Collier glanced at Antony. Was James the reason
he was so determined to win the boy over? To find
redemption in this youth who was now his brother
through Catherine? A waste of time, Collier told himself, and returned his attention to the ride.

A half hour later, Antony veered toward a border-
ing wood. "There is a stream there," he shouted. "We
can refresh ourselves and the horses."

Collier looked to the trees. Did someone lie in
wait? He couldn't imagine Antony coming along simply for the ride. He slid his hand over the hilt of his
sword and dagger. Now if only he had eyes in the
back of his head.

As they neared the wood, they slowed.

Collier listened. Birds overhead. Small animals
skittering over fallen leaves. The silence of trees. Just
like a wood ought to sound. Deceptively so?

Antony led the way, and shortly the stream came
into sight. He dismounted and guided his horse forward.

Collier followed. He watched the boy lower himself beside the stream, then looked over the surrounding wood and tree tops. Nothing unusual, but that did
not mean they were alone. He knelt beside the stream,
splashed water over his face, and quenched his thirst.
Throughout, he felt Antony's gaze.

Collier wiped his face on his tunic and looked to the boy. Antony's eyes were nearly as hard as Catherine's had been when Collier had first come to Strivling. "Eventually you are going to have to accept the Yorkists, Antony," Collier said.

The boy cocked his head. "Like my sister? She is weak."

"You think so?" Collier stood. "And here I thought her the strongest woman I had ever known."

Antony also stood. "Strong? I can think of other words for her, but that is not one of them."

Brother or not, Antony was going to pay the price if he uttered any of those words. Collier stepped toward him. "You do not know Catherine."

"I know she is a traitor. That in wedding you, she turned from King Henry."

"And do you know why she wed me?"

Antony's laughter was harsh. "No doubt, you know well how to please her."

Collier grabbed the boy and shoved him against the tree behind. "She did it to save you and your family," he spoke between clenched teeth. "That you would not be attainted as Montagu threatened if she did not wed me."

Antony's eyes grew large. "I . . ." He swallowed. "I did not know."

Collier pushed the boy away, and in the next instant heard the low chirp of a bird. It stood out from the others. Just like in the movies.

Antony's startled gaze swept the wood.

"Expecting someone?" Collier asked.

His answer was the whistle of an arrow. Though it was surely meant for him, it skimmed his shoulder and pinned Antony's sleeve to the tree behind.

Walther?

Collier wrenched the boy forward. "Come on!" Dragging Antony after him, he ran toward the horses. In the next instant, the war cries rising from the trees caused Antony's horse to bolt.

"Damn!" Collier cursed. Not needing to look around to know the enemy was converging on them, he threw a leg over his horse and reached a hand to Antony. "Get up behind!"

The boy stared at him, then glanced over his shoulder.

An arrow rushed past Collier, narrowly missing him, but the next grazed his cheek. "Choose," he growled.

Antony's gaze wavered, then he slapped his hand into Collier's.

Collier swung the boy up behind and jabbed his heels into his horse. They were away, and in pursuit were at least half a dozen riders.

To avoid the rain of arrows, Collier wove his horse in and out of the trees. Then they were on open ground. Trickier. With Antony holding tight to him, Collier spurred the animal in the direction of Toller.

What chance had they of escape? he wondered. Without the added weight of Antony, it was possible, but with him?

He glanced over his shoulder. Although those the boy had brought against him did not seem to be gaining, neither were they falling back.

Collier closed his mouth against the curses he was tempted to spew and bent low in the saddle. As with everything worth doing well, focus was the key to doing it best. Single-mindedly, he pushed the horse in search of its limits. It responded beautifully. Beneath his hands and the press of his thighs, the animal gave. And gave more.

The land sped by. The hills rose and fell. The sun crept higher. And finally Toller came into sight.

"They have turned!" Antony shouted.

Gone? Perhaps. Perhaps not.

A few minutes later, Collier sped his horse over the drawbridge. "Lower the portcullis!" he bellowed.

Hardly had he said it when the gate began its descent. Toller's men-at-arms had not been lax in their duties. They had seen what transpired and been ready for it.

Collier halted his mount in the outer bailey and swung around.

Wary, Antony met his gaze.

Had the boy a good deal less pride, Collier thought he might have been reduced to tears, but not Antony Algernon, defender of King Henry and hater of Yorkists.

Collier thrust the boy off the horse. Though it was the least he wanted to do to him, it satisfied a bit of his anger.

On his back in the dirt, Antony stared at Collier.

"Next time you try to kill me," Collier said, "do not inconvenience me by having me save your neck." Beneath the gaze of those in the bailey and on the walls, he urged his horse toward the stables.

Quentin was waiting. "You . . . had a good ride, my lord?"

A more foolish question he could not have posed, Collier thought as he looked into eyes that held enough fear for both him *and* Antony. Had he known what the other boy intended? No, Collier didn't think so.

Leaving the squire's query unanswered, Collier dismounted and tossed the reins to him. Then he patted a hand across the horse's neck to its great jaw. "I am indebted," he said.

With a toss of its head and a roll of its liquid eyes, the destrier whinnied.

There was nothing quite like discovering a oneness with a horse, Collier thought—except, of course, the greater oneness to be found with a woman. Catherine. "Rub him down and see he gets extra feed," he instructed Quentin.

"Aye, my lord."

Collier turned.

"My lord, there is something I must tell—"

Impatient, Collier waved the boy's words away and strode across the bailey.

The hall was unusually quiet when he entered. No fire to warm the chill from the room. No servants. No Lewis Algernon.

Collier's mind jumped back to when he had earlier passed through the hall and thought the old man asleep. Had he guessed wrong? Was this what Quentin had tried to tell him?

He took the stairs two at a time, and at the landing was met by hand-wringing servants.

"What has happened?" he asked.

"'Tis Lord Algernon," a woman said. "He—" As if realizing the mistake she made in referring to the old man as the lord of Toller, she averted her gaze.

A path to the lord's solar opened for Collier. He strode down the corridor and knocked on the door.

Tilly admitted him. She must have read the question in his eyes, for she shook her head. "He is quite ill, my lord."

Collier stepped into the chamber.

Lewis Algernon lay propped against pillows in the middle of the huge bed. Leaning over him was a man Collier surmised to be the physician, and in a chair alongside the bed was Lavinia. Catherine and Eustace stood opposite, and the older knight, Sir Mathis, was before the hearth.

Catherine met Collier's gaze.

He saw sadness in her eyes, but also acceptance. She had known her father did not have much time left to him, and now that his days were closing, was prepared for his passing.

Suddenly, she frowned.

Collier realized he had forgotten about the arrow that had grazed his cheek. Surely it had left blood on his face.

The physician straightened from the bed. "There is naught to do but wait," he said. "It could be a day, mayhap as long as a sennight."

Eyes half-lidded, Catherine's father stared forward. Although he appeared to be conscious, it was questionable as to whether or not he was cognizant.

"He is to remain abed," the physician said.

Meaning he would no more occupy the lord's high seat. Collier knew there was no reason he should feel for the old man, but he did.

Without warning, Antony burst into the room and lunged past Collier. "Father!" He clasped one of Lewis's hands between his and urged the old man to respond, to look at him. But Lewis continued to stare forward.

Antony stilled, then turned on Collier. His cheeks were stained with tears. "You told them, didn't you?" he demanded.

Lavinia looked up. Her face was also moist with tears. "Told us what?"

Antony gazed at Collier with disbelief.

Collier pulled the door closed. "Return to your duties," he ordered the servants, and walked to his chamber.

*   *   *

In the quiet of the world he was trapped in, Lewis Algernon contemplated the bits of conversation that had filtered into his consciousness. Not much of it made sense, but he *had* figured out one thing: Antony had tried to kill the Yorkist and failed.

So why was Antony still alive? Gilchrist could not have had stronger justification for slaying the boy. A true Yorkist, and even a Lancastrian, would have done so, especially if the offender was heir to the properties the usurper had taken for himself.

Catherine's husband was strange indeed. If King Henry's bid to regain his throne was truly over with, was the Yorkist worthy of ruling Toller and its people? Perhaps, but first he would have to better his knightly skills which Sir Mathis said were sorely lacking. But the older knight would see to that.

Lewis's weary heart grew heavy for his son. Antony would have to make his own future. He only hoped the boy did not choose wrong.

Catherine wiped the blood from Collier's cheek. "Why did you not leave him in the wood?" she asked.

So, Antony had confessed. . . . Collier looked at Catherine. "He would have been forced to turn outlaw. I wanted him to have a choice."

"But he sought your death. Why do you care what becomes of him?"

More than once he had asked himself the same question. He shrugged. "He is too young to know better."

"He is almost a man."

Perhaps in this day and age, but only because medieval society forced adulthood on children regardless of whether or not they were ready for it. "Almost," he said.

Catherine sighed. "Ever I am owing to you."

"Your knight in shining armor, eh?"

"My what?"

"Your . . . champion," Collier tried again.

A smile eased her mouth and smoothed her brow. "That you are."

He liked it when she smiled. It was as if a light went on inside her. But he wanted more than smiles from her. He wanted to feel her silken skin against his, hear her sweet moans, taste her soft mouth . . .

She must have sensed it, for she hurriedly turned to the table and the pot of salve there.

More time? Collier wondered. How much more did she need?

"The lord's high seat is yours now," she said as she applied salve to his cheek. "You should sit there this eve."

He sought her gaze, but she would not give it to him. "It is not the high seat I want."

She looked at him.

"I want *you*, Catherine."

She started to draw back.

Collier caught her arm. "Night after night I am left aching for want of you." He pulled her between his thighs. "When are you going to let me touch you again?"

She stared at him a long moment, then released her breath. "I want you to, but . . ."

But still his secret stood between them, not to mention her fear of abandonment. Unfortunately, until he told her the truth about his past—or was it his future?—there was not much he could do to calm her fears. If only he could trust her. Collier released her and stood. "I'll be back late," he said, starting for the door.

"Where are you going?"

"The village of Tipping."

"But what of the rebels? They may still be out there."

He looked over his shoulder and saw the worry etched on her brow. "I doubt it." It was not likely they would expect him to leave the castle so soon following their attack. "But in the event they are, I shall take an armed escort with me." He opened the door.

"But 'tis near noon."

Collier nodded. "It will be dark when I return. Do not wait up for me." He stepped into the corridor and closed the door.

They were waiting for him. He should go.

Instead, Antony stared at the flicker of light from deep within the wood below Toller. Did they think him a traitor like his sister? Likely, for what else were they to believe? Choose, Gilchrist had demanded, and Antony had taken the Yorkist's hand and fled. But did that mean he had deserted King Henry? That he was now on the side of the usurper?

The thought turned his belly bitter. Never. If not for the Yorkists, his father would not be nearing death. And one day Toller would have been his. Antony cursed himself for not having stayed in the wood this morn. For not having joined the rebels. So why hadn't he?

Gilchrist.

"Damn you," he muttered. He wanted to hate the Yorkist with all the hate his sister once had for the enemy. And more. But Gilchrist was nothing like those who had taken Bamburgh Castle—who had humiliated Antony and the others who'd defended the fortress in the name of their king. He was different.

Though he wore his stolen title lightly, he had already earned the respect of many of the castle folk. He was not rash, seemed fair in settling disputes, praised Antony's swordsmanship, and took none of the opportunities that came his way to belittle him. Then, this morn, he had wasted precious time to give Antony a choice. Time which could have cost him his life. And afterwards, he had not carried tale to anyone else of what had happened.

Antony remembered the look on his mother's face when he had admitted what he had done. Horror. The fear that had risen in Catherine's eyes and the anger that had shortly replaced it. Eustace's childish awe. Their father's empty gaze.

He picked out the fire in the distance. What was he to do? More, what would *they* do to him? Fear rising, he latched on to the Lancastrian pride his mother had angrily denounced. He must not forget what he stood for. Regardless of what the rebels planned, he must go to them.

Antony swung away from the window.

"Catherine says King Henry will not be king again," Eustace spoke from the bed.

Antony faltered. He had thought his younger brother was asleep. "Catherine is a traitor. Do not forget that."

"She seems . . . kind."

"Is that what you are going to say to King Henry when he has her drawn and quartered—and you with her?"

The boy fell silent.

"Go to sleep, Eustace." Antony walked to the door.

20

An urgent knock awakened Catherine. She lifted her head from the pillow and peered through the darkness. It wouldn't be Collier, for even if he had returned from Tipping, he would not knock before entering their chamber. Tilly, then? Had something happened?

She tossed the covers back, and a moment later threw open the door. There stood Eustace, his face anxious. "What is it?" she asked.

He caught his bottom lip between his teeth and lowered his gaze.

"Eustace?"

"I . . ." He shifted foot to foot. "It's Antony. He has . . ."

"What?"

He looked back at her. "He has gone."

Although Catherine knew the answer, she asked, "To the rebels?"

"I think so."

She had so hoped that Antony's having chosen to return to Toller when the rebels had attacked meant he would finally come around, but it seemed not. "Then he has decided the way of the Lancasters," she said.

"Can you not stop him?"

"Stop him?" Catherine shook her head. "Antony must decide for himself, Eustace."

Tears rolled into the boy's eyes. "He is my brother. I do not wish him to leave."

Catherine felt torn. Though she doubted there was anything she could do to turn Antony from his path, the trust Eustace had placed in her made her wish she could.

"Please, Catherine," he pleaded.

If only Collier was here, but he was not. And even if he were, what would he do? Antony had betrayed him once already. Would he give the boy another chance? Nay, it would be asking too much of him, and rightfully so. It was best she dealt with it herself. "I will try," Catherine said, "but I make no promises."

A tearful smile turned the boy's mouth around. "Thank you, Catherine."

"How long ago did he leave?"

"Mayhap five minutes."

Then he might still be within the castle walls. Knowing it would be a waste of time to dress, Catherine donned her mantle over her chemise and pushed her feet into slippers.

"God speed," Eustace said as she stepped past him.

Careful not to disturb those sleeping in the hall, Catherine slipped out of the keep by way of the kitchen. She kept to the shadows as she traversed the inner and outer bailey looking for Antony, but it seemed he had gone.

Wrestling with whether or not she should continue her search, she saw again Eustace's pleading eyes. A moment later, she turned toward the postern gate. It was unguarded, and the bar that secured it had been pushed aside—by Antony, no doubt.

Catherine pulled her hood over her head and stepped through the gate. Outside the walls, she paused to study the land sloping away from Toller, and was shortly rewarded with a glimpse of a figure heading toward the wood. Antony had a good lead on her, but if she ran . . .

The moonlight from a cloudless sky was both a blessing and a curse. Whereas it allowed Catherine to keep sight of her brother, it also threatened to reveal her to the castle guard.

Ahead, Antony was nearing the wood. Although Catherine wanted to call to him, she feared her voice would carry to the castle walls. Desperate, she forced her legs to reach farther.

At first, she thought it was blood pounding in her head, but as the reverberation grew louder, she realized the sound came from outside herself. She looked left and saw the approaching riders, black against the indigo sky.

Her heart leapt. Was it Collier returning from the village, or the Lancastrians? Either way, it boded no good. If it was Collier, then Antony's betrayal might be revealed. If the rebels, Catherine faced capture and punishment, especially if Walther was among them.

Would she make it to the trees ere the riders were upon her? Suddenly the wood seemed far away. Her lungs beginning to burn, she groped for the strength to speed her to the wood, but there was not much more to be had.

*   *   *

He would tell her, Collier decided. All of it, and if she didn't believe him, then he had done all he could. Now the question was how to go about it.

With the silhouette of Toller rising in the distance, he searched for the words. Unfortunately, they proved as elusive as he had known they would. It was simply unbelievable. Why, even he still had moments when he questioned the reality of having traveled five hundred years into the past.

"My lord!" Sir Mathis shouted.

Collier looked to where the knight pointed, and a moment later saw that which had caught Mathis's eye. Though it was too dark to identify who stole toward the wood, Antony came first to mind. And if not the boy, then one of the rebels. If he had known for certain it was Antony, he would have let him go, but he didn't. "Let's go!"

Veering left, Collier and the half-dozen men he had taken with him to Tipping converged on the man as he neared the wood. A few moments later, they surrounded him.

"Show yourself," Collier commanded.

The figure whirled around. "Collier! I . . . I feared 'twas the rebels."

Not a man at all.

A murmur of surprise rose from the others as Collier stared at the cloaked figure of the woman who had betrayed him. The woman he had been about to tell his dangerous secret to. A Lancastrian.

With anger the only thing left to him, he urged his mount forward, leaned down, and tossed back the hood of her mantle. "Hello, *wife*."

The moonlight on Catherine's upturned face reflected an uncertain smile that immediately fell away. "I know what it must look like, but—"

"Leave us!" Collier ordered their audience.

Sir Mathis and the men-at-arms turned their animals toward Toller.

"It seems I have inconvenienced you," Collier said.

Catherine laid a hand to his knee. "You do not understand. I—"

"But I do understand. Completely."

She shook her head. "I beseech you, let me explain."

"You mean *lie*, don't you? Nay, Catherine, I do not wish to hear it."

The outrage that transformed her face was as genuine as any he had ever seen. But then, she had fooled him into believing he could give her his confidence. A confidence that might have seen him burned at the stake.

He reached a hand to her. "Now, if you are ready to return to Toller . . . "

She jumped back. "You speak of 'trust'! I have shared things with you I have never shared with another, and what do you give me in return? Naught!"

It was true, but surely it was part of the trap she and the Lancastrians were laying for him. Gain his trust, then find some way to use it against him.

Catherine pulled her mantle open to reveal the thin chemise that was all she wore beneath. "And what do you think of my attire, *husband*? Is it not perfect for a late-night rendezvous with your enemy?"

What *was* she doing wearing only her chemise? Collier wondered. The day she had gone down into the underground, she had eschewed her woman's garments in favor of those of a man. But if she was not going to meet the rebels, what other explanation was there for her flight into the wood? What reason would she have offered if he had allowed her to? No doubt a fantastic lie, he told himself.

Catherine dropped the mantle closed. "Believe what you will. I do not care." She swung around.

Collier stared at her back a long moment before following. "Come onto my horse, Catherine," he said as he overtook her.

She refused him her gaze. "I prefer to walk."

And nothing was going to convince her otherwise, he realized. Very well. As she would have it.

Collier was tired of the silence that had filled the hours since he and Catherine had spoken their last words on the night past. Side by side they had laid awake until dawn had finally stretched across the sky. Then, each avoiding the other, they had risen and dressed, attended mass, and afterward come down to meal. Not a single word.

His anger having calmed somewhat, Collier looked up from the simple meal of cheese and bread. "How is your father?" he asked, knowing Catherine had checked on him and her mother following mass.

She did not immediately respond—as if she had no intention of doing so—but after a while, she turned her cool eyes on him. "The same as yesterday."

"And your mother?"

The corners of her mouth tightened. "Faring well." She lifted her goblet and focused her attention on it.

Silence descended again.

Collier shifted in the chair he occupied beside the lord's high seat and looked past Catherine to where Eustace picked at his food. "Antony is not coming down?" he asked.

The boy looked up, then quickly away.

"He is abed?"

Eustace popped a crust of bread into his mouth and chewed it for all it was worth.

Disquiet rising, Collier waited for him to swallow, then asked, "Where is your brother?"

The boy reached for a piece of cheese.

"Eustace, where is Antony?"

"Likely practicing his sword," the boy muttered.

Collier doubted that. He stood. When the others in the hall also started to rise, he waved them back to their seats and stepped from the dais.

None in the inner bailey had seen Antony, nor in the outer bailey. As for the training yard, it was empty as was to be expected for this early in the morning.

Collier acknowledged what he had not wanted to until that moment: Antony had left Toller and gone over to the side of the rebels. But it was more than the boy's betrayal that stung, it was its bearing on Catherine's flight into the wood last eve. Had she, perhaps, left the castle in an attempt to stop her brother? Was that what she had wished to explain to him? It would certainly account for her poor choice of clothing.

With the feeling he had made a terrible mistake, Collier turned toward the keep, but as he did so, one of the men-at-arms caught his eye and nodded toward the stables.

Collier walked to the dimly lit structure. From the far end of the stables came the sound of movement. Peering into the shadows, he focused on the figure bent over the water trough.

It was Antony, his bared back to Collier. Then he had not left Toller, meaning—

Suddenly, Collier understood the reason Antony bathed in the stables rather than the keep. From the waist up, his back was a mass of bruises and scratches, and his arms as well. Obviously, he wanted none to see what he could not easily explain away—punishment for having returned to Toller rather than joining the rebels. But last night Antony had changed his mind and gone to them after all, only to be sent back. No doubt, to spy on his Yorkist lord.

Collier halted five feet from him. "Is his name Griffin Walther?"

Antony's shoulders tensed, and for a moment he did not move. Then, coming to life, he snatched his tunic from the ground, dragged it on, and turned.

Collier did not need to see Antony's chest to know it was as scored as his back, but at least his face had fared better. Only a few scratches and a bruise over his left eye.

"What do you want?" Antony demanded.

Though there was challenge in his eyes and the jut of his chin, he was also frightened.

"Tell me who did it," Collier said.

Antony stared at him a moment, then wiped his forearm across his damp brow. "I do not know what you speak of."

Collier took a step nearer him. "I speak of the one who dragged you behind a horse. Was it Griffin Walther?"

"Who?"

"Walther," Collier repeated.

Antony propped his hands on his hips. "Never heard of the man. As for being dragged"—he nodded to the stable behind—"'twas my own horse that did it. As you know, he's a skittish animal."

Looking closer, Collier saw that the horse within was the same which had fled yesterday when the rebels had come out of the wood. Skittish or not, the animal was not responsible for Antony's injuries—at least, not directly.

"Perhaps we ought to set you up with something a bit more tame," Collier suggested. "An old mare perhaps."

Antony surprised Collier with an indifferent lift of his shoulders. "If it so pleases you, *my lord.*"

Whatever had transpired these last hours before dawn, it had been enough to reestablish Antony as a Lancastrian. He'd had some sense beaten into him—unfortunately, the wrong kind.

Damn, but he was fighting a losing battle. "It does please me," Collier said, and turned away. He felt the bore of Antony's gaze all the way to the stable door.

Outside, the bailey was beginning to stir to life. The smithy was setting his fire, the carpenter had thrown open the shutters of his shop, and the lad who tended the chickens was tossing grain to the hungry birds. But all of it blurred against the need filling Collier. He had to speak with Catherine. *If* she would speak to him.

Lavinia looked up from where she sat on the edge of the bed. "He is resting well," she said.

Catherine noticed the shadows beneath her mother's eyes. "You should also rest. Go to my chamber and lie down. I will sit with Father."

Lavinia shook her head. "'Tis all the time I have left with him."

She had said the same thing earlier this morn when Catherine had offered to relieve her. "Very well," Catherine said, knowing it was useless to argue with her. "Would you have me stay with you?"

"'Tis not necessary. When he awakens, I will send

word." Obviously, she wanted to be alone with her husband.

Respecting her mother's wishes, Catherine turned away.

"Are you well, daughter?" Lavinia asked.

Catherine looked over her shoulder. "Aye, just a bit tired. I did not sleep well last night."

"Mayhap . . ." The sadness etched around Lavinia's mouth eased. "Could it be you are with child?"

Catherine shook her head. Her menses had come and gone since the one night she and Collier had spent as husband and wife. Thankfully. "I do not think so."

Obviously, Lavinia would have been pleased to learn she was going to be a grandmother—regardless of whether or not the child was born with the sight. Sorrow returning to her face, she looked at her husband. "I will send word when he awakens."

Her mother's pain deepening her own, Catherine closed the door. As she traversed the corridor, footsteps on the stairs warned of another's approach. A moment later, Collier appeared atop the landing.

She averted her gaze and started past him.

"Antony is returned," he said.

Wondering if she had heard right, she halted. "Antony? But he . . ."

"I know. It seems the rebels have sent him back to keep an eye on Toller."

Then Collier had learned Antony was missing only to discover him returned. Catherine looked away. "I see."

He placed his hands on her shoulders. "You were trying to stop him last night, weren't you? That's the reason you left Toller."

"So now you are willing to listen to my lies, hmm?"

"I am sorry. So sorry."

Catherine pretended nonchalance. "Do not feel badly about it, for eventually I would have betrayed you just the same. I am a Lancastrian, after all, and naught can change that."

Pain flashed across his face. "I know I hurt you, and I certainly deserve your anger, but—"

"Now I am the one who does not wish to hear it." Catherine shrugged off his touch. "I've work to do." She had taken only a step down when she paused. "You will send Antony away?"

"I haven't decided."

Catherine shrugged. "You probably should. After all, you *are* seriously outnumbered."

True, Collier admitted as she turned down the stairs. He was a single Yorkist among a hundred hating Lancastrians. The little he had gained with Catherine these past weeks was lost, thanks to his hasty conclusion last night. All because of his distrust of women.

Long after she had gone, Collier remained atop the stairs. Although part of him urged him to forget his love for Catherine and seek his return to the twentieth century, a greater part of him refused to. He had allowed Aryn to walk out of his life, and in doing so, had lost her forever. Now there was Catherine, and if he walked away from her, there would be nothing left but emptiness.

Whatever it took, he would win her back.

21

They were given no warning of his coming. With a stride so long and angry that few in the hall had time to stand before he was upon them, Edmund Morrow ascended to the dais. His eyes pinning Catherine where she had risen, he slammed the ledgers down in front of her. The impact caused the contents of the trenchers to slop across the tablecloth.

"Where is it?" Morrow demanded.

Catherine knew what he referred to, but did not understand why he didn't know where it was himself. Beside her, she felt Collier's tension as surely as if she touched him.

Then he had not given the money to Morrow as he'd said he would. Had he kept it for himself? The thought alarmed her, but more, the implications. She glanced at him. Was he a thief? A liar?

"Where?" Morrow asked again.

As distant as she and Collier had grown since his

accusations a sennight past, and as angered as she remained in spite of his attempts to right the wrong he had done her, she could not reveal him. "I do not know what you speak of, my lord," she said.

Morrow leaned across the table and thrust his face near hers. "I speak of the money that is missing from Strivling's coffers. Three hundred pounds."

"Three hundred?" But it had been eight hundred. Collier must have changed the entries, but then why had he not taken all of the money off the books? It made no sense. She stole a glance at him.

Trust me, his eyes seemed to say.

Yet he did not trust *her.* "It is as I told my husband when he inquired into it—I know naught of the whereabouts of the money, nor was I aware Strivling ever possessed such wealth."

Morrow shifted his gaze to Collier.

"I searched, my lord," Collier said, "but there was no money to be found."

Morrow considered him a long moment, then looked back at Catherine. "If not you, then who *would* know of it?"

She could not prevent the words from passing her lips. "Why, 'twould be the man in whose seat you now sit. Lord Somerton. Such a shame your Montagu had not a care for who fell beneath the fire of his siege. *He* could tell you."

Was it regret for what had happened at Strivling which came and went in Morrow's eyes? Or only regret that the old baron could not tell him where the money was?

"If you are lying to me, Catherine Algernon, and I learn you put Strivling's money into the hands of the Lancastrians, I vow your punishment will be harsh. Most harsh."

"Does such money exist, and *if* the Lancastrians possess it, I swear 'twas not given to them by me." Then she added, "And I am Lady Catherine *Gilchrist* now . . . my lord."

He cocked an eyebrow. "So you are."

Sensing a lull in his anger, Catherine looked past him to those at the surrounding tables. They waited, wary of this man who was now their baron—except Antony, who stared at her with something in his eyes that stirred her unease. She did not ponder it long, for it was time to play the lady of Toller. "You would join us, my lord?"

Morrow seemed to notice for the first time that the high seat sat empty. "You were expecting me?" he asked.

"Nay, my lord," Collier said, "but you are welcome at Toller."

Undoubtedly, he wondered why Collier had not claimed the highest place for himself, but he did not ask. Instead, he lowered himself into the lord's high seat. As baron of Highchester, it was due him during his stay at Toller, as was the lord's solar. If he intended to stay the night, which was fairly certain since darkness was descending, then her father would have to be moved.

Regaining her seat, Catherine nodded to the serving women who awaited her direction.

Trenchers and tankards of ale were brought for Morrow and his men, and though talk resumed, it was noticeably strained for the first half hour. Finally, Toller's people began to relax in the presence of their new baron.

Grudgingly, Catherine admitted that Edmund Morrow did not seem as unpleasant as she had first thought. He did not harass the women servants, smiled occasionally, and listened intently to the answers Collier supplied him with regards to the state of Toller. Perchance he would make Highchester a good baron after all.

The meal lasted longer than usual, but at last it drew to a close. "You will stay the night, my lord?" Catherine asked as Morrow rose from the chair.

"Aye. We will leave early morning."

"I will see that your chamber is readied." She stepped down from the dais and started across the hall. Barely had she set foot on the stairs when Collier intercepted her.

"Do not move your father," he said in a low voice. "Prepare our chamber for Morrow."

"But surely he will wish the lord's solar for himself."

"I will speak with him about it. We will take Antony's and Eustace's chamber."

Catherine couldn't believe Morrow would agree, but she conceded. "Very well." As she turned away, Collier stayed her with a hand to her arm.

"Catherine . . ."

She looked down at his strong, tanned fingers against her sleeve. Though she fervently wished she felt naught, there was no denying the heat that flushed her skin.

"Thank you," he said.

She met his gaze. Knowing he referred to her not having told Morrow about the money—trusting him again when he did not trust her—she nodded.

"I will explain it all," he said. "Wait up for me." Flashing a grin that made her catch her breath, he turned back into the hall.

After he left, Catherine noticed Antony standing back from the others, watching.

What was he thinking? she wondered. What mischief would he make of this day? She sighed. Doubtless, Collier was going to regret he had not sent Antony away.

Finally, Collier had something to hang his hope on. Catherine had not revealed him.

"Why did you not tell me what you had found in the books?" Edmund asked.

Collier looked into the shadowed planes of his ancestor's face. He had known this was what Edmund wished to speak to him about when he had asked him outside. However, there was no need to tell him that what he believed missing from Strivling's coffers far exceeded three hundred pounds. It could serve no purpose other than to make Edmund more determined to discover its whereabouts.

"As there was no money to be found, it was not uppermost in my mind," Collier said. "Then, with your return to Strivling so sudden, and our departure equally so, I forgot to mention it."

Edmund stared at him.

Was he believed? Collier wondered. Or did Edmund think he had taken the money for himself? If only he could reveal where the coin was hidden, but he could not.

Finally, Edmund asked, "You think Lady Catherine speaks the truth?"

"I do. There was no opportunity for her to deliver the money to the Lancastrians. Either it was smuggled out during the siege, or it never existed."

"What of her escape? She could have taken the money with her then."

"She had not gone far when I discovered her missing

and went after her. I saw her before she saw me, and she was carrying nothing."

"Hmm." Edmund fell silent. "I do not know why I trust you, Gilchrist," he said some minutes later, "but I do. I pray you will not disappoint me."

Collier bowed his head. "I am ever loyal, my lord."

"Aye, loyal, but what of your judgment?"

"My judgment?"

"You act the commoner you no longer are by eschewing the high seat. For what purpose?"

"Out of deference to my wife's father," Collier said. "The old man is dying and hasn't many days left." For certain, Edmund was not going to like what he said next. "I have allowed him to remain in the solar with his wife, Lady Lavinia."

It was a very long moment before Edmund spoke again. "A lord who does not sit in the high seat? Nor take the lord's solar for himself?" He shook his head. "I have given you a castle, lands, and a title, yet you do them no honor."

Collier realized he had offended Edmund. "I suppose it is the common in me," he said, "but I fail to see what harm there is in allowing an old man to die with respect. My dinner will taste no better if I sit in the high seat, nor will my sleep be more restful in the lord's solar."

Edmund stepped near him. "If you do not claim what is yours, these people will think you weak and try to take it from you. *That* is the harm of it."

At first, Collier blamed Edmund's words on medieval thinking, but then he reminded himself that he had been like-minded with his business dealings of the twentieth century. He had always believed in a show of force, in giving no quarter, and that there was no place for compassion in business dealings. So what had changed his attitude?

He did not have to search far. It was Catherine. Loving her even though his feelings were not returned—and might never be.

"Have you naught to say?" Edmund asked.

Collier met his gaze. "As you have said yourself, I do not fit, my lord. I see things differently. All I can do is ask you to trust me in this."

"And if you fail me?"

Would he? With every day that passed, he was more and more accepted by these people. No longer did he feel their hatred, nor see it in their eyes. No, though he may have failed with Catherine, he was definitely making progress with Toller's people. "Upon my word," Collier said, "I will not fail you, my lord."

Edmund was thoughtful for a long moment, then nodded. "I will hold you to it." He turned back toward the keep. "Any more sightings of the rebels?"

Collier walked beside him. "None." Knowing Edmund should be apprised that the Lancastrians were in the vicinity, he had sent word of last week's attack. However, he had not mentioned that Antony had been behind it.

"Word has reached me that it is Griffin Walther who leads them," Edmund said, "and that he is trying to raise an army."

"Trying?"

"Aye, but without funds, he cannot possibly gather enough men to do more than harass us."

They started up the steps of the keep.

"I have decided to take Lady Catherine's brother with me when I return to Strivling," Edmund said.

Collier halted. "Antony?"

"I need a squire."

"But his loyalties—"

"Lie with the Lancastrians. This I know."

"Then why choose him?"

"He is strong, determined, and though young, he thinks like a warrior. In short, he is worthy."

"But if you cannot trust him, what good is any of that?"

"Time and a firm hand should bring him to the side of the Yorkists," Edmund said. "He will learn his place."

Collier felt pulled in opposite directions. Should he tell Edmund of Antony's role in the attack? If he was going to take the boy as his squire, he ought to know. But then, how would Edmund react to learn of Antony's Lancastrian activities? What punishment would he mete out? "I cannot be certain, my lord," Collier said, "but I suspect Antony had something to do with the attack last week."

Edmund considered him a moment, then said, "I would be surprised if he did not."

Then there was something he was not saying. "Yet you would still make him your squire?"

"Should he fail me, he will lead me to the rebels." He smiled. "You see, my friend, some good comes of every ill."

Then Antony was to be used as bait?

"'Tis as a squire I want Antony," Edmund said, as if reading Collier's mind. "In that I speak the truth. However, does he betray me, I will not be above taking advantage of that betrayal."

It was probably for the best, Collier conceded. If Antony remained at Toller, he would eventually cause more trouble.

A quarter hour later, Collier entered the room Antony and Eustace shared, but which was to be his and Catherine's this night.

"Morrow has taken our chamber?" she asked from a chair before the hearth.

Collier strode forward. "He has."

Catherine's worried brow smoothed. "Was he angry when told my father occupies the solar?"

"He was not pleased."

"I did not think he would be." She clasped her hands in her lap. "I thank you, Collier."

He halted alongside the chair opposite her. Although she would find out soon enough, he had to tell her about her brother. "Morrow intends to take Antony with him to Strivling."

Her eyes widened. "Whatever for?"

"He wants him for his squire."

Catherine stared at him a long moment, then said, "You asked him to take Antony?"

"No. I was as surprised as you when he told me of his plans."

"Does he know about the attack? That Antony was behind it?"

"I told him only that I suspected his involvement."

"And still he wishes to make him his squire?"

"He believes he can turn Antony's loyalties."

"And if he cannot?"

"Then Antony will lead him to the rebels."

She drew a deep breath. "I see."

They both knew it far more likely Antony would betray Edmund than come over to the side of the Yorkists.

For what seemed a very long time, nothing more was spoken between them, then Catherine stood and walked to the bed. "What about Strivling's coin, Collier?"

He did not know how he was going to tell her, only that it was time to tell her everything. Time to trust. "I will explain," he said, "but first I need to tell you about Aryn."

She turned. "Aryn?"

"Yes."

She shook her head. "'Tis not necessary."

"But it is." He steeled himself for the pain of what he was about to say. "I lost her because I didn't tell her I loved her, nor did I show her." Memories of the day she had walked out on him returned to Collier. "I didn't trust her, just as I haven't trusted you. Worse, I lied to her."

Catherine looked puzzled.

Would she believe him? Collier wondered. "The only reason I'm here with you is because, after learning of Aryn's death, I pleaded for a second chance with her. You were it, Catherine. My second chance."

"Just because I look like—"

"I am not from here."

"Of course not."

She misunderstood. "What I mean is that I am not of your world. Not of this time."

"This time?"

"The fifteenth century."

Her eyebrows drew together sharply. "What do you speak of?"

Of course it was unbelievable. It had been the same for him when he had come through her portrait and found himself attired in medieval dress. He had been so certain it was only a dream. "I'm from the twentieth century, Catherine. I was born five hundred years from now."

Catherine could only stare at him. What was he talking about? Was he jesting? Surely. Otherwise it could only mean he was . . . mad?

"It's true," he said.

"You are telling me you are not even born, and yet here you are? You jest, Collier Gilchrist."

There was no laughter in his eyes. Instead, they were intense. Serious. "If you can dream of the future, why is it inconceivable that I am *of* the future?"

Still it did not seem possible. Was he mad, then? Lord, she prayed not, but what other explanation was there?

"My name is Morrow," he said. "Collier Gilchrist Morrow."

Catherine stepped back, as if she'd been dealt a blow. "Then you and Edmund . . ."

"Are related. Through him I was born, though not for another five hundred years."

A nervous laugh spilled from Catherine's lips. "What you are saying is impossible. Such things do not happen."

"But it did."

She held up a staying hand. "I do not wish to hear any more of this nonsense, and neither should you speak of it to anyone else."

"Just as your father did not wish you to speak of your dreams?"

Her breath snagged. It was true. "I . . ."

Collier motioned to the bed. "Sit down and I will explain."

She hesitated before lowering herself to the mattress.

Collier strode to the window. "When I was growing up, there was a picture that hung in the library of my home—a landscape painted in the sixteenth century. On the surface, it was hardly deserving of display, but because of its age it was worth a great deal of money. Thus, my father liked to show it."

He was silent a long moment. "One day when I

was about ten, I was in the library reading. Something drew my attention to the picture, and it was then I saw a stain of red on it. Upon closer inspection, I discovered it was not a stain at all. The top layer of paint had peeled away." He looked over his shoulder at her. "The red was of a rose, Catherine. A Lancastrian rose."

Something fearful crept over her skin.

"My father brought in specialists, and it was determined that the original painting was of the fifteenth century. But though restoration was attempted, the top layer of paint would not be forced. By the time I was sixteen, enough of the paint had come away to reveal an unfinished portrait of a woman. However, most of her features remained hidden."

Catherine wished he would tell her no more, but he continued.

"As the picture had been brought out of my family's ancestral home—Strivling Castle—my father believed the lady to be the one legend said had held Strivling against the Yorkists during the Wars of the Roses." He captured Catherine's gaze. "Her name was Catherine Algernon, and she died defending the winch room when a mercenary named Walther turned her sword on her."

Catherine jumped to her feet. "I . . . I will listen to no more."

In an instant Collier was at her side. "Is it not your dream, Catherine?" He gripped her shoulders. "The one you had before I came to you that night?"

"I do not believe in such things—will not believe in such things!"

"Then how do you explain it? You told me all your other dreams have come to pass, except the one of your death. My coming changed that. I asked for a second chance with Aryn and was brought backward through time. To be with you."

She shook her head. Lord, let him not say what she feared he might.

"The night I received news of Aryn's death, the rest of the landscape fell away to reveal Catherine Algernon staring out at me with the face of the woman I had loved and lost."

Catherine began to tremble. She remembered having come upon him in her chamber when he had stood over the portrait. Hearing him say he would find Aryn. "I am not Aryn," she declared.

His eyes swept her. "You are in her image, and sometimes I see glimpses of her in you, but no, you are not Aryn. Time and circumstances have made you different."

"But you are saying I will live again. In this other woman. 'Tis not the teachings of the church, Collier!"

He sighed. "I know. But it is a prayer answered. A tip of God's hand, if you will."

"I cannot believe He would do such a thing."

Something darkened Collier's eyes. "When you fell into the sea, I made a promise that never again would I question God's existence if only He would help me reach you. And when I could stretch no more, and you were lost to me, your hand came into mine."

She recalled it herself. The water closing around her, dragging her under. And just as she'd acknowledged her life was forfeit, she felt the strength of Collier's grip.

He cupped her face in his palm. "Although I came to find Aryn—prayed she was somewhere beneath your hate—it's you I have come to love, Catherine. As I have never loved before."

He seemed so sincere. So certain of what he said.

As loudly as her mind rejected the possibility of Collier having come across five hundred years to be with her, Catherine's heart whispered that just maybe it was possible. If so, it would explain so much about him that made no sense: his peculiar speech and behavior, his unusual facility with letters—despite his strange spellings—and numbers, and that he did not act the man of lowly birth he claimed to be. More, it explained how he had known she should have died in the winch room, and how his arrival had changed that. Had changed her dream.

Panic gripped Catherine as she realized she was beginning to believe. With a gasp, she wrenched out of Collier's hold and put the length of the room between them. "I would rather think you mad," she said.

A wry smile slanted his mouth. "For a while, I thought so myself, but I'm not mad. It really happened. And now you understand why I couldn't tell you."

If not mad, then deceiving her, she decided. Aye, he had constructed this incredible tale to explain away his thievery of Strivling's wealth. "What of the coin?" she asked.

"It's in the storeroom—returned to its hiding place where it was forgotten when you died at Walther's hands. If you'd like, I will show you when next we go to Strivling."

Catherine moistened her lips. "If what you say is true"—and it couldn't be—"why would you not give it to Morrow as you told me you intended? Or keep it for yourself?"

Collier thrust a hand through his hair. "Although I have not always succeeded, I have tried to keep history as closely the same as possible. True, I irreversibly changed it by giving you back your life, but for what other reason would I have been brought back? As for the coin, I don't know what happened to it in that other past—whether Edmund found it, or another, or if it still lies buried in the twentieth century—but whatever its fate, it had to be returned to its hiding place."

"Then why would you change the entries in the ledgers?"

He shook his head. "I did not. Obviously, my ancestor does not know his numbers very well."

It seemed Collier had an answer for everything. Was what he said possible? That she had been reborn in another time and place? That his love for this other woman had resurrected her from the dead?

"I insisted on leaving your portrait behind for the same reason as the coin," he said. "It's how I got here, Catherine. Through your portrait."

Catherine looked longingly at the bed, wanting to bury her head beneath a pillow and not come out for a good, long month.

"There is more I need to tell you," Collier said. He swept a hand to the chair. "Please, Catherine."

A struggle between her heart and her mind ensued, but finally she took the chair.

Over the next hour, Collier paced the chamber, speaking of Aryn and how he had met her, telling her of his climbing accident, his resultant addiction to what he called "painkillers," and of his struggle to purchase Strivling Castle only to lose it to another. He told her of Aryn's anger upon discovering he had lied to her about the painkillers, the treatment he had gone through in hopes of winning her back, the letter that had been waiting for him when he had come home from the treatment center, her portrait drawing him into the past. . . .

It explained so many things. So many that Catherine wanted to believe it was all true.

Looking tired, Collier lowered himself into the chair opposite her and closed his eyes.

Catherine's gaze was drawn to the sword on his belt. It was the one he had told her had been set beneath her portrait all those years in the future. The same which Walther had taken from her, and in that other past had turned on her. How could she not believe Collier?

"That is my secret, Catherine." He looked at her. "That is what I could not tell you or anyone else. Not even Edmund."

And now she understood why—providing what he told her was the truth. "What of King Henry?" she asked. "Is it true what you said? That he will not be king again?"

"His reign is over, but he will return. Providing my presence has not upset the course of events, six years from now he will regain the throne, then Edward will unseat him one last time."

Although part of Catherine wanted him to elaborate, the other did not. But there was something she needed to know. "If what you say is true," she said, clinging to her shredded doubt as if it were all the sanity left to her, "what happened in that other past? After I died."

He sighed. "There is not much I can tell you beyond the legend of Catherine Algernon."

Her a legend . . . "But what do you know?"

"As with now, Edmund Morrow was awarded the barony."

"And Toller? My family?"

It was a long moment before he answered. "I sent Walther from Strivling, and though he has joined with the Lancastrians again, it was not to have been that way."

She swallowed. "What are you saying?"

"Toller was to have been his. Griffin Walther's."

That was saying enough. Fear for what would have become of her family swept Catherine.

Collier leaned forward in his chair. "It's different now," he reassured her. "Though I shouldn't have interfered further with the course of time, your family is safe."

"What about where you come from? Is there no one who will miss you? Who will question your disappearance?"

"No."

"What of your mother? Your father?"

"My father is dead."

"I am sorry."

He was silent a long moment, then said, "As for my mother, I have not seen her for twenty years—not since she walked out on my father."

"Walked . . . out on him?"

Collier shrugged. "He was not a pleasant man to live with. My mother finally had enough and decided to trade him in for a new life. She never looked back."

Catherine didn't understand anything about "trading husbands in," but she felt Collier's pain even if he pretended not to feel it himself. After all, she also knew the pain of abandonment. "So she left you with your father."

"And my older brother as well—James."

"Is your mother the reason you did not trust Aryn to tell her you loved her?"

Irritation snapped Collier's eyebrows together. "Playing psychologist, Catherine?"

"Psy . . . psychol . . . ? I do not know," she said,

wondering whether or not she should be offended. "Am I?"

Almost instantly, the displeasure cleared from his brow. "You are, but you're also right. My mother had every right to leave my father. In fact, she should have left him sooner. Still, the fact that I never heard from her again caused me to distrust women—even Aryn whom I had planned to marry."

"And what of your brother? Will he not miss you?"

He laughed. "More than likely he will rejoice."

"Rejoice?"

Collier's gaze grew distant. "When we were younger, we got along well in spite of our father's efforts to pit us against each another. However, once we were brought into the family business, things changed. It was 'outdo or be outdone.' Overnight we went from being brothers to adversaries. The old man couldn't have been happier."

"But your father is dead now."

"Yes, but his legacy is not." Collier's jaw hardened. "You see, James is the one I lost Strivling to."

His own brother? Catherine slipped out of the chair and dropped to her knees before him. "I am sorry," she said.

He searched her eyes, then reached forward and caressed her cheek. "So am I. If there were some way I could make things right with him, I would."

A sudden thought struck Catherine. If all Collier had told her of traveling through time was true, then could he return to his own time? More, did he wish to? "Will you stay?" she asked, dreading his answer.

"Does this mean you believe me?"

"I wish to."

It was something, Collier told himself. Not enough, but more than he'd had this past sennight of near silence. "I came back for you, Catherine. I would not leave without you."

"*Can* you leave?"

"I don't know. The night you came upon me in your chamber, I felt the pull of your portrait, but it lacked the strength which had first propelled me through it." He felt a shudder of fear go through her.

"Do you wish to leave?" she asked.

He shook his head. "It has been difficult fitting into your world, and I do miss the modern conveniences I was accustomed to, but more and more I grow content with this life."

Her shoulders sagged as if with relief, but tensed a moment later. "Are you certain 'tis me you love, Collier, and not Aryn, whom you see in me?"

He smiled. "It's you, Catherine. Though Aryn will always have a place in my heart, you *are* my heart. I want to spend my life with you."

When she lifted her gaze to his, tears sparkled on her lashes. Would she finally declare her feelings? Collier wondered. Would she speak the words of love he so needed to hear?

Instead, she leaned forward and pressed her mouth to his.

Though he was disappointed, Catherine was too sweet to ignore. Gently, Collier urged her lips apart and touched his tongue to hers.

A short while later, they came together with a hunger so great they did not bother to remove their clothes. Amid the twisted garments they sought one another, found pleasure in the places they uncovered, and cried out when their bodies met like thunder to the sky.

Afterwards, Collier held Catherine, stroked her, and when she caught her breath, began to rouse her again. And so it went until, finally, neither could give any more.

"An unfinished portrait of Lady Catherine was found in her chamber," Edmund said, looking down at Collier from atop his destrier.

Collier nodded. "I thought it best to leave it behind."

"You do not wish it, then?"

"Doubtless, King Edward would not approve of a portrait of my wife which so strongly proclaims her a Lancastrian."

Edmund chuckled. "Ah, the red rose. It could be painted over."

"It *would* be a pity to waste such a fine piece of canvas." Collier hoped Edmund would think so himself. "But I would rather start anew."

"I understand."

Actually, he did not, but then, he wasn't supposed to. "What will you do with it?" Collier asked.

"I had it carried to the storeroom." Edmund shrugged. "Mayhap the canvas can be used for something else."

A landscape, though it would not be painted in Edmund's lifetime.

Edmund looked around. "What did Antony say when you told him?"

Collier followed his gaze to where Antony was ascending to the saddle of the palfrey he'd been reduced to. Before him stood Catherine, her mother, and Eustace.

"That he accepts no Yorkist as his lord," Collier said, which was putting it mildly. In truth, Antony had raged when told Edmund wanted him for his squire. Knowing it would be useless to try to reason with him, Collier had left him to it. But though the boy was no longer raging, he was still angry.

"And so we shall see," Edmund said.

So they would.

Beneath her mantle, Catherine hugged her arms to her against the crisp morning air.

In spite of Antony's unkempt golden hair and the malice in his eyes, he was handsome, she thought as she looked at him astride his horse. Very soon he would have many a maid falling at his feet. If he lived that long.

She glanced at her mother. Lavinia's eyes were swollen from the tears she'd wept upon being told Antony was leaving. As for Eustace, he was controlling his emotions admirably well—with the exception of that lower jutting lip.

Catherine stepped to Antony's side. She knew he would reject her, but still she laid her hand over his. "God be with you," she said.

He jerked his hand away. "Waste not your prayers on me, Sister. *I* am not the one who needs them."

Hurt swept over her. She hardly knew him, but still she felt for him, and she needed to warn him. "Hate me," she said in a low voice, "but do not throw your life away on foolish gestures, Antony. Henry's reign is over." These were almost the same words Collier had spoken to her, she realized.

He gave a mocking smile. "Be prepared, Catherine, for you will surely answer to King Henry for this day." He wheeled his horse around and trotted the animal to where Morrow's men awaited their lord.

Catherine refused to allow her shoulders to sag beneath the burden settling upon them. She would be strong. Not for Hildegard or anyone else. But for herself and Collier.

She looked to where he stood alongside Morrow. Dark hair sweeping off his brow and curling over the neck of his tunic, shoulders broad and straining the seams, and large hands expressive as he spoke, he looked all the man her betrothed had never been.

Nay, Collier was not born to the sword as many a warrior of this "medieval age" was, nor did he act the noble, but he was more worthy than any man she had ever known.

As she watched, Morrow leaned down from his destrier and said something to Collier.

The corners of Collier's eyes crinkled and his teeth flashed white. Then, as if feeling Catherine's regard, he glanced her way.

What that smile did to her heart and her hopes for the future. She reveled in the glow warming her. It was beautiful. Thrilling. But also frightening, for nothing in life had prepared her to feel anything like this. It went beyond desire. It filled all the empty places inside her which no one, and no thing, had ever filled.

Was it love? Collier had said he loved her, and she knew he was waiting to hear the same from her, but was that what she felt?

Morrow's shout reminded her of where she was. She looked up as the baron and his men guided their horses out of the bailey onto the drawbridge. Antony trailed behind.

"You did this. You sent him away!"

Catherine turned toward the tear-filled voice.

Hands clenched at his sides, Eustace stood before Collier. "I hate you!" he said, and ran from the bailey.

"Eustace!" Lavinia called.

Her mother had lost much weight this past sennight, Catherine realized as she watched Lavinia hurry after Eustace. She looked fragile, as if a slight breeze might blow her over. She certainly did not need the burden of dealing with her younger son's anger.

Catherine caught up with her mother in the inner bailey. "I will go to Eustace," she said. "Return to Father."

"I . . ." Her shoulders sagging, Lavinia nodded.

Catherine took her mother's arm and together they climbed the steps to the keep.

22

For the briefest of moments, Catherine weighed the option of the dreaded chore of sewing against seeking out her husband. Not surprisingly, the latter won out. She could use some fresh air.

Upon inquiring into Collier's whereabouts, she was pointed to the training yard outside the castle walls. Thus, she traded the fresh air for the dust stirred by soldiers practicing their arms. Somewhere amid the haze, was Collier.

Noticing Eustace where he straddled the upper rail of fence, Catherine walked to him. However, he was too intent on the melee to realize he was no longer alone.

"You have seen my lord husband?" she asked after some time had passed and he had yet to acknowledge her.

Eustace looked down at her. "I have not," he said, and turned his attention back to the yard. It was more than a sennight since Antony had gone to Strivling, but Eustace's anger was no less felt.

With a sigh, Catherine searched the yard, and shortly picked out Collier among the soldiers. His opponent was a man smaller than he, but more experienced. However, the longer Catherine watched, the more she realized Collier's skill had developed beyond his ability to defend himself. True, the soldier fought better, but more than once Collier forced him on the defensive.

Catherine smiled. She had known Collier was practicing, determined as he was to master the sword, but she would not have guessed he would progress so rapidly. But then, neither would she have believed he could climb a cliff face with naught to hold him to it but his fingertips. For a man not yet born, he was truly remarkable.

Abruptly, she drew her thoughts to a halt. Though more and more she believed Collier's story and the remarkable tales he told her when they lay in bed at night, she continued to hold onto her doubt.

"Did you see that?" Eustace exclaimed, pointing to the household knights.

The younger knight swiped at the back of his tunic as if he had landed in the dirt. Several feet to the right of him lay his sword and, standing over it, Sir Mathis.

"Sir Laurence swears he will one day better Sir Mathis," Eustace said, "but he can never get close enough."

Catherine knew her brother was in awe of these men who lived their lives on the edge of a sword. As a child, she had loved to watch the soldiers practice, and from time to time, the men had humored her by permitting her to handle their weapons—not that she had become proficient with them, but she had understood the power of a finely-honed blade, the point of a spear, and the flight of an arrow. Only after Edward had taken the throne from Henry had she come to understand the true horror of weapons.

She looked back at Eustace. Soon he would don the raiments of war and ply his sword for the gain of another—just as those who had defended Strivling had done. Their deaths still burdened Catherine.

"'Tis an exciting thing to watch," she said.

Eustace was too caught up in it to pull his gaze away. "Aye. Someday I will wield arms myself, and then I shall smite my enemies."

"The Yorkists?"

"Of course."

Catherine sighed. "'Tis far different from this, Eustace. This is play, not war."

He regarded her a long moment, then asked, "Is it true you raised a sword against our enemy?"

"Aye, and it was a foolish thing to do."

"Because you are a woman."

She should have expected that. "No. Because the battle was long lost. I allowed pride to guide me rather than reason." And she had been living for Hildegard.

"Antony told me you have turned your back on King Henry."

Had she? "Only on his war." As Catherine had come to realize, and Collier had confirmed, there was naught but bloodshed to be gained from it.

Catherine followed Eustace's gaze and saw it was Collier he had fixed on, and that Sir Mathis stood before him now.

"Antony told me 'tis the Yorkist who made you a traitor," Eustace said.

Antony talked too much and hated too deeply.

"He told me 'tis by the bed Gilchrist holds you."

Anger spurted through Catherine. How dare Antony speak such to his younger brother! "And do you believe everything your brother tells you?"

"He is the only one who tells me anything. And now he is gone."

The sorrow in his voice calmed Catherine's ire. He was lonely—at that awkward stage when he was no longer a child, yet many years from becoming a man. And though his father still lived, he was unable to offer the encouragement and reassurance his younger son needed. Eustace might as well be fatherless.

Hurting for him, Catherine returned her attention to the yard and was surprised to see that both Collier and Sir Mathis held quarterstaffs—rods spanning six-and-a-half-feet and weighted at both ends.

Sir Mathis intended to instruct Collier? Catherine wondered. The knight was staunchly Lancastrian and unwaveringly loyal to Lewis. So why the interest in Collier? Did he hope to humiliate him?

Collier also wondered at the knight's purpose. Few words had passed between them since the man had offered advice on swordplay weeks back. So why now his offer to show how a fight was fought?

"Grab it in the middle," the knight said, demon-strating. "And place your other hand a quarter of the way from the end." Then he assumed a half-crouched stance and beckoned Collier forward. "Now come."

A few moments later, their staffs crossed.

The knight thrust Collier away, rotated his staff, and countered with a blow that forced Collier back a step. Then he thrust again. "The trick," he said, meeting Collier's gaze between the angle of their joined staffs, "is to spin the staff"—he did so, and slammed it against Collier's—"each time shifting your grip quarter-to-quarter."

He steadily pressed Collier backward, moving so rapidly it was all Collier could do to block the jabs and thrusts.

"Look for the opening," Sir Mathis said, and a moment later stabbed the weighted end of his staff toward Collier.

Collier swung his staff down, blocking the blow that would have knocked his legs out from under him.

Immediately, Sir Mathis engaged him again. "When your opponent is recovering from one blow, deliver another." He did so. "Do not let him rest." He swung high, narrowly missing Collier's hand where he held the staff. "*Then* you will have him." He lunged forward, slid his left hand down the staff, joined it with his right, and swung like a batter to a baseball. His quarterstaff landed in Collier's gut. "And that is how 'tis done."

Maintaining his hold on the staff, Collier fought his way past the ache. So *that* was how it was done.

"Position!" Mathis forewarned.

Collier sucked a deep breath and raised his staff.

Around the yard they fought, each step and blow followed by the soldiers in the yard and those on the walls.

They were taking bets, Collier realized when he saw the soldiers digging in their purses. Unfortunately, that glimpse left him vulnerable. A moment later, with his shoulder aching fiercely, he resumed his position.

Do not let him rest, the knight had said. Very well. Rather than attempt to better Mathis, Collier studied his moves as the knight wore himself down. His opportunity would come soon, he was certain.

Sooner than expected. Slow to recover from a meeting with Collier's staff, the knight left his belly open, and a moment later Collier found his mark.

With a grunt, Sir Mathis seated himself in the dirt.

A groan rose from the onlookers. Obviously, most had favored the older knight.

A hand pressed to his belly, Sir Mathis looked up at Collier. Then, surprisingly, he grinned. "You learn quickly, my lord. I must needs remember that."

Collier reached a hand out to him.

Sir Mathis grabbed his wrist and stood. "You will do, Lord Gilchrist," he said.

Would he? Collier wondered. If—no, when—the need arose, would he be capable of defending Toller?

Sir Mathis jutted his chin to a point beyond Collier. "Tomorrow, the quintain."

Meaning the knight was taking it upon himself to ensure Toller's lord was worthy. "I'm game," Collier said.

Clearly, Sir Mathis did not understand the modern expression.

"Tomorrow," Collier restated.

The knight inclined his head and strode from the yard.

"You fought well."

Collier turned at the sound of Catherine's voice. He had not known she'd come to the training yard.

"'Twas quite a display," she said, halting before him. "Methinks very soon the garrison will accept you."

"That is what I'm working toward."

"You need a bath, husband."

As he was well aware of. From head to toe he was covered in filth and sweat. Of course, as with all his baths since he'd arrived in the fifteenth century, it would be accomplished with a basin of tepid water

and a hand towel. What he wouldn't give for a stinging hot shower followed by a long soak in a tub. The
twentieth century was not *all* bad.

"Come." Catherine laid a hand to his arm. "I will
see that a bath is drawn for you."

"As in a *real* bath?"

"Of course."

"In a tub?"

"We *do* have one at Toller. You thought we did
not?"

As he had not seen one, he'd assumed Catherine
was also bathing herself with a basin and towel. "I
was beginning to wonder," he said.

She laughed. "Toller is not *that* backward. Why,
we even have a pulley to hoist the water abovestairs."

A pulley . . . not at all backward, Collier thought
wryly.

"How do you do it in your time?" Catherine asked.

Even if he were an expert on plumbing, which he
certainly was not, it would take much explaining.
"First the bath."

"Then the tale?"

"If you truly wish to hear it."

"I do."

However, it was not the subject of twentieth-century
baths that Catherine broached once Collier was settled
in the wooden tub. Staring at him where he sat with his
head back against the tub edge and his eyes closed, she
gloried in the feelings surging through her. Was it the
same as Collier felt—loving her with a love beyond that
which he had known in another time and place?
Loving her, Catherine. Not merely the image of Aryn?

Whatever it was, it grew a longing in her. She
leaned forward and brushed her mouth across his.

He opened his eyes.

"I . . ." How did one go about telling their husband they wished to make love? It could not possibly be proper.

Collier smiled. "You wish to join me?"

In the tub? Even if there *was* room for both of them, a bath was not what she wanted.

"I was thinking . . ." She lifted a shoulder. "Perhaps you might wish to come out."

He shifted his legs beneath the water. "I would prefer it if you came in."

Something in his voice told her it was more than a bath he was offering. When she swept her gaze over him, she realized that beneath the water he was erect. As she stared at him, he grew even more so. But surely he couldn't mean—

"It would be best if you removed your clothes," he said.

Catherine met his dark-eyed gaze. He *did* intend to make love to her in the bath. The thought of it caused her pulse to quicken and heat to diffuse her skin.

"Should I help you?" he asked.

With a shake of her head, she began removing her clothes. Beneath Collier's stare, her hands felt clumsy—uncertain—but finally the last of the fastenings gave way.

She stepped into the tub and Collier pulled her onto his lap.

Feeling his male member hard against her backside, she shuddered. She wanted him inside her. Wanted to be one with him again. "Collier," she said.

"Shh." He urged her back against his chest. "I want to show you something."

The water rose precariously near the lip of the tub as Catherine eased her head back against his shoulder.

Slowly, Collier's hands began to move over her— circling her breasts, feathering her sides, spanning her abdomen, pressing the outsides of her thighs, then the insides.

Now? Catherine wondered. She felt him strain against her, but he did not touch that place of hers that ached.

Turning his breath into her ear, he glided his hands back to her breasts and began rolling her nipples between his fingers.

Catherine's ache deepened.

"You like that?" he asked.

"Aye."

"And this?" Lightly, he traced the shell of her ear with his tongue.

Her breath catching, she nodded.

He nipped the lobe of her ear, then pulled her chin around. His mouth came down hard on hers. Hungry. Seeking. His tongue pressing inside and claiming all.

Catherine tried to kiss him back, but he consumed her. His lips seemed everywhere at once—her mouth, ear, neck, and shoulder. His hands spun silken webs of desire over places he had touched before, and those he had not. His fingers thrilled and left fire in their path. He roused her, made her burn, caused her to cry out, and yet not once did he touch her woman's place.

Catherine wanted, yet did not. Was satisfied, yet was not. She felt drunk, as if her veins ran with wine. Weak, as if Collier had already moved inside her and wrung pleasure from her. But he had not. Had he? As long as he didn't let go of her, it didn't matter. As long as he didn't stop touching her.

"Are you ready, Catherine?" he asked, his voice coming to her as if from far away. Almost a whisper.

Ready? For what?

A moment later, she had her answer.

Collier pushed inside her, stilled, then withdrew and came to her again.

Catherine was deluged with sensation. Dizzying. Exhilarating. Overwhelming. She threw her arms out and gripped the sides of the tub.

Collier touched her womb, settled there a moment, then slid an arm around her waist and began rocking his body into hers.

Each thrust carrying her that much nearer to the place only he could take her to, Catherine tried to speak his name. She could not. From somewhere outside herself she heard Collier groan and the sound of splashing water, but it soon diminished— as if all else but the joining of their bodies had ceased to be. Higher and higher she spiraled, her breath growing shallow, her pleasure coming faster. Perfect. And then every one of those sensations culminated into one and burst over her.

It was not like the other times she and Collier had made love. This went deeper than that. More satisfying.

Feeling as if she were a leaf drifting to earth, Catherine reveled in the tremors of her descent. Gradually, she became aware of Collier at her back. She heard his breathing, smelled his masculine scent, felt the heat of his body that warmed her as the bath water no longer could.

She sighed.

"We will have to bathe together more often," Collier murmured.

She looked over her shoulder into his half-lidded eyes. "I would like that."

His grin was lopsided.

"Did you . . . ?" Catherine began, but trailed off as embarrassment swept her. It was not something a lady asked.

Collier pulled her around. "I did—with you." He stroked a hand up her back.

It was hard to say, but she said it. "I wish to do the same to you, Collier."

"Hmm?"

"Touch you as you touched me. Pleasure you."

His eyes opened wider. "You *have* pleasured me."

"But 'twas of your doing."

"I assure you, Catherine, you had no small part in it." He chuckled. "Still, I would not be averse to putting myself in your hands."

She would never be merely a possession to him—chattel. "Now?" Catherine asked.

Laughter rumbled up from his chest. "If it so pleases you, my lady. But may I suggest something more comfortable?"

Not only had the bath water cooled, but its volume was reduced to less than half.

Catherine nodded.

Collier handed her out of the tub, and a short while later lay back on the mattress.

Slowly at first, but growing bolder with each passing minute, Catherine began to explore him.

An hour later, her backside cradled against Collier's front, she entreated, "Tell me another of your tales."

"Another, hmm?"

"Aye." These past nights he had delighted her with tales of things called "automobiles," that roamed the roads without horses to pull them, "planes," that carried people into the sky like birds on the wind, and "radio" and "tell-a-vision," that sent voices and moving pictures across the world and into people's homes. All unimaginable, but he said it was so.

Collier tightened his arms around her, and over the next hour related a fantastic tale about something called "computers" and "surfing the Internet."

23

The dream feathered her brow, whispering of life, bright and new as the morn. Innocent eyes. Sweet laughter. Skin as soft as down. And its scent . . . like sunshine. Then it flew away.

When Catherine opened her eyes, she was surprised to discover Collier sleeping beside her. As he was always up before dawn, it was the first time she had awakened to find him still abed. But then, not until the early morning hours had either of them gotten any sleep.

Remembering the things he had made her feel, the places he had taken her to, and the words he had spoken, she smiled. Never would she have believed she could be so happy. Nor that anyone could love her as he loved her. She slid a hand over his chest.

He stirred, but did not awaken.

It wasn't just the night they had shared which was responsible for his exhaustion. He was overworked. With no news of the Lancastrian rebels, and Antony gone from Toller nearly three weeks, life was beginning to resume its normal pace—or as normal as it could considering what had been visited upon these lands during the war. There were disputes to be settled, rents to be collected, supplies to be bought, and a multitude of other responsibilities Collier took upon himself. Although it meant Catherine saw less of him, the outcome was that it had gained him acceptance as the lord of Toller.

Feeling a sharp pang of hunger, Catherine guessed it was late morning. She considered rising and going belowstairs for something to eat, but instead drew her hand up Collier's chest, over his shoulder, and laid it alongside his jaw.

He needed a shave, but, as usual, would put it off for as long as possible. He so hated having the beard scraped from his jaw, even though she hardly ever cut him. She eyed the nick on his chin. It had healed, but was lighter than the surrounding skin. Remembering the incident, she grimaced. He'd muttered something about an "electric razor," but hadn't explained.

Catherine sighed. There was so much about his world she would never understand, but at least he seemed content in hers.

"Good morning," he said, his voice husky.

She looked into his eyes. They were more gray than usual, the sunlight having narrowed his pupils to pinpoints. "I think 'tis nearer noon," she said with a smile.

He pulled her naked body against him. "Then perhaps we shouldn't bother rising."

"Stay abed all day? But I am almost sick with hunger."

He caressed a hand down her back and slid it around her belly. "Perhaps you're pregnant."

Catherine had only a moment to thrill to his touch, then the dream flew back to her. Her breath caught. Could it be? Never had she known such a dream. So beautiful. So precious. So unlike the horrors her sleep had always visited on her.

"What's wrong?"

She finally breathed. Meeting Collier's concerned gaze, she said, "I dreamed."

His brow furrowed.

"Nay." She shook her head. "'Twas not like that. It was a . . ." She searched for the words. What to call it? "It was a real dream. Like other people's dreams." She remembered gurgling laughter, the feel of soft skin, the warm scent that had filled her. "I dreamed of a babe, Collier."

A smile sent the worry from his face. "Our child?"

"I . . . think so." She conjured the round little face she had seen. "It had your eyes. Do you think—" She touched her belly. Would she soon grow round with his seed?

"If you dreamed it, then it must be," Collier said.

Must it? "But never have I had such a dream. Those things I see in my sleep are only to be feared."

Collier's smile slipped away. "You are saying you have never had a pleasant dream?"

Though she had told him of the sight, she had not told him all of it. "None that I can remember." And not even the dream of her death had been as clear as the joyous one she had awakened from this morn.

"Perhaps the sight is changing," Collier suggested.

Dare she to believe it was no longer a curse? Catherine's next thought swept away the budding hope. Had it been a girl child? Mayhap the dream was not as joyous as it had appeared, but spoke to her of ill to come—that the babe she bore Collier would be cursed with the sight.

"Catherine?"

She had been looking through him, she realized. "What if 'tis a girl?"

He chuckled, deep and warm. "My ego does not demand a son. I am not so macho I would be displeased if you gave me a daughter."

"Macho?"

"I would love the child just the same."

Aye, he would. "But if 'tis a girl, she might be born with the sight. Mayhap what I saw in this dream was to be feared after all."

Collier was thoughtful a long moment, then asked, "Is that how it is passed—through the female line?"

"It seems to be."

He pushed up on an elbow. "If it is a girl, and she has the sight, I will not send her away as your father did you. Just as I will not send you away. I give you my word."

Tears sprang to Catherine's eyes as she fought to form words which she had long denied. To tell him of this thing that filled her heart so full it felt it might burst. But it would not be spoken.

Collier brushed his mouth across hers. "Whatever happens, we will deal with it—together."

Bathed in the warmth of his gaze, Catherine nodded. He would not fail her.

Collier sat up. "And now that I've lazed away the morning, it is time to rise." He stretched.

Catherine also sat up, but Collier pressed her back down. "Get some more sleep," he said.

"But I am rested."

"A few more hours will do you good."

Catherine smiled. "Though I may be with child, it does not mean I am unable to see to my daily chores—many months from now, perhaps, but certainly not at this time."

"I know, but I would prefer it if you rested."

She did feel a bit tired. . . . "There is much to do," she protested.

"It will keep."

It *would* be nice to lie abed another hour—but only that. "I should check on my father."

"I will do it."

"I am hungry."

As if knowing he'd won, Collier tucked the covers around her. "I'll send Tilly up with a tray."

Catherine sighed. What more was there to argue? "Very well."

Collier walked to the chest and began searching through his meager choice of clothing.

He had said nothing when her first attempt at sewing for him had failed. She really ought to try again, she knew, but the memory of that failure was still fresh, as well as the embarrassment. All Collier had done was reach across the table, and the seams of his tunic had burst. He had made light of it, saying something about having to watch his "calories" more closely, but the pitying looks the castle folk had turned on him had made Catherine vow she would never again take up a needle. But she would.

As Collier pulled on his braies, he reflected on the briefs he'd left behind in the twentieth century. He had thought he would become accustomed to the loose fitting undergarments of this time, but still he missed his elasticized briefs. It was not much better than running around naked.

He pushed his feet into boots, and as he straightened, flexed his aching shoulders and rolled his head on his neck. His muscles were taut from the night spent on the lumpy bed. Yet another thing he missed—his orthopedically correct mattress.

At the door, he looked over his shoulder, and that was all it took for thoughts of his twentieth-century world to flee. For several minutes he stared at Catherine, her face gentled in sleep and a bloom of color in her cheeks that he did not remember having been there before. He smiled. Aye, this was what he wanted—more than anything or anyone else. And the child he prayed she carried.

Collier had never given much thought to having children. In fact, in his other life he probably wouldn't have missed them if he'd never had any. But girl or boy, sight or not, he wanted the child Catherine dreamed of. He wanted to see what she had seen. Hold the little one. Glimpse immortality in its eyes. In fact, he wanted it so badly it caused a dull ache in him.

Remembering his assurances to Catherine that he would check on her father, he closed the door and strode down the corridor.

Lewis Algernon had surprised everyone by lingering well past the time the physician had said he would. In fact, he had begun to show signs of improvement. Still, Collier knew the old man would not sit in the lord's high seat again. However many days he had left would be spent in bed.

Collier knocked. No answer. Likely Lady Lavinia had gone to the chapel as she was wont to do when her husband slept. But even as Collier pushed the door inward, he sensed something was wrong, and a moment later the feeling was confirmed.

The old man lay on the floor several feet from his bed, on his belly with one arm outstretched. It looked as if he had been trying to crawl to the door.

Fearing the worst, Collier rushed forward and gently turned him over.

Lewis's aged face was still, but a moment later he drew a wheezing breath and peeled back his lids.

His passing was upon him, Collier realized. "Lord Algernon, I am going to return you to your bed."

Lewis fixed his gaze to Collier's. "M . . ." he tried to talk. "My . . ." Entreatingly, he laid his hand on Collier's forearm.

Collier knew what he wanted. His high seat. Though he had thought the old man would not sit in it again, it seemed he would do so one last time. "I will take you," he said.

Although Lewis had obviously been of a good height and build before his stroke, his withered body lifted easily from the floor. Collier turned toward the door.

Lavinia stood there. Her eyes sad, she stared at her husband. "'Tis time, isn't it?"

"It is," Collier said.

She stood unmoving a long moment, then stepped aside.

With Lavinia trailing behind, Collier carried the old man down to the hall.

The servants looked up from their tasks, and in the time it took Collier to cross to the dais, their ranks swelled from four to ten or more.

Feeling watched, Collier lowered Lewis into the lord's high seat.

It must have taken all of the old man's strength to hold himself upright, but he managed.

"Bring your lord a blanket," Collier ordered a servant.

"Lord Gilchrist?" Tilly said.

Collier looked around.

"You would have me fetch Lady Catherine?"

"Aye."

By the time the servant returned with the blanket, several of the castle garrison and the two knights had appeared. All knew this would be the last time Lewis Algernon presided over Toller's hall.

Feeling uncomfortable as a Yorkist among Lancastrians whose lord was nearing death, Collier turned away. Hardly had he done so when he heard a loud grunt. He looked over his shoulder.

The old man met his gaze.

"My husband wishes you to sit beside him," Lavinia said.

Wondering what the old man wanted, Collier lowered himself to the chair. "My lord?"

Lewis closed his eyes a moment, but when he opened them, there was a spark in their depths. "To . . . "

Collier leaned near him. "Toller?"

It was only a slight movement, but Lewis nodded.

"I will take care of your people, Lord Algernon," Collier said, guessing that was what the old man asked.

"La . . . vi . . . "

"And your wife." A movement off the stairs caught Collier's eye—Catherine, and walking beside her, her younger brother. "And Eustace as well."

"An . . . "

Antony. "Whatever I can do for him." It was a hollow promise, for what *could* he do for the boy?

Lewis surely knew it as well. He turned his attention to Catherine and his younger son as they stepped up to the dais. "Ca . . . ine."

Her mouth trembled with emotion.

"Of course," Collier said, "and the child she carries."

Lewis swept his gaze to Collier. Stricken.

He understood the old man's fear. It was the same as Catherine's. He laid a hand to Lewis's arm. "I will let neither of them go."

Lewis searched Collier's face, then closed his eyes.

Collier waited, as did the others in the hall.

Finally, the old man began tugging at the ring on the hand that lay useless in his lap. He pulled it off. Shifting his body toward Collier, he held it out to him.

Collier stared at the signet ring of the lord of Toller.

"You," Lewis said.

Collier looked into the old man's eyes.

Lewis motioned with his chin.

"'Tis yours now, husband," Catherine said. "You would do my father honor by accepting it."

Memories of his own father returned to Collier. Winton Morrow had died without any dignity. In his hospital bed, the cancer having taken its toll on his body, he had loudly berated his sons for a business decision they had made without consulting him. He had called them irresponsible, unworthy of the name "Morrow." Collier and James had stood through it, but when their father had started cursing them, and the woman who had bore them, they had walked out. Winton Morrow had died alone with none to mourn him.

"You are worthy," Catherine said, settling her hand to his shoulder. She had come around the table.

Collier looked into her blue eyes which he could almost swear shone with love.

She nodded to the ring. "Take it."

The old man thrust it nearer Collier.

It symbolized Lewis's acceptance of this Yorkist to rule his people, Collier knew. But why? Why when

his hatred and resentment had been so strong the day
Collier had come to Toller? What had changed the
old man's opinion? Catherine?

He was keeping Lewis and the others in the hall
waiting. It was time to take his place as the lord of
Toller. "I thank you, Lord Algernon." Strange emotions bottling in his throat, Collier reached forward.

Lewis dropped the ring in Collier's palm, met his
successor's eyes, and slumped back in his chair. He
was exhausted.

Collier looked from the old man to Lady Lavinia.

She nodded.

Beside his mother, Eustace stared at Collier with
large, moist eyes.

The servants and soldiers gathered throughout
the hall watched Collier, but it was not resentment he
felt from them. They were waiting for him to put the
ring on.

Collier swung his gaze back to Catherine.

Though she grieved for her father, she managed a
smile.

He lifted the ring between thumb and forefinger,
studied it a moment, then slid it on his hand. It fit.

A hushed murmur going around the hall, the old
man looked up at Collier. With a barely perceptible
movement, he nodded as if with approval and closed
his eyes.

Lewis Algernon lingered a quarter hour before
finding his final rest.

"I did not dream of his death," Catherine said as she
walked beside Collier.

"Nothing?"

She shook her head. "I do not understand it."

"You dreamed of our child," he reminded her.

In spite of the sadness of the day—her father having been laid to rest only minutes earlier—a smile curved her lips. "I did, and 'twas most wonderful."

"Then your dreams *are* changing."

"That they are the good of things and no more the bad? I pray 'tis true, Collier. That this curse is lifted."

As he did himself.

"And that I will bear you a son."

"Girl or boy, the child will be loved," he assured her once more.

Her eyes were soft like the blue of the sky. "I know."

Were they alone, Collier would have taken her in his arms. With a sigh, he glanced at Lavinia who walked at the head of the procession of mourners returning to Toller.

The woman's sadness was felt by all. Not only was her husband dead, but last evening the messenger sent to Strivling had returned with word of Antony's refusal to attend his father's burial. On the surface, Catherine's mother had taken the news well, but shortly thereafter had withdrawn to her chamber. This morning, her puffy eyes had proven her tears of the night before.

There was going to be trouble before long, Collier knew. Not for one moment did he doubt Antony would lead Edmund to the rebels. So how was he, Collier, to keep his promise to Lewis Algernon to watch over his reckless son?

He sighed. It was going to be a challenge.

Antony waited, and as he waited, his thoughts turned once more to that which he had obsessed over since learning of his father's death.

The ring.

It was said Lewis Algernon had taken it off his hand and given it to Gilchrist—in doing so showing his acceptance of the Yorkist as lord of Toller. This was what stood out more clearly in Antony's mind than anything else, even more than the death of his father. He was betrayed by the very one whose loins he had sprung from. The man who had promised that he, Antony Algernon, would one day be lord of Toller. All lies.

Although, in the end, Catherine had forsaken the Lancasters, Antony now understood how she had been able to do what she had done in defending Strivling. Simply, her hate had been that strong. But not as strong as Antony's had grown, for *never* would his hate of the Yorkists fall to a lovesick heart.

"Whelp!"

Antony looked around.

It was Griffin Walther who stood before him, sneering. The man who had first been on the side of the Lancasters, then the Yorkists, and now again the Lancasters. A vile mercenary, but nevertheless useful, for it was he who now led the band of more than a hundred rebels determined to put King Henry back on the throne. And he who had given Antony a very close and painful look at the floor of the wood.

Respect him? Antony did. But he also hated him.

"You keep the king waiting," the mercenary said.

Antony started. "King Henry?" He was here? Was this the reason he had been summoned from Strivling this eve?

Disgust pulled Walther's sneer higher. "Surely you do not think I refer to Edward?"

"Of . . . of course not." Antony stepped away from the stream. "I did not know the king was here."

"Go!" Walther jerked his head toward the largest of the tents erected in the deep wood.

The king wished to see him—Antony Algernon. A mere squire. His heart pounding with sudden excitement, Antony hurried forward, and in his haste tripped over one of those curled up before the camp fire. The man's curses followed him to the king's tent, but Antony hardly heard them.

A large and rather ugly man stood before the tent. Fleetingly, Antony thought him familiar, but he had other things to attend to. Namely, King Henry.

The man threw back the flap and motioned Antony inside, then followed. A moment later, Griffin Walther also stepped within.

The tent was nothing like what Antony expected. No fineries as befitting a king. No velvet cushions or thick-piled rugs. No platters brimming with unimaginable delicacies. But for a smoking lantern, a bowl of withered fruit, and two men—one standing, the other sitting on the ground and huddled in the folds of a blanket—the tent was barren.

"I am Sir Richard Tunstall," said the man who stood. "Come closer."

Wondering if Walther were playing a game with him, Antony took an uncertain step forward.

"Is King Henry still your sovereign?" Sir Richard asked.

Antony nodded. "As God is my witness."

"Then kneel."

Antony lowered his gaze to the man who sat before him. *This* was King Henry? This man with dull, heavily lidded eyes, an angular face that made him look as if he had not eaten in months, a small head which sat more bowed on his neck than erect, and brown hair that sprang unkempt from his scalp? This the king of England?

As if to confirm it, the man in question nodded.

Antony knelt and bowed his head.

A hand touched his shoulder.

He looked up into sorrowful eyes.

"I am your king, Antony Algernon," the man said, his voice so soft as to be hardly heard.

Then it *was* him? Was his appearance a result of these past months spent as a fugitive—moving from safe house to safe house just ahead of those who sought to take him for Edward? Even so, Antony could not help his disappointment. He had imagined King Henry to be a giant of a man much like the one who had ushered him into the tent. Not a man who was more likened to a beggar than one worthy of wearing the crown of England.

"I was much aggrieved to hear of your father's passing," King Henry said.

Only because he did not know that Lewis Algernon's loyalties had shifted during his last days, Antony added to himself. But no need to tell him. It would only reflect badly on himself.

"I share your sorrow," the king added.

Sorrow. Antony looked down so that his anger could not be read in his eyes.

There followed a long moment of silence, then the king asked, "You know why I have summoned you?"

Antony collected himself and returned his gaze to Henry's. "I do not, Your Majesty."

The king tried to smile, but it was a sickly attempt. "Sir Griffin has told me you were present when Morrow came to your sister, Lady Catherine, and demanded to know the whereabouts of Strivling's wealth."

"Aye, Your Majesty, I was there." And on that very night had stolen out of Toller to bring word to

Walther. He had not known the significance of the missing money, only that it was a great deal and *had* to be important.

"What was Lady Catherine's response?"

Surely Walther had told him. "She said she knew naught of it."

A movement pulled Antony's gaze to where Henry's hands had come out from beneath the blanket. As if agitated, he clenched right hand over left, reversed it, then again.

"And the sum?" King Henry asked.

"Three hundred pounds, Your Majesty."

The king shifted his gaze past Antony's shoulder.

Was it Walther who captured his regard, or that large man? Antony wondered.

A nervous tic pulling at the corner of his mouth, the king looked back at Antony. "You are certain it was only three hundred?"

"'Tis what Morrow said, Your Majesty."

Henry fell silent a moment. "Then your sister still holds it for me."

"I . . . I do not think so, Your Majesty. She has turned traitor—"

"Or pretends to have done so."

Was it possible? "I wish it were true, Your Majesty, but for certain my sister has forsaken thee for her Yorkist lover."

Again, King Henry glanced past him. "I thank you, young Antony. You have been most helpful. And now, I give you your leave to return to Strivling."

Leave? But he was ready to join the rebels. Ready to fight for the right of the Lancasters—even if the king looked hardly capable of raising himself from the ground. "If it so pleases you, my king, I would stay with you."

Henry patted his shoulder. "You best serve me at Strivling."

Antony's heart sank. The thought of spending one more day in the service of Edmund Morrow turned his saliva bitter. But there was nothing for it. "Aye, Your Majesty." He stood and began backing his way out of the tent.

The large man swept the flap open for him.

"Antony?" The king's voice reached him by a slender thread.

Antony looked back at him. "Your Majesty?"

"If . . . when . . ." King Henry blinked several times. "When the time comes, I will send for you."

Meaning he would be a part of the reclaiming of these Northumbrian lands? Of England? His spirit revived, Antony said, "I thank you, Your Majesty."

Antony stepped into the cool night air and looked up at the stars. Very soon England would be Lancastrian again. He had to believe it. Trying to ignore the doubts pressing in on him, he turned his thoughts to knighthood. Perhaps King Henry himself would confer it upon him. Imagining it—the grand ceremony, the fastening on of spurs, the presentation of his knightly sword, the collée delivered by the king's own hand—he started back toward Strivling.

Henry looked from one man to the other. Although his enemies said he was witless and oblivious, he felt the animosity between these two men. And understood it—most especially the great man's hatred. If Walther had not proven so useful in gathering men to the Lancastrian cause, Henry would never have accepted him back to his side, but he needed the mercenary.

"You are sure 'twas eight hundred?" he asked, looking at the great man with eyes that burned for sleep.

"Aye, Your Majesty. Either Morrow is mistaken, or he holds the other five hundred pounds. *And* the household valuables."

Those valuables would be worth a good deal themselves, Henry acknowledged before returning his thoughts to the money. Though, in truth, he would have been pleased to lay hands to even a hundred pounds, he needed far more to even begin raising an army. "And if Morrow does not have it?" he asked.

"Then Lady Catherine must have hidden it all."

A derisive laugh broke from Walther. "Methinks the whore has given it to Gilchrist."

The great man's nostrils flared and hands clenched into fists. "Lady Catherine would not do that."

The mercenary swung his gaze on him. "God's blood, you are a fool—"

"I will not abide swearing!" Henry raised his voice. It sickened him to hear men take the lord's name in vain.

Walther bowed his head. "I beg your forgiveness, Your Majesty."

"'Tis God you should ask pardon of."

"And that I will do, Your Majesty."

Henry nodded. God in his heavens would be pleased. Now what had he wished to say before Walther had blasphemed? He stumbled backward through his thoughts which, more and more of late, were difficult to keep ordered. Only to himself would he admit it, though.

The money. Catherine. Aye, that was it. "I need Lady Catherine," he said.

Walther smiled. "So you shall have her, Your Majesty."

Soon, Henry hoped. He was exhausted running from his enemies. Tired of relying on the generosity of those who secretly continued to support him. Sick of pitying eyes. And weary of wondering what was being said of him.

But to be king again without a worry in the world, to have his fair queen, Margaret, at his side willing to take all his burdens upon herself—

"Your Majesty?"

Henry looked up at Sir Richard, his chamberlain and companion these past months.

"You should try to sleep now," Richard said.

Henry looked around. Walther and the great man were gone. Had Richard given them their leave? He must have. Thinking he must be quite tired not to have noticed, Henry laid down. "You are a good man, Tunstaill," he murmured.

"Ever your loyal servant," Richard replied.

Proven time and again.

Henry pulled the blanket over the lower half of his face and closed his eyes. Although he knew God looked favorably upon those who foreswore the comforts of this world—that suffering was good for the soul—his thoughts strayed to the huge canopied bed that had been his before Edward had stolen the throne from him. Now he was reduced to the floor of the wood and a coarse blanket to warm him.

If Margaret could see him now, she would rage at the indignity done him. A vision of her rising before the backs of his eyelids almost made Henry laugh. But it wasn't funny. Was it?

Henry clutched the blanket closer against the chill. A few minutes later, in the midst of his prayers, he fell asleep.

24

"Cy va, cy va, cy va!"

The shout cleaving the air, the riders veered sharply right. Through the wood they sped, around bramble, over fallen trees, and through a stream that sprayed bitingly cold water on them. But they hardly noticed, their minds firmly set on that which ran from them.

Desperate, their prey turned off its path and disappeared from sight, but only for a moment. Then, once again, it was before them.

"Cy va, cy va, cy va!" the shout rang again, urging the dogs on.

Making a great noise, the hounds gathered speed as they raced up the incline with an enthusiasm that had not flagged during the past hour of the chase. They smelled blood, and would likely taste it very soon.

Although Collier had never been enthusiastic

about hunting, he found this medieval form exhilarating. The elements were essentially the same, but that this was not just sport separated it from the gentlemen hunts he had always thought pretentious and a waste of good time. Once the great stag was brought down, it would feed the castle folk well for days, and its hide could be used for boots and gloves to weather the coming winter. Strange how necessity changed one's way of thinking. Strange how these past months had changed him.

He looked sideways at Catherine. Riding astride, she kept effortless pace with the others, among them, Sir Mathis, Sir Laurence, and Eustace, who was doing his best to keep up. Twenty in all.

Catherine met Collier's gaze, flashed him a smile, then raised the ivory horn suspended from a cord around her neck. She blew a series of piercing notes to mark the progress of the hunt.

Collier wondered if she was pregnant. This morning when she had insisted on accompanying him on the hunt, she had confirmed that her time of month had not arrived—it now being a week past due. However, as she was not always regular, and had yet to suffer any signs of pregnancy, she had seen no reason to stay behind. And even if she were with child, as her dreams these past weeks continued to indicate, what harm in a ride so early in her pregnancy?

When Collier had continued to express reservations, Catherine had indignantly informed him she was no stranger to the hunt—that once she had even dispatched a boar herself.

No argument left to him, Collier had agreed she should come along, and now that he saw her joy, was glad she had.

Ahead, the hounds disappeared over the swell of

wooded land. Within moments, their frenzied baying proclaimed the stag's flight at an end.

The hunting party paused atop the rise.

Surrounded by nine hounds, the great animal swung its antlered head side to side, threatening to gore any that came any nearer.

"Hallali!" Sir Mathis cried.

Given the command for the final attack, the dogs eagerly closed around the stag.

Though a doe would easily have been felled, not this great beast. It kicked its hind legs, slashed with its fore legs, and stabbed at the hounds with lowered antlers.

One of the dogs' yelps turned pained. It limped away. Then a second was tossed through the air and into the path of the approaching riders.

Sir Laurence skirted the mortally wounded hound. "Son of a sow!" he cursed the stag.

Hunting dogs were a precious commodity, Collier had learned—nearly as well-loved as falcons, and better cared for than servants.

The young knight raised his hunting spear. "You will sell your life dearly for this," he vowed, and pressed his heels into his horse's sides.

"'Tis Lord Gilchrist's," Sir Mathis shouted.

During the previous hunts, Collier had deferred to whomever wished to take down the animal, and had learned from their successes and failures. Here now was his chance to use the bowskill Mathis had been instructing him in.

As it was only a matter of time before another of the dogs fell to the wrathful animal, Collier spurred his horse ahead of the others, and at sixty yards dismounted. He drew an arrow from the quiver at his waist, notched it on the bowstring, and started forward. At forty yards, he halted. Near enough for the arrow to fly straight without dropping, yet far enough to loose another if he overshot, as was his tendency. He positioned himself. Body turned to the side. Bow held at the full length of his left arm. Feet straddled and heels in line with his target. Head turned sharply left. String drawn back to the angle of the jawbone. The stag sighted over the pile of the arrow. The arrow loosed. Reaching for another.

Had the stag not swung sideways to butt at one of the hounds, the arrow would have found its mark—the breastbone. Instead, it embedded itself in the animal's shoulder.

"Damn!" Collier cursed. Suffering was not what he had in mind. He sighted the stag a second time, but as he did so, the enraged animal broke from the hounds and headed straight for him.

Collier corrected his aim to take the stag's flight into account, and released. He overshot.

Heart pounding, adrenaline constricting his blood vessels, he wrenched another arrow from the quiver. If he even had time to draw again, this one must find its mark, else the stag would be upon him with its great antlers ready to gore him.

He heard Catherine's fearful cry, followed by Sir Mathis's shout. Collier was raising his bow when another released an arrow. It caught the stag broadside, but though it slowed the animal, it did not stop it. Still it came.

Focus, Collier ordered himself. Fifteen yards. Draw. Ten yards. Sight. Five yards. Release.

Two yards from where he stood, the stag fell dead.

Once again, Collier was watched over.

A single long note on the horn—the Blowing of the Death—pierced the wood.

Collier turned.

Her face drawn with fear, Catherine stared at him from atop her mount. But it wasn't she who had blown the horn. It was Eustace.

A glimmer of excitement in the boy's eyes, he suddenly grinned. And here Collier had thought him incapable of anything more than a scowl.

Seeking to reassure Catherine, Collier started toward her.

"Well done, my lord!" Sir Mathis extolled.

A murmur of assent rose from the others.

Collier glanced at the older knight. Across his saddle lay his bow. For certain, it was he who had shot the arrow which had slowed the stag. Collier was indebted. He inclined his head in silent acknowledgment and strode to Catherine.

She summoned a trembling smile.

Collier lifted her from her horse.

Staring at him through thick lashes, she said, "I feared for you—that I might lose you."

He pushed aside a tendril of hair fallen over her brow. "And would that be so bad?"

She lowered her gaze. "I . . . I could not bear it."

Then she loved him? What he wouldn't give to hear her say the words. Would she?

"My lord, the quarry awaits," one of the men called.

Had Catherine been going to profess her love, the moment was past.

Disappointed, Collier turned to those who had dismounted in preparation for the ritualistic cutting up of the animal. As before, most of the organs would be given to the hounds, with the right forefoot presented to Collier as the lord of the hunt. The remainder would be conveyed to Toller's kitchens.

Collier looked up at where Eustace had yet to descend from his mare. "You wish to help?" he asked, nodding to those gathered around the stag.

The boy eagerly bobbed his head up and down. "Aye, my lord."

My lord. That was a new one. Though thus far Eustace had appeared unmoved by Collier's ability to manage Lewis Algernon's estate, he was awed by the downing of the stag. Not surprisingly, Collier supposed, but still it was frustrating to be measured more by his facility with weapons than what had made him a sizable fortune in the world he had left behind.

"Come down from there," Collier said.

Eustace bounded out of the saddle. "I am ready." He patted the dagger on his belt.

"Then go."

Eustace hurried past him.

"You will stay here?" Collier asked Catherine.

She looked to where the stag lay. "Aye, but I would have you bring me the heart bone."

"The heart bone?"

"You know naught of it?" she asked, then smiled with understanding. "'Tis found in the stag's heart and thought to have medicinal properties. Thus, it is often given to a pregnant woman."

Collier laid a hand to her waist. "And are you?"

"I believe so."

Though Collier wanted to sweep her into his arms, instead he leaned forward and stole a kiss. "The heart bone, hmm? Sounds superstitious to me."

"It is, but still I wish it."

Collier pulled his dagger from its scabbard. "Then you shall have it."

*   *   *

The walls were silent. Where there should have been castle folk eager to greet the hunting party whose success was proclaimed by the contents of the rumbling cart, only two were visible—one between the battlements, the other atop the gatehouse. None upon the lowered drawbridge.

Collier drew in the reins and raised an arm to check the progress of the others.

Bathed in the soft glow of twilight, Toller appeared harmless, but that might be the harm of it. Once more Collier scanned the castle walls in search of those who were conspicuously absent. Where were they?

"Something is awry," Sir Mathis murmured.

Collier looked at the knight who had brought his horse alongside.

Brow furrowed, Sir Mathis scrutinized Toller. "Aye, very wrong." He met Collier's gaze. "We should retreat, my lord."

A tightening in his belly, Collier said, "Take Eustace up with you."

The knight turned his horse.

Collier looked to where Catherine sat astride her mount.

Disheveled from the ride, her large, unblinking eyes no less blue for the waning of day, she asked, "What is it?"

"Walther," he said. He knew it as surely as he breathed.

"Nay."

He held out his hand. "Come onto my horse."

She reached to him.

Collier pulled her up behind. "Hold onto me."

She wrapped her arms around his waist and pressed herself against his back.

"Retreat!" Collier shouted, wheeling his mount around.

The hunting party turned. A moment later, the silence rose to thunder as twenty horses bolted across the land they had minutes earlier passed over at a leisurely pace. Then, suddenly, the thunder doubled, and trebled.

Over the far hill came horsemen. Twenty. To the left, twenty more. To the right, yet another twenty. Their trap was sprung, and at the center lay their prey.

Collier dragged on the reins and looked around. There was only Toller, but hardly was the thought upon him when he saw the gathering of men through the portcullis. Walther's men, no doubt.

Surrounded, with nowhere to go, the others also reined in.

What had happened to Toller's men-at-arms? Collier wondered. Had they been lured back to their Lancaster roots and let Walther in? Or had they resisted and now lay dead?

"Collier?" Catherine asked.

He glanced over his shoulder into her fearful eyes. For certain, there were two things Walther wanted: revenge against Collier, and the life denied him when Collier had come between him and Catherine.

Collier's mind raced. He had to protect her, but how? Damn it! He felt helpless. But he wasn't. If there was one thing he could do better than any of these fighting men, it was ride. The horse was worthy, and if need be, there was also his sword. He closed his hand around the hilt.

As if awaiting their cue, the others drew their swords.

Though they must know it was the Lancastrians

who rode toward them, it seemed they stood with their Yorkist lord.

But the numbers were too great. Twenty against sixty or more. It would be a bloody mess with likely nothing to show for it. "Lower your weapons," Collier ordered.

The men looked at one another.

"We go alone," Collier said. "Hold firm to me, Catherine, and stay low."

Her arms tightened around him.

Collier waited and watched, and as the rebels neared, decided on his course—a break in the front bearing down on them. He spurred the horse forward. Gripping the sword in one hand, the reins in the other, he leaned down and melded with the animal. One body. One force.

The rebels swept inward, but their efforts to close the gap were for naught.

With time to spare, Collier guided the horse between the riders. As he passed beyond their reach, he loosed a triumphant shout. By the time the rebels came about, he would have the lead needed to escape. Before dawn, he and Catherine would be at Strivling.

But it was not to be. Having been thwarted once before by Collier's horsemanship, Walther was this time prepared. In the distance, another wave of riders appeared, bows drawn and ready to release their deadly missiles.

Collier did not need to see Walther's face to know who rode at the fore. There was none else it could be. "God almighty," he muttered. There was no way out. Now the quarry, he realized it must have been the same for the downed stag. Still, the animal had fought to the death.

Were he alone, Collier thought he might do so

himself, but there was Catherine to consider. And their unborn child. God willing, there would be another opportunity for escape, but this was not it.

He halted the destrier.

Catherine looked around Collier. "Walther," she breathed.

"Say nothing," Collier said as he returned his sword to its scabbard. He wanted to give the mercenary no reason to seek immediate reprisal. The more time they had, the more opportunities that would come their way.

As Walther neared, his mouth stretch into a self-satisfied smile. "'Tis Lord Gilchrist and his fair wife, Lady Catherine," he drawled. "A pleasure, indeed."

Against his back, Collier felt Catherine tense. Wishing there was some way to reassure her, he looked to the sword and dagger on Walther's belt. Though within reach, how quickly could either be had? But they didn't need to be had. Not as long as the arrows of Walther's men were notched and ready to kill.

Walther came alongside Collier. "You look hardly surprised to see me," he said, then laughed. "But you knew I would be back, didn't you?"

Collier maintained his silence.

With a knowing nod, Walther pulled the sword from the sheath at Collier's waist. Feigning interest, he turned it this way and that, fingered the heavy pommel, then eyed Collier around the blade. "I have something for you, Gilchrist," he said.

A moment later, he swept the butt of the sword toward Collier.

Collier threw up an arm to block it, but he wasn't quick enough. The pommel struck his temple with a loud crack.

Darkness and light burst upon him—like fireworks

at midnight. Hearing Catherine's cry and feeling her arms tighten around him, he struggled to rise up through the mire of unconsciousness, but it pulled him to its depths. Deeper and deeper.

"Catherine," he formed her name on his lips, but his voice was lost to him.

Collier was falling, and there was nothing Catherine could do to prevent it. Holding on, she followed him to the ground. Though she landed hard, she scrambled onto her knees and bent over Collier.

Blood flowed from the head wound Walther had inflicted, but he breathed.

Catherine jumped to her feet and swung around. "Bastard!" she spat.

Walther began to laugh. Coarse, vulgar laughter that was like a slap to the face.

Catherine gave no thought to what she did, nor what might happen to her. She grabbed her dagger from its sheath and leapt forward.

This time it was Griffin Walther's flesh her blade sank into. His shout of pain, not Collier's. But her victory was short-lived. Hardly had she embedded the blade in the mercenary's thigh when his hand closed around hers and wrenched the dagger from his leg.

"Slut!" he hissed, spraying spittle over her.

Catherine strained backward.

Walther tightened his grip and pulled her toward him.

The bones in her hand felt as if they might snap, but she would not cry out, Catherine vowed.

Walther stared at her, eyes blazing with hatred.

More than anything, he wanted to slay her, she saw, just as he had wanted to do in the winch room. She looked to his hand upon Collier's sword. He would use it against her, just as he had done in her dreams—

The sudden realization that it *was* the same sword sent fear spiraling through Catherine. Although she'd had no dream to forewarn her of this day, was that other dream finally coming true? A different time and place, but otherwise the same?

"This time you are mine, Lady Catherine," Walther spoke through clenched teeth.

Then he also remembered the winch room. "And this time 'tis you who bleeds," she reminded him.

His lips lifted into a hideous smile. "Not as you shall bleed, *my lady*." He squeezed her hand tighter.

The pain was excruciating. "Then be done with it!"

His nostrils flared. "I would, but first there is someone who wishes to speak with you. And your lover." He jutted his chin to where Collier lay.

Then Collier was safe, if only for a while longer. Relief washing over her, Catherine momentarily forgot her pain.

"God's blood!" Walther shouted. "Where is he?"

Startled, Catherine followed his gaze. All that remained of Collier was the impression his body had made in the grass. He had escaped? But how?

Walther turned in the saddle. "Where did he go?" he demanded.

Bewildered silence.

"Did none see him rise?"

His men looked at one another, then shook their heads and offered helpless shrugs.

Unease rose within Catherine. Impossible. Here in the vast open with Walther's men looking on, Collier could not possibly have fled unnoticed, nor would he leave her. She knew he would not.

"Fools!" Walther shouted. "Idiots!" He pinned Catherine with his feral gaze. "Where is he?"

She feared the answer to his question. Feared it

straight through her heart. But as desperately as she had cleaved to her doubt these past weeks, she knew now that Collier had spoken true when he had told her he'd traveled across time to be with her.

Please God, she sent a prayer heavenward, *do not take him from me. Not now that I have begun to love.* Finally, she had admitted it, but the joy that should have been hers was lost without the man she ought to have spoken the words to long ago.

"Where?" Walther demanded.

Hurting as she had never hurt before, she met his gaze. "You think I would tell you?"

He thrust Collier's sword beneath his belt, then tore the dagger from her clenched fingers and grabbed a fistful of her hair. "Tell me!" He pressed the edge of the blade to her cheek.

What? That Collier Gilchrist—Morrow—could be found five hundred years from now in a world where people flew and light could be had at the touch of a button? But if it was so, what of the portrait? Collier had said it was how he had come backward through time, and yet it had been left behind at Strivling. The sword, then? Something beyond it? Whatever it was, it had taken him back. Catherine felt as if she might break into a thousand pieces. *Please God*, she silently beseeched. *Please*.

Through her tears, Walther's repulsive face rose before her.

"You think I would not?" he threatened, pressing the blade deeper.

"He is gone," Catherine said, a chill sweeping her. More painful words had never been spoken.

The vile curses the mercenary spewed were but a whisper against her anguish. Did she die this day—

But nay, there was the child. That growing in her

which was of Collier. If never she saw him again, still she had someone to live for. To love. Though it would not be enough, she gathered strength from it and looked into Walther's flushed countenance. "Surely your liege awaits," she said, wondering who wished to speak with her.

Walther thrust her back. "Aye, and when he is done with you, you are mine."

"I will never be yours!"

Again, that sickening smile. "Bring her!" he shouted, and started toward Toller.

25

He had been here before. Through this same vortex that had first transported him into the medieval world of Catherine Algernon. It could mean only one thing.

Collier shouted Catherine's name. Reached through the darkness for her. Prayed as he had not prayed since the day he had nearly lost her to the sea. And then there was the ground. He slammed into it with such force he was certain he had broken every bone in his body. He lay there a long time, not wanting to open his eyes for fear of what he would see—where he would find himself—but there was no denying it. He had returned.

He peered at the ceiling overhead. Though vaguely familiar, it was not his bedroom at the manor house. Perhaps he had not left the fifteenth century after all.

Praying it was so, he flexed his hands, shoulders, and legs. No broken bones, but his head throbbed fiercely. He pressed fingers to his temple and came away with the blood Griffin Walther had drawn. Walther who had Catherine.

Collier sat up. It was not the clamor of chain mail that met his ears, but the soft rustle of nylon. He looked down at the jogging suit and white leather running shoes he wore. "Nay!" He shouted, and slammed his clenched hands against his brow. "God . . . no!" It hadn't been a dream. He had been there—with Catherine—and she was in danger. He had to get back to her.

"Collier? Is it you?"

He knew the voice, slurred as it was, but it was not one he would have expected. He looked around.

Sprawled in a chair, his tie loosed and his shirt freed from the waistband of his pants, James stared at him through half-hooded eyes. As for his slurred speech, the bottle of Scotch on a nearby table accounted for that.

"Where am I?" Collier asked.

His face reflecting intense discomfort, James tried to sit forward, but he was drunk. He slumped back in the chair.

Collier stood. Damn, but the room was familiar! "Where?" he asked again.

James chuckled. "I would say you are in my dreams, Brother. What do you think?"

How strange his accent, Collier reflected. Yet only months ago it had also been his. He looked back at James. So what was his brother doing drinking? Though in his younger days he had been known to imbibe to excess, Collier had thought he had gotten it under control. But then, he knew as little about his

brother's life these past years as James knew of his.
"What is this place?" he asked.

"My castle, of course." James panned a limp hand
out before him. "Magnificent, isn't it?" His arm fell
back to his side and lids fell closed. "Damned money
pit."

Strivling. Now Collier knew why the room was
familiar. Although the layers of five hundred years had
removed it from its medieval roots, this was the lord's
solar. He crossed to his brother's side. "I have to get
back," he said. God, he prayed he could get back.

James's eyes remained closed. "Back?"

"To Catherine."

"Ah, so she's part of this dream, too. Didya know
she bears an uncanny resemblance to that American
girl you were dating? What was her name?"

Collier grasped his brother's shoulders. "Look at
me!"

James grinned, but did not open his eyes. "Damned
vivid dream. Or maybe it's a hallucination, hmm? I
have been drinking."

"I assure you this is all very real," Collier said.

"You been drinkin' too? You sound . . . different.
Strange."

Just as James sounded to him. "I need your help."

"*My* help? This has to be a dream." James squinted
at Collier. "A rather nasty looking cut you got there.
It'll take a few stitches to close that one up."

"Did you hear me?"

"Hear you? Not something I care to admit. You
see, you don't exist anymore. Down at Scotland Yard,
you're just another missing person. Dead for all they
care." He clenched his hands. "Sons-a-bitches."

Unbelievable as it was, there was no mistaking the
pain in James's voice.

If only he could explain it to him, Collier wished. If he could make things right with him just as he had longed to do when he had found himself in the fifteenth century. Now wasn't the time, though. Perhaps on the drive to London—

"For a while they thought it was me who offed you," James said. "Bloody hell, they probably still do. Just don't have the evidence. No body, you know."

What had happened these past months? Collier wondered, but then told himself he had no time to speculate. Catherine needed him. "I've got to get to London. Where are the keys to your car?"

"London? Whatever for?"

Though he wouldn't understand, Collier said, "I need the portrait of Catherine Algernon." If there was any chance of him returning to her, that was where it lie.

"It's not in London."

"What do you mean it's not in London?"

"Not in London."

Even drunk, James was his usual infuriating self. "Listen to me—"

"Behind you." James nodded past Collier's shoulder. "I brought her home to Strivling."

Collier turned.

Above the mantel hung the unfinished portrait of Catherine Algernon—looking no worse for his travel through it and back.

He started across the room.

"Is it really you?" James asked.

Collier looked around.

There was focus to James's eyes that had not been there before, as if through his drunken stupor he was considering this might not be a dream after all.

"Aye—yes," Collier corrected himself. "This is not a dream, James."

"You're . . . sure?"

"Positive."

This time James succeeded in sitting forward. "Where have you been?"

There was only the truth, but perhaps it would be more easily accepted with the alcohol James had consumed. "With Catherine Algernon."

James snorted. "I may be drunk half out of my mind, but even I know you can't have been with a woman who's five-hundred-years dead. I'd say this obsession of yours has gotten quite out of hand."

"If there was time to explain it, I would"—Collier stepped toward the portrait—"but I must return to Catherine immediately."

"And how do you propose to do that?"

James was humoring him. "I went through the portrait once to find her, I pray I can do so again."

"Through . . . the portrait?"

"It sent me five hundred years into the past to the time of Catherine Algernon." Collier reached toward the red rose clasped between Catherine's hands.

"Are we talking time travel here?"

"I suppose that's what you would call it."

James chuckled. "If you didn't come out of this bottle, all I can say is you're going to need some pretty extensive counseling, Collier."

The unseen force which had dragged at Collier months back when he had come upon the portrait in Catherine's chamber was still. Despair unfolding, he drew a steadying breath to keep from releasing the emotions that tensed him tight as a loaded spring. Think, he commanded himself. How had he done it the first time?

"Collier?" James asked.

Collier looked to the ceiling. Once again he would be asking for a miracle. He closed his eyes.

Surprisingly, James allowed him his quiet. Collier prayed for another chance with Catherine. Prayed that, once again, he could deliver her from Walther's clutches, and that their unborn child would know him. But in the end, there was only silence.

"I hate to tell you this, but you're still here."

How long had it been? Collier wondered. A half hour? An hour? More? Battling emotions drawn so taut it was only a matter of time before they snapped, he drew a deep breath, and in doing so was assailed by an aroma he had almost forgotten. He looked up.

James stood in the doorway, envelopes and a cigar jutting from his shirt pocket, and a cup in each hand. Although his stance was broad to counter the effects of alcohol, he appeared to have sobered somewhat. "Coffee?" he asked.

Collier looked at the heat wafting above the rims of fine china.

"It's my fourth," James said. Swaying slightly, he stepped into the room and held out one of the cups.

Collier accepted it. Black. The only way his brother drank it. Though he himself had always added a good dollop of cream to his coffee, Collier took a swallow of the hot liquid. It always smelled better than it actually tasted. No wonder he hadn't missed it.

"Aspirin?" James asked.

Collier considered the bottle his brother produced from his pants pocket.

"You look like you could use a couple," James said.

His head still throbbing from where Walther had struck him, Collier set his coffee on a nearby table, accepted the bottle, and took two of the pills.

"Catherine Algernon did not die in the winch room," James said unexpectedly.

Looking around, Collier found his brother staring at the portrait. If the changes to the past had manifested themselves in the present time, how was it James recalled that other past? "No," Collier said, "she did not die there."

James shook his head. "Perhaps I am going mad, Collier, but was that not the legend of her—that she died defending Strivling against the Yorkists?"

"It was, but I changed that."

James looked over his shoulder.

Collier met his bloodshot gaze. "I *did* go back to the fifteenth century."

Though doubt reflected in James's eyes, he nodded for Collier to continue.

"After I learned of Aryn's death, I—"

"I found the letter from her mother."

Collier remembered crumpling it in his hand, but what he had done with it he couldn't say. "I pleaded for another chance with her, and when I looked up, Catherine's portrait was revealed to me. There I saw Aryn."

"I knew it. I knew they looked the same." James seemed to be warming to the idea. "And the sword—which, by the way, no longer exists—what of the blood on it?"

It no longer figured into the past because it had not killed Catherine. "In my grief and anger, I seized it by the blade and cut myself."

"Then what happened?"

There was so much to explain, and it looked as if he was going to have plenty of time to do it. But perhaps in doing so he might hit on the key to returning to the fifteenth century, Collier thought. The possibility kept him sane as he began to relate his fantastic tale.

An hour later, he ended it with his final confrontation with Walther. Not knowing whether or not he was believed, he waited for a response.

"You must love her very much," James finally said.

"I do."

"Have you told her?"

"Aye."

"And she feels the same for you?"

Again that ache. "I believe so, but she hasn't said."

James nodded. A few minutes later, he began to speak of the past months. He pulled out newspaper clippings detailing Collier's mysterious disappearance, and that speculated on James's involvement. He spoke of the interrogations he had been put through at Scotland Yard. The letters he had written to relatives inquiring into their knowledge of Catherine Algernon. However, none but he recalled anything other than the new past Collier had made. No one knew anything about Catherine meeting her end in the winch room. She was no longer a legend.

James straightened from the mantel. "If everything you say is true—and God knows it would explain so much—why me, Collier? Why am I the only one who remembers things as they truly were? You know as well as I there's no love lost between us."

His words took Collier back twenty years to a time when they had still been brothers. Before their father had determined they should be rivals. Emotion tightened his throat. "You're wrong," he said.

"What do you mean?"

"I don't hate you, James. And I don't believe you hate me. It's our father we've been battling all these years, not each other."

As if suddenly uncomfortable, James averted his gaze.

"Perhaps I was returned to this time to make things right with you," Collier continued.

In James's haste to remove the cigar from his shirt pocket, one of the envelopes behind it fell to the floor. He didn't notice. "What's there to make right?" His voice was gruff. "You have your life. I have mine."

"That's not the way it should have been."

James fumbled with the wrapper and a moment later jammed the cigar between his teeth. "And how should it have been?" he asked, speaking around it.

Collier nodded to the cigar. Although James rarely lit up, he had taken Winton Morrow's habit for his own. "Our father made us over in his image. We should never have allowed it."

James pulled the cigar from his mouth and eyed it.

"I'm not staying," Collier said. "Somehow I'll find a way back to Catherine. I just want you to know I regret the wrongs I did you, and that I consider you my brother." And now the hardest to say of all. "I love you, James."

James stared at him a long moment. Then, his eyes brightening, he swallowed and looked away. "I've definitely had too much to drink," he muttered, "or perhaps not enough." He stepped past Collier to the table.

As Collier watched, his brother poured himself a generous glass of Scotch. "Are you an alcoholic?" he asked.

James paused with the glass halfway to his lips. "Wondering if I have the same problem as you?" he said, suddenly defensive.

Collier knew what he referred to. Several of the newspaper articles James had shown him had headlined Collier's addiction to painkillers. As if uncomfortable with the subject, James had not commented on it. So was it a problem? Collier could not remember the last time he had thought of the painkillers, let alone craved them. "It's under control," he said.

James's laughter was dry. "Well, this was under control, too"—he raised his glass—"until you disappeared."

"I'm sorry to have put you through this," Collier said. "I really am."

James contemplated him a long moment. "Determined to break me of all my vices, hmm?" he said, attempting humor where there was none.

"Somebody has to."

James set the Scotch glass on the table and dropped into the chair. "So how are you going to get back?"

As Collier looked toward the portrait, the envelope that lay before the hearth caught his eye. He picked it up. "From Geraldine Morrow," he read aloud the return address.

"Came in this afternoon's mail. You remember dear old Great-Aunt Gerry, don't you?"

"Isn't she the one who used to tell us stories about Catherine and the fall of Strivling?"

"The same. Go ahead, open it and see what she has to say now about the legend of Catherine Algernon."

From his tone, Collier knew James expected the dotty old woman to beg off knowledge of Catherine having died defending the winch room—the same as the others whom he had received responses from.

Collier tore open the envelope and began to read. The first few paragraphs consisted of idle chat, but finally she answered the question James had put to her.

In response to your recent letter, there is very little I can tell you about Catherine Algernon, for not much is known of the lady. Apparently, once Strivling fell to Lord Montagu, she was forced to wed a Yorkist by the name of Gilchrist and sent to live at Toller Castle. Though it was hoped she would settle down and pose no more of a threat to King Edward, it was not long before Lancastrian rebels seized the castle and clashed with the army of our ancestor. Edmund won the day, and when the dust settled, Lady Catherine was discovered missing.

Missing? Collier's heart clenched. For certain, Walther was behind Catherine's disappearance. He forced himself to read the remainder of the letter.

What became of Catherine is unknown, but it stands to reason she was behind the rebel forces entering Toller.

How wrong Geraldine was. But of course it would appear that way.

As for her Yorkist husband, it is believed he died in the conflict, for nothing else is known about him. If I can be of further help, dear James, do write. I will continue to pray for you and the safe return of your brother. As ever, Geraldine Morrow.

Collier lowered the letter. Catherine needed him. How was he to get back to her?

"Knows nothing of Catherine Algernon, hmm?" James said.

Collier crossed to his brother and handed him the letter. "She says Catherine disappeared from Toller after Edmund recaptured it from the Lancastrians."

James quickly read the letter. "You think it was Walther?"

"Has to be."

"So how are you going to get back?"

Collier looked to the portrait. "Through there." Now that things were as right between him and his brother as he could make them, surely there was nothing to hold him here?

"But how?" James asked.

"I don't know, but if I make it back, the coin . . ."

"You think it's still there?"

"If it is, you should have it."

"I could certainly use it."

Wishing they had more time together, Collier stared at his brother a long moment. But Catherine was waiting for him. He started to turn away.

"Collier?"

"James?"

"What you said, it . . . it goes for me as well."

A tightness in his throat, Collier nodded. Amazing how much he had learned to feel these past months. In loving Catherine, he had discovered emotions he would never have believed himself capable of. "I won't forget you," he said.

"Same."

Feeling as if a weight was lifted from him, Collier turned to Catherine's portrait. God willing, he would be with her again soon. He only prayed there was still time.

But a half hour later he was no nearer to being returned to the fifteenth century, and James had fallen asleep beside his bottle of Scotch.

Wanting to rage—to shout out his anger, frustration, and pain—Collier clenched and unclenched his hands. Think! What was missing? The sword came to mind. But no, it had lost its significance when he had prevented Walther from taking Catherine's life. Hadn't it? He had cut his hands on it prior to his first journey through time, and then Walther had struck him with it just before his return journey. A coincidence? Fiercely, he prayed it went beyond that, for, according to James, the sword no longer existed.

Collier pounded a fist against the mantel. "God, what more will it take? I love her. Have told her so. She—"

She hadn't told him.

Sightlessly, Collier stared at the hearth. Was that it? Not until he'd lost Aryn had he admitted he loved her, but when finally he had, he'd been granted a second chance. Was that what it would take? For Catherine to speak the words—providing it was love she felt for him?

Feeling beaten, but unwilling to give up the fight to return to her, Collier grasped the mantel and pressed his forehead to it. "Love me, Catherine," he pleaded across five hundred years. "Please love me."

26

Northern England, August 1464

She'd had to wait two hours. Finally, with night upon Toller, Catherine stepped into the hall.

Walther, with a slight limp from the injury she had done him, walked ahead of her.

In spite of the great number of people present—the castle folk, Toller's men-at-arms, and the rebels who stood watch over them—it was silent within.

Catherine located her mother near the dais, on one side of her Eustace, on the other, the household knights. They were safe, for now. So who wished to speak with her? She swept her gaze to the high table, and in the next instant stumbled to a halt. In disbelief, she stared at the great man who stood before the dais.

He returned her gaze. Impassive, but very much alive.

Could it be? She had been told he had died in the

confrontation with Montagu's men, and that Griffin Walther was the one who had delivered the death blow. So what was he—

"Surprised?" Walther asked.

Catherine looked at where he had come to stand beside her.

"So was I," he said, making no attempt to conceal his regret, "but I assure you, he and I are not finished."

Meaning that though Walther sided with the Lancasters, he would not be satisfied until Severn was dead, as he should have been months ago.

Catherine returned her gaze to the knight. And suddenly, she knew. It was he who had sent the missive to her at Strivling. "S" for Severn.

Walther pulled her forward. "Come. You keep the king of England waiting."

The king? Startled, Catherine looked to the high table and saw the one she had not heretofore noticed—dwarfed as he was by Severn's greater presence.

Clothed entirely in gray, right down to the broad-toed shoes that were fit more for a countryman than one of royalty, the man watched from the lord's high seat as she crossed the hall beside Walther.

This was King Henry? This sickly-looking man who appeared as if he would be better abed? Although it was his queen, Margaret, whom Hildegard had often spoken of with such veneration, Catherine had envisioned the man to be far different from the one who occupied her husband's place at table.

Collier. Pain, deep and tearing, stole Catherine's breath. How was she to live without him? She carried his child, but still there was a place inside her which would ever be empty. Of course, if Walther had his way, she would not have much time to suffer.

Abruptly, Catherine shut out the pain. She would not die this day. Somehow, she would escape the fate Walther planned for her and bear the child she and Collier had made. Somehow.

Without regard to her footing, Walther towed Catherine up to the dais.

She nearly made it without mishap, but on the top step fell to her knees.

"Sir Griffin," King Henry spoke sharply, "'tis a lady you mistreat so. Have a care."

Was the king of a kindly disposition as she had heard it said? Catherine wondered. Of course, Hildegard had called it weakness.

The mercenary bowed his head in deference. As he assisted Catherine back to standing, his fingers pressed hard into the flesh of her upper arm.

She wrenched free. He would be angry, she knew, but she couldn't stand his touch any longer.

"Lady Catherine, Your Majesty," Walther presented her, his voice tight.

She smoothed her skirts, then did as any subject would when coming before their king. She bowed. Forget it was Edward who wore the crown now. Forget Henry's reign was at an end. Forget that in loving Collier she had, in effect, gone over to the side of the Yorkists. If she was to survive, she could not afford to alienate the only one who might be able to help her.

"Arise, Lady Catherine," Henry said.

She straightened.

In the brief moment the king held her gaze, Catherine saw the weariness of his soul in his eyes.

"Where is Lady Catherine's husband?" Henry asked Walther.

"He . . . disappeared, Your Majesty."

"Disappeared?"

"I felled him and—"

"I ordered that none was to be harmed," Henry interrupted. He colored slightly, but that seemed the extent of his anger.

"He attacked me, Your Majesty. I had to defend myself."

"You lie!" Catherine exclaimed, knowing she spoke out of turn, but unable to help herself. "My lord raised not a weapon against you, but you struck him down."

"This from a woman turned traitor but for that gotten between the Yorkist's legs," Walther scorned. "She is a whore, Your Majesty. She—"

"I will not tolerate such vulgarity, Sir Walther," Henry reprimanded. "You will cease this instant."

The mercenary swallowed. "My apologies, Your Majesty."

Henry inclined his head. "Now tell me, how did Gilchrist escape you?"

"I do not know, Your Majesty. One moment he lay on the ground, and in the next . . ." Walther raised his palms. "He was gone."

"What do you mean 'gone'?"

"Vanished. As if he had never been."

Henry regarded the mercenary a long moment, then murmured, "And they say I am mad."

The words were not lost on Catherine.

King Henry sighed. "No matter." He turned his attention to her. "You know why I have come?"

It had to be the money and valuables. Though Severn had not known where she kept them hidden, he had known of their existence. And that, did Strivling fall, it was to have gone to the Lancasters. "I do not, Your Majesty," she said.

He leaned forward. "I have come for the wealth of Strivling. Where is it?"

What if she were to tell him? Would it really make the difference Collier feared it might? Would it be enough to put Henry back on the throne when it was Edward whom Collier told her was destined to hold it? Should hold it?

"'Tis mine," King Henry said. "Lady Hildegard vowed that if Strivling fell to the Yorkists its monies would be delivered into my hands."

Which was the promise Catherine had done her best to keep the day she had ventured into the underground, and nearly died for it. She steeled herself for the king's fury. "This I know, Your Majesty, but I fear 'tis gone."

Out of the corner of her eye, she saw Walther's hands clench.

Henry stared at her a moment, then beckoned to the man who had stood silently beside him. "Sir Richard," he said.

Where was the king's anger? Catherine wondered.

"And who has stolen it from our king?" Sir Richard asked.

Catherine met his gaze. "Methinks it was Montagu." After all, he would have taken it had he known of it—would have used the lives of the castle folk to force her to divulge its hiding place.

"You *think* he took it," Sir Richard said. "You do not know?"

"I . . . the coffers were empty when I came for them."

"Then he found where you had hidden them."

"He must have."

Sir Richard looked past her. "Antony Algernon, come forward."

Antony? He was here? No word had come from

Strivling that he had fled to the side of the Lancasters. But then, perhaps he had only just done so.

Eyes averted, her brother stepped up to the dais and came to stand next to Catherine.

"Were you not present, Antony, when Edmund Morrow came to Toller and demanded to know the whereabouts of three hundred pounds he discovered missing from Strivling's books?" Sir Richard asked.

"I was."

"Was there not in excess of eight hundred pounds in Strivling's coffers, Lady Catherine?"

She swallowed. "I believe so."

"And you think Montagu took the entire sum and the valuables?"

"I do." Hardly had Catherine said it when the muttering of the king drew her attention back to him.

His lips were forming words she did not understand, and his gaze was intent on the thumbnails of the hands he clasped before his face. Henry seemed not to be listening, as if he were not even present.

"Then what of the three hundred pounds that is unaccounted for?" Sir Richard asked, showing no awareness of the king's peculiar behavior.

Did he think she had given five hundred to the Yorkists and kept the three hundred for herself? Catherine wondered. "'Tis eight hundred pounds missing from the books," she said. "Edmund Morrow does not know it. Methinks he is unlearned in numbers."

It was several moments before Sir Richard spoke again. "Be it so, you are saying Edmund Morrow's overlord, Montagu, said naught of the money he took from Strivling?"

"Why would he? Montagu is a greedy man. Obviously, he wished it all for himself."

Walther could no longer contain himself. "She speaks untruths, Your Majesty!"

Roused from his stupor, Henry blinked.

Walther took a step toward the high table. "She and her Yorkist lover have hidden the money. I am certain of it!"

It took Henry a moment to gain his bearings, then he held up a silencing hand and pulled Catherine into his tired gaze. "Are you loyal to me, Lady Catherine? Or is it this Yorkist you side with?"

How was she to answer him? "I do not stand with Edward," she said, hoping that in his state of mind he would not notice her evasiveness.

"What of Gilchrist?" he asked, crushing her hopes. "Do you stand with him?"

Collier who stood with the Yorkists. "He is my husband, Your Majesty."

Annoyance lit Henry's lackluster eyes. "I ask again, Lady Catherine, do you stand with your Yorkist husband?"

He gave her no choice. "I do."

The king still did not rise to anger, but seemed merely disappointed. "Then 'tis true. For the sinful pleasures of the flesh you have forsaken me."

He was so wrong. Tears pricking the backs of her eyes, Catherine said, "Nay, Your Majesty. Though you would condemn me for it, I . . ." She took a deep breath. "I love Collier Gilchrist." Hurting all the more for speaking the words aloud, she wondered if this was how Collier had felt when he finally declared his love for Aryn. Such pain. "For love I stand with him."

Henry looked up. "But he is not here to stand with. This man you say you love—this Yorkist—has left you to your fate, Lady Catherine."

And what was that fate? "Could he return, he would," she said. She was certain of it.

The king shook his head. "You have been deceived, Lady Catherine, and have thus deceived me. I will have my eight hundred pounds. Be it in your hands, Gilchrist's, or Montagu's, I will have it."

What was he threatening? Catherine wondered. The lives of the castle folk as Montagu had done? If so, what was she to do? Though she might save Toller's people by divulging the whereabouts of Strivling's wealth, what of the lives that would be forfeit when Henry used it to mount an attack against Edward and his supporters? She would merely be trading lives for lives.

"Sir Griffin," Henry said, "take Lady Catherine from the hall that she might think on her loyalties this night."

Did he know what he did in sending her with the mercenary? Did he know what Walther was capable of? Likely. Though Catherine had begun to believe Henry would not resort to such means, it seemed that was what he intended.

Walther bowed. "Your Majesty." Then, once more, his hand fell to Catherine.

As she was drawn past her mother, Catherine met Lavinia's anxious gaze, then Eustace's. They feared for her.

"Sir Severn," Henry called. "You will also accompany Lady Catherine."

Relief swept Catherine. Regardless of Severn's feelings for her now that she was declared a Yorkist, one thing was certain: the great man would do her no harm, and neither would he allow any other to harm her.

Feeling Walther's rancor in the stiffness of his step, Catherine turned her thoughts to escape.

*   *   *

A soft landing. It was about time. Rising from the hay
that had cushioned his fall, Collier realized that, once
again, he wore medieval garb. He was returned—to
the stables, no less.

By the dim light the moon cast between the slats of
wood, he descended from the loft. It was quiet here,
the only sounds those made by the horses in their
stalls.

Ducking the unshuttered windows, Collier crept to
the doorway and paused to listen. Walther's men
were out there. To reach Catherine, wherever she
was, he must get past them.

He felt across his waist. He had his dagger, but
that was all. No matter, he also had his fists. He
pulled the dagger from its scabbard and looked
around the doorway.

Fifty feet out, a soldier leaned against a water
trough. He appeared to be dozing.

Collier picked out the others and planned the order
in which he would take each man down. Of course,
crossing from the outer bailey to the inner would
prove another challenge entirely. From what he could
make out, there were at least a dozen men before the
portal. But he would worry about them when he got
there. Crouching low, he stole from the stables.

With a muffled grunt, the first soldier fell to the
blow Collier landed with the hilt of the dagger. The
two after him cooperated just as nicely. However, as
Collier advanced on the fourth, the snapping of a
branch underfoot alerted the soldier to his presence.

The man looked around, but even as he opened his
mouth to sound the alarm, Collier shoved his fist into
it. The soldier staggered backward. Knowing it might

not be enough, Collier struck him again, this time with the hilt of his dagger. The soldier dropped to the ground.

Collier dragged him into the shadows of the smithy. Now he had to get past those stationed before the inner bailey. Could he simply walk past as if one of them?

Suddenly, he felt cold steel press into the flesh of his neck.

"Drop your weapon," a voice rasped near his ear.

Although Collier's first thought was to resist, he knew it would only gain him a slashed throat. Dead, there was nothing he could do to save Catherine. He released the dagger.

Still holding the blade to Collier's throat, the man at his back came around and flashed the smile of Edmund Morrow.

Relief washed over Collier.

"I thought it was you," his ancestor whispered, lowering his dagger. "Who else would leave a trail of senseless men?" Edmund retrieved Collier's dagger and handed it to him. "I know 'tis not likely you will need it, but should you . . ."

Collier turned his hand around the hilt. "How did you learn Toller was taken?"

"Young Antony, of course."

Of course. Where Antony had failed Edmund as a squire, he had more than made up for it by leading his lord to the Lancastrians.

"Henry is thought to be within," Edmund said.

King Henry? God, but this wasn't supposed to be. Henry was supposed to be keeping to the safe houses. Walther's amassing of rebel forces must have brought him here.

"And now we will take Toller back," Edmund said,

"and perhaps even deliver Henry into Edward's hands." He jutted his chin toward the outer wall.

Collier looked around.

"My men," Edmund said. "Are you ready?"

"Ready."

His massive bulk engulfing her in his shadow, Severn came to stand over Catherine.

There was something he wished to say to her, she knew, and she had no doubt as to what that might be. She looked up from where she sat before the hearth in Eustace's chamber. "I thought you dead."

The knight's wiry eyebrows rose. "As did Walther."

Thus, the reason for the intense hatred Catherine felt emanating from them this past half hour. When pressed, Collier had told her what the mercenary had done when he had come out of the pit—needlessly putting Severn through with his own sword. Fortunately for Severn, he was a man of enormous proportions.

"You appear to have mended well," she said.

Severn's nostrils flared. Likely, it was only by a slender thread he held himself from slaying Walther. He searched Catherine's face, then changed the subject. "Lady Hildegard would have been disappointed."

Disappointed in the one who should have given her life to defend Strivling. Who should never have wed a Yorkist—not even to spare the lives of her people. "I know," Catherine said. "Hildegard would have had all of England fall before admitting her wrong."

"Wrong?"

Although Severn had been the old baron's knight, it was Hildegard he had been loyal to. He had revered the woman as if she were the worthiest of warriors. And would likely have revered Catherine had that other past come to be.

"How long have you been with King Henry?" Catherine asked.

"Since shortly after I stole half-dead from Strivling."

Though she could not see around Severn to where Walther stood near the door of the chamber, Catherine knew the mercenary was listening to their exchange. "That long, and yet you do not know how Hildegard could have been wrong?"

The big man's gaze narrowed.

"Come, Severn," Catherine chided, "even the mercenary knows Henry is unfit to rule England. Had Walther not been sent from Strivling in disgrace, he would never have sided with so weak a man."

For the briefest of moments, she sensed that Severn also thought Henry incompetent, but stubborn Lancastrian pride would never allow him to admit it.

Appearing beside Severn, Walther lowered his hating gaze to Catherine. "I am going to take great pleasure in cutting your traitor's tongue from your mouth," he snarled.

"Traitor?" Catherine repeated. "You are hardly one to call another such."

"At least I know what I am, Lady Catherine, and I make no excuses for it."

And what was she? A woman who had turned her loyalties from the Lancasters, but not to the Yorks. Rather, to a man who had taught her to love. "Were I such a coward as you," Catherine said, "I would not be so proud of it."

Anger flushing up from his neck, Walther drew back his arm.

Severn caught it midair and thrust his face near the other man's. "Keep your distance, knave," he growled, "else I shall forget King Henry believes he needs you."

Walther stared at Severn, then jerked his arm free and turned away. The scabbard of his sword riding alongside Collier's sword, he strode to the door.

Severn lowered himself to his haunches beside Catherine. "Where is the money, Lady Catherine?"

She swallowed. "As I told King Henry, methinks Montagu took it."

"Never would you have allowed the bastard near it."

"And I did not. He surely found it on his own."

Severn laid an urgent hand upon her arm. "To Lady Hildegard I gave my word I would protect you, but do you not speak the truth, I will be unable to keep my vow."

Catherine drew a deep breath. "I am sorry, but there is naught I can tell you."

He rose slowly to his feet. "God be with you."

And her child, Catherine prayed. As Severn turned away, she pressed a hand to her belly. It seemed her dreams as she had once known them were truly over, for she'd had no inkling of this terrible day. All her dreams in recent days had been of the child Collier had left her with. Collier. She wanted to cry.

Suddenly, a clamor arose from without. Exultant shouts. The ring of steel. The cries of death. Booted feet pounding the stairs.

Could it be? Had the Yorkists come? Catherine looked from Severn to Walther and saw from their expressions that the same thought ran through their minds. Had Antony led Morrow here?

"The king!" Severn shouted. He drew his sword and started for the door.

Her heart speeding, Catherine stood.

Walther also pulled his sword from its scabbard, but it was Catherine he turned his gaze on.

"Leave her," Severn said, throwing the door open. The sounds of struggle in the hall below grew louder. "King Henry requires us."

Obviously, Walther would have preferred not to rally to the king's side, but he was in no position to refuse Severn. He pulled the key from the door.

Catherine knew what he intended. "Nay," she cried, running forward.

Walther smiled. "We would not want you to be gone when we return." He stepped into her path and thrust a hand to her chest.

She fell backward. "Severn!" she called.

"'Tis best you remain here, my lady," the knight responded.

Walther closed the door and turned the key in the lock.

It would be a waste of strength to attempt to budge the planked door, Catherine knew. She looked around her. To her knowledge, there were no secret passages here as there were at Strivling. That left only the windows— and nothing below them but a sheer drop. Still, Catherine ducked into an embrasure and looked out.

Small fires lit about the bailey illuminated Yorkist against Lancastrian, and cast their long shadows over the walls. Who would be the victor? she wondered. Yorkist, she prayed, and in the next instant reflected on how different her life was from three months back when she would rather have died than be ruled by Edward. Collier had changed that.

Pretending she didn't ache as badly for him as she did, she straightened from the window. How was she going to get out of here?

27

Toller's weaponless men-at-arms stood uncertainly among the melee, their eyes fixed on Sir Mathis who had positioned himself to the side of the dais in front of Lady Lavinia and Eustace.

They were waiting to see which way the senior knight would go, Collier realized. Which way *would* he go? Would Mathis side with the man who had been ushered from the lord's table when Edmund's forces had broken into the hall? Or would he stay the course set by Lewis Algernon?

As Collier knew it might be believed he had fled, he began fighting his way toward the dais using the sword he had appropriated from a fallen soldier. But not once did he draw blood.

Suddenly, a Lancastrian soldier lurched into his path and slammed his sword against his opponent's—a young man-at-arms whose wounds spread crimson down his sleeve and tunic. Clearly, it was only a matter of moments before Edmund's man fell.

Collier lunged forward, and a moment later, the Lancastrian reeled backward.

His knuckles aching, Collier retrieved the soldier's sword and stepped past the wide-eyed man-at-arms. It was then, across the distance, that he met Sir Mathis's gaze.

The knight grinned and gave the signal Toller's men were waiting for. They were Yorkist now.

Collier had to fell two more soldiers before he made it to Sir Mathis. "Where is Catherine?" he asked, thrusting a sword into the man's hand.

"Abovestairs."

"Walther?"

"King Henry sent him and another with my lady."

Fear constricting Collier's heart, he demanded, "And what of Henry?"

The struggle in the knight's eyes bespoke his uncertainty. Though he accepted Yorkist rule, he was loath to reveal the man he had once been loyal to.

Collier stepped nearer Mathis. "Trust me in this," he said. "I no more wish Henry dead than you."

Though puzzlement creased his brow, the knight nodded. "Methinks he fled abovestairs. There can have been no other course for him."

True, for Edmund's men had covered all exits when they had converged upon the hall. Unfortunately, that meant Henry would be trapped up there. Collier released a harsh sigh. He was going to have to work a miracle of his own to put time back on track. "What of Antony?" he asked.

"He is with Henry."

A miracle indeed. Collier looked to where Lady Lavinia clutched her younger son against her. "The tapestry," he said, nodding to the wall hanging behind the dais. "Get behind there and stay put until I call you out."

Lady Lavinia took Eustace's arm and ushered him into hiding with her.

"Come," Collier said to Sir Mathis, and started toward the stairs.

The soft click was "like music to her ears"—as Collier might have phrased it. Releasing her held breath, Catherine pulled the needle from the keyhole. At last she had found a use for the abhorrent object other than stitching. She started to rise from her knees, but in the next instant, the door slammed inward and knocked her back. Gasping, she looked up at Walther.

"Nay!" she cried, scrambling backward. She had been so close. So close!

The mercenary yanked her to her feet.

Desperate, Catherine reached for the sword beneath his belt—Collier's—and pulled it free. Its grip was warm, as if Collier's hand had recently been upon it, but no more had she drawn the weapon back when Walther slammed his forearm against hers.

The sword flew from her hand.

Catherine wanted to scream, to kick, to pummel her fists against the cur. And so she did.

"I have not the time for this," Walther snapped, evading her knee which she had targeted for his groin.

She settled for raking her nails down his cheek.

Bellowing, Walther bunched his fist and drew his arm back.

Instinctively, Catherine clapped a hand over her abdomen.

The blow never came. Instead, there was silence, and

a moment later, laughter. Wicked. Triumphant. "So we've a little traitor in the making, eh?" Walther said.

Dread overcoming her, Catherine dropped her arm to her side. For certain the miscreant would try to use her pregnancy against her. She met his gaze. How she hated his smile—that vile thing that was surely of the devil.

"You think me with child?" She injected as much incredulity into her tone as she could feign. "I assure I am not."

"You lie beautifully, my lady," Walther said, then landed his hand to her abdomen.

With a cry, Catherine jumped back, leaving him clutching the material of her gown.

"Try me further," Walther said, "and I will cut Gilchrist's seed from your belly."

She swallowed. Could he be so evil?

"Do we understand each other?"

She nodded.

"Better." Confident that he had her under control, Walther released her. "Now come."

Catherine preceded him out of the chamber. There, on the landing above the stairs, Walther's men struggled to hold back those who sought to recover Toller.

"To the chapel," Walther said.

She turned opposite the landing, and at the far end of the corridor pushed open the door to the sacred place. As she stepped within, her gaze fell to Severn, then to Antony beside him. For the brief moment her brother allowed it, Catherine held his gaze. He was fearful. Lost. His dreams of glory were eroding with each passing minute.

King Henry lay prostrate at the altar with Sir Richard hovering nearby.

Walther ushered Catherine farther into the chapel. "King Henry," he called.

The king did not move. His muttered prayers were the only evidence he still breathed.

"Get off the floor, man!" Walther shouted. "We haven't much time."

Still the king paid him no heed.

Walther strode forward. Clearly, he intended to drag Henry to his feet.

Sir Richard stepped into his path. "You will not lay hands to the king," he warned.

"Do we not leave now, the Yorkists will certainly lay hands to him," Walther snarled, "and by the morrow, your beloved king's head will be on Edward's plate."

It was Henry who answered him. "Young Antony says there is no way down from here." He sat back on his heels.

Eyes widening with disbelief, Walther swung his gaze to Antony. "Surely there is a hidden passageway."

Antony shook his head. "There are only the stairs to the hall."

Walther was silent a long moment, then he began to smile. "And up to the rooftop. Aye, that is where we will go."

"But there is no way down," Antony protested.

"Is there not?" Walther strode to the altar. Paying no heed to the holy cross, he tore the cloth from beneath it. The relic clattered to the floor. "We will fashion ourselves a rope and climb down." He held up the altar cloth.

Eyes bulging and mouth working uselessly, King Henry could only stare.

Catherine glanced at the door behind. Could she make it out of the chapel? If so, what of the Lancastrians beyond?

"Do you cause me to chase you, Lady Catherine, I

vow you will pay tenfold," Walther said, and reached for the fine material that draped the walls.

"St. John!" Henry finally managed. "'Tis the House of the Lord you desecrate."

The mercenary tore down a panel of the material and reached for another.

"Wait!" Antony said. "We can use the rope that draws the water abovestairs."

A light entered Walther's eyes. "Good lad. Fetch it and meet us on the roof."

Avoiding Catherine's gaze, Antony skirted her and hurried from the chapel.

"Are you with me?" Walther asked Henry.

"I stay," the king said. "God will protect me."

"As he protected your throne?"

"The Lord tests me, that is all. He will surely deliver me from the Yorkists."

The mercenary laughed. "You fool of a man! Idiot! Stay here and die if that is what you wish, but do not expect me to die with you." He started toward Catherine.

Although Walther's words must surely have cut him, Henry's face remained impassive.

"Your Majesty," Sir Richard said, "it may be the only way."

"I stay," Henry said, more forcefully.

"What of your queen?" Sir Richard reminded him. "What think you she would do?"

Henry blinked. "I . . ."

"Queen Margaret would go with Sir Griffin," the knight said.

With Henry reconsidering his decision, Walther drew his sword and thrust Catherine ahead of him.

"You do not need me," she protested.

"I do not," he agreed. "Just the coin. And you are going to tell me where 'tis."

"But I cannot climb a rope!"

"Then you are going to learn."

Out of the chapel and down the corridor, Catherine searched for some way to escape Walther. There was the dagger beneath his belt, but he would be on her before she could drag it free. And it was too great a risk considering his threat to her child. She looked to the landing ahead that was defended by Lancastrian soldiers. Perhaps the Yorkists would break through, forcing Walther to leave her side to defend himself.

As Catherine sidestepped Walther's soldiers, she caught a glimpse of the men on the stairs below. The Yorkists, who easily outnumbered the Lancastrians, appeared to be making good progress as they fought their way upward. And among them was one whose face was familiar. Sir Mathis.

Catherine did not call to him as she wished to, for Walther's sword was at her back.

"Hurry!" he barked.

Catherine began her ascent and, shortly, with Walther, King Henry, Sir Richard, and Severn following, stepped onto the torch-lit rooftop.

Antony awaited them. "The rope is secure," he said. "We will lower ourselves into the garden, and from there make our way to the postern gate."

Walther leaned into the embrasure the rope dangled from. "Well done," he said. "You might make a soldier yet, Antony boy."

Severn stepped forward. "I shall go first, and King Henry after me."

"You may trust I shall ensure the rope remains secure," Walther said.

"*I* will tend the rope," Sir Richard said, brooking no argument, "and be the last to follow."

Beginning to feel the cool night air, Catherine

wrapped her arms around herself and watched as Severn ascended to the embrasure. A moment later, he disappeared from sight.

Shoulders stooped, King Henry reached for the rope.

Was he capable of the descent? Catherine wondered. He seemed so frail. So weary.

"Halt!"

The deep voice with its peculiar accent spun a song around Catherine's heart. She had thought never to hear it again.

Sword in hand, Collier stepped onto the roof beside Sir Mathis.

"Collier!" Catherine cried. She had no more than put a foot forward when Walther yanked her back.

"Stand back, Gilchrist," he shouted, "else I'll cut yer babe from her belly. I swear it!" He pressed his sword to her abdomen.

Collier had thought his fear could not be greater than when he had nearly lost Catherine to the sea, but it was. Halting, he looked from the mercenary to Catherine's fearful face. After all they had been through, he was not going to lose her now. There was a way. There had to be a way. He clenched his hand tightly on sword "indomitable," which he had recovered minutes earlier from Eustace's chamber.

"We are going over the wall," Walther said. "Do you try to stop us, Catherine's death and your child's will be upon your conscience."

Her fate would be no different if Walther was allowed to take her from Toller, Collier knew. She would disappear and undoubtedly be murdered. He looked to Antony who stood to one side of Walther, then to the two opposite. Sword drawn, a knight had positioned himself before one whose hooded head was all that was visible of him.

King Henry? It must be. Fortunately, the first duty of the knight would be to protect his king. Thus, he was not likely to move from his place other than to defend Henry.

"What do you wish to do?" Sir Mathis asked.

What needed to be done. "Come," Collier said. Fixing his gaze on the mercenary, he put his sword before him and started forward.

Walther swept the blade to Catherine's neck.

She cried out.

As much as Collier feared for her, he did not stop.

Suddenly, Antony lunged toward Walther.

"Let her go!" the boy shouted.

God! Collier silently cursed. Now was not the time for Antony to feel the flutter of brotherly love.

Walther dealt with Antony swiftly. Retaining his hold on Catherine, he swept his sword forward and caught the boy across the shoulder.

Antony clapped a hand to the wound and dropped to his knees.

"Whelp!" Walther spat, then looked back at Collier. "I have warned you, Gilchrist!"

"You have," Collier said, continuing forward, "and now I issue a warning of my own: do Catherine harm and your death will be the longest and most painful any man has ever known." It was true. Though he had believed he could never take another's life, he would kill Walther, and be justified in doing so.

Dragging Catherine with him, Walther backed toward the embrasure. "You think I fear you? You who chooses fists over the sword? A man who cannot tolerate the drawing of blood?"

"Things change," Collier said. "This time I will kill you, Walther. I swear it."

The mercenary's eyes narrowed.

"Unless you release her," Collier added. "In which case, I will allow you and the others to leave."

"Just like that?" Walther laughed. "Your whore of a wife lies better than you."

Twenty feet from the mercenary, Collier halted. In an attempt to reassure Catherine, he met her gaze.

Her steadfast eyes shined with something it seemed he had waited forever for, and in that moment, Collier knew it was so. She loved him. It was that which had brought him back to her. Strengthened by her love, he sought the man behind the knight.

The one whose destiny needed to be put back on track stared at him.

"King Henry, I presume," Collier said.

After a long hesitation, the man inclined his head.

"I have no quarrel with you," Collier said. "I want only my wife."

"And in exchange you would allow the king his freedom?" asked the knight who stood before Henry, disbelievingly.

Precisely. After breaking through the Lancastrian defense on the stairs and coming upon his sword, Collier had ordered ten of his men to hold the upper floor and sent the remainder back to the hall. True, he could not hide that Henry had been here, but where he had disappeared to . . .

"When all quiets," Collier said, "I will see that your king and the rest of you are escorted to the postern gate."

He felt Sir Mathis's astonished gaze turn on him.

"He lies!" Walther exclaimed. "Does he not murder the king, he will deliver him into Morrow's hands."

King Henry stepped alongside the knight. "Are you a man of your word, Gilchrist?" he asked.

"I am."

"Do you believe in God?"

Collier glanced at Catherine. "I do."

"Then in His name I would have your word."

"As God is my witness," Collier said, "you and your men will be delivered safe from Toller."

As if savoring the words, Henry closed his eyes. When he opened them, he addressed Walther. "Release Lady Catherine."

Walther shook his head. "Surely you are not fool enough to believe this Yorkist?"

"Nay, I am no fool," Henry said. "And yes, I do believe him."

"What of the coin?" Walther demanded. "'Tis she who possesses it."

"Even if Lady Catherine holds it, I would not trade my life for it. Would you? Now release her."

Disgust curled Walther's lips. "Nay." Holding Catherine with his sword, he reached behind and put a hand to the embrasure.

Collier weighted his back leg and watched for the right moment. It would come, he was certain.

Henry took a step toward Walther. "I have ordered you to release her," he said more sharply.

"And I am done taking orders from a degenerate." The mercenary put a foot up on the embrasure. "Come, Lady Catherine, we shall see how quickly you learn the rope."

Although it was not the moment Collier had hoped for, he could not allow the mercenary to pull Catherine into the embrasure with him. If Walther fell, he would certainly take her with him.

Collier sprung toward him. A moment later, he saw he had read the man right. The mercenary prized his depraved life more highly than the satisfaction of taking Catherine's. Releasing her, Walther swung his sword up.

Their blades met.

"Get back!" Collier shouted to Catherine as he stared into Walther's eyes—looking for the mercenary's next move as Sir Mathis had instructed him. There it was.

As Catherine scrambled away, Collier fended off Walther's downstroke, then turned his blade around the other's and forced their swords up.

"My lord?" Sir Mathis called.

"Nay," Collier said. *He* would deal with Walther—as he should have done months back.

Issuing a low, guttural sound, Walther stumbled back against the embrasure. At a disadvantage with the wall behind him, and the injury done his leg as evidenced by the bandage, he pushed Collier's sword off his and sidestepped.

But Collier was unwilling to give up his advantage. He followed and delivered another blow.

"I see you have been practicing," Walther said as he deflected the blade intended for his arm. He thrust his weight forward to free his sword, then sliced toward Collier's thigh.

Collier jumped back, swung, and caught the edge of Walther's blade with his own. He had to kill him, he knew. It was the only way to ensure the man never again threatened Catherine. All he needed was the opening to do so.

It presented itself minutes later when Walther staggered beneath a thrust of Collier's sword. In the next instant, the mercenary's sword sailed out of his hand.

Collier swept his blade to Walther's chest. He had to do it. For Catherine. For their children. For all others who might cross this man's path, and those having already crossed it—the serving wench, Sara, who had been in the wrong place at the wrong time. The knight, Severn, his life so violently taken. And those unknown who surely lay cold in their graves.

"You cannot do it," Walther said. "You're a coward, Gilchrist. A coward!"

Though it went against all Collier had ever believed in, he would have done it, for there was none more worthy of death than the mercenary. But as he leaned into his blade, a giant of a man rose up between the battlements and seized Walther.

Severn? Collier did not believe his eyes. The knight was dead. Wasn't he?

Walther cried out as he was dragged into the embrasure, scrambled for purchase as he was lifted, and flailed as he was carried above the big man's head.

"And now I give you your due," Severn rumbled.

"Nay!" the mercenary shouted. A moment later, his protest turned to a scream of terror, resounding off the walls as he fell to his death.

In the silence that followed, Severn met Collier's gaze. "He'll not bother Lady Catherine again," the big man said.

No. Providing Walther did not have nine lives as Severn did. Collier turned and sought the one he would have killed for.

Catherine straightened from where she knelt beside Antony. A moment later, she was in Collier's arms.

They searched each other's face.

"You came back," Catherine said. Tears filled her eyes. "I thought I had lost you forever."

Collier shook his head. "I am with you for always."

She smiled. "I love you. But you know that, don't you?"

"I do."

"I should have told you sooner. I—"

Collier covered her mouth with his. It was the sweetest kiss ever. He and Catherine had been granted a second chance to right the wrongs of their lives. To find love. To make a future together. A future with the promise of roses.

"I will not forget this day, Sir Collier—what you have done."

With dawn reaching fingers across the sky, Collier looked into the face of a man history had not been kind to. "It would be better if you did," he said.

After a thoughtful moment, King Henry said, "You are no Yorkist, are you?"

As it was Edward's claim to the throne Collier supported, he had considered himself one, but he really wasn't. He pressed Catherine's hand in his. "I am neither Yorkist nor Lancastrian, Your Majesty. I want only what is best for England."

A great sadness filled Henry's eyes, then tears. He looked down. "'Tis as it should be," he murmured.

More than anything, Collier wanted to warn Henry of what lay ahead. To urge him to flee this land and live out the remainder of his days in peace, but he could not. "You have served England well," he said. "I am certain one day you will do so again."

When Henry looked up, a grateful smile was on his mouth and in his eyes. "You are truly a man of God, and though you would have me forget what you do, I will not."

Unfortunately, that could mean trouble.

Henry laid a hand to Collier's arm. "Do not fear," he said. "None but these present will ever know."

Collier looked to the others: Catherine, Severn, Sir Richard, Sir Mathis, and Antony whose eyes were cast down. Though it was obvious the boy wished to remain at Toller, he had chosen a path which he could not turn from. Like King Henry, he would ever be running from the Yorkists.

Collier removed the ring Lewis Algernon had given him. It belonged to another. "Antony," he said.

The boy met his gaze, then shifted it to the ring.

"It is yours," Collier said.

Antony blinked.

"Take it."

After another hesitation, Antony reached for it.

"If you need anything . . ." Collier said.

Antony slid the ring on his finger. It was loose, but one day it would fit.

"We should go, Your Majesty," Sir Richard said.

Henry nodded.

As he and the others pulled the hoods of their mantles over their heads, Catherine touched Antony's arm. "Godspeed," she said.

His eyes were sad. "Would that I could be an uncle to your child. That I could right the wrongs I have done you."

"You have," she assured him, "and we will certainly be together again."

Clearly, Antony did not think so, but he said, "That we will."

"Lady Catherine," Severn said.

She turned.

From the shadows of his hood, he smiled. "You are worthy, my lady. Truly worthy."

Catherine slipped her hand out of Collier's, stepped forward, and kissed the great man's cheek. "As are you, Sir Severn."

A few minutes later, King Henry and his entourage slipped through the postern gate and back into the pages of history—a history Collier had done his best to put right.

Sir Mathis caught Collier's eye, gave an approving nod, then turned into the bailey that had hours ago been rife with battle.

"You think they will be all right?" Catherine asked.

Would they? Collier thought so. "Aye."

She slipped her hand into his. "It has been a long night, husband. Methinks I would like to rest for a while. Would you lie with me?"

Collier looked into her blue eyes. "I can think of nothing I would rather do."

28

It had not been a dream. Not found in the bottle of Scotch he had awakened beside a week ago.

Staring at the name, James sat back on his heels. Yesterday he had broken into Strivling's storerooms that had long ago been sealed off. It had taken him several hours to locate the stone and pry it loose, but even when he had looked upon the treasure within, he had still doubted—had told himself it was far more likely he was telepathic than that his brother had traveled back through time.

But what he had found in the shadow of the ruins of Toller Castle confirmed it. He traced the weathered letters with his fingertips. *Lord Collier Gilchrist of the White Rose, A Man of God and Much Beloved, Died August* . . . Anxious, James brushed away the dirt and peered closer. *Died August, 1514.* For a moment, he had feared his brother might have died during the conflict with the Lancastrians. Instead, Collier had lived to roughly eighty years of age, a very old man by the standards of the Middle Ages.

Swallowing emotion, James pressed his hand against the headstone and closed his eyes. Was it his imagination, or did he feel a presence beneath his palm? He so wanted to believe.

He drew a deep breath and opened his eyes to look upon the headstone beside Collier's. *Lady Catherine Gilchrist of the Red Rose, A Legend in Her Own Time, Died June, 1514.* Two months before Collier.

James bowed his head. It was a long time since he had shed any tears. A very long time. Born of sadness, but also happiness, they threatened to spill forth. "So sorry, Collier," he said, praying his brother could hear him. "I do love you. And I miss you."

Sometime later, a shadow fell across James and roused him from where he sat on his haunches before the headstone.

"You are trespassing," a woman said. "I must ask you to leave."

James looked up. The sun at the woman's back spun a halo through her golden hair and outlined her feminine figure. Unfortunately, the bright light prevented James from making out her features.

"Who are you?" he asked, squinting up at her.

Though she had to know of his discomfort, she did not move from where she stood. "Who are *you*?" she tossed the question back at him.

"James Morrow."

"Ah," she said, as if she had heard of him. And she likely had, considering the amount of media exposure he had been subjected to these past months.

"What is your business at Toller, Mr. Morrow?"

As he obviously couldn't tell her he had come to visit his brother who had died five hundred years ago, he struggled for an answer. "Just researching a little family history," he said. "I am a . . . descendant of Collier Gilchrist." He gestured to the headstone.

"Really?" Her tone said she didn't believe him.

"Really," James said, and asked again, "And you are?"

Finally, she stepped away from the sunlight. "Pagan Algernon." Her large brown eyes coolly assessed him.

Normally, her unusual first name would have grabbed his attention, not to mention her beauty, but it was her surname that stole the limelight. He had not known there were any Algernons left. In fact, he distinctly remembered Collier's unsuccessful attempt years past to dig up a trace of the family. Could it be this woman had arisen from an altered past?

"This is my land you are trespassing on," she said. "I would like you to leave."

His thoughts speeding ahead of him, James stood. "You are descended from Catherine Algernon."

Eyes narrowing with displeasure, the woman said, "Not directly."

Of course not. Were she a direct descendant of Catherine's, she would not have retained the surname of Algernon, for Catherine and Collier's offspring would have been Gilchrists. "Who, then?" James asked.

Her lips compressed. She was not going to tolerate much more of him.

"I don't mean to pry," James said, hoping to defuse the situation. "It's just that I have some questions about Collier Gilchrist—and Toller—which you might be able to shed some light on."

She stared at him a long moment. "Toller is not for sale, Mr. Morrow."

Was that what she thought he was here for? The reason for her antagonism? James looked to the ruins in the distance. "There is not much I could do with it if it were," he said, hoping a little humor would lighten her mood.

Wrong. It drew her delicately arched eyebrows together and warmed her face with color. "Mr. Morrow, my dogs do not like you, and I cannot say I do myself. I really think it would be best for you to leave."

Dogs? James looked left of her, then right.

There they were. Two Dobermans. Except for their gleaming eyes and quivering jaws, they stood as still as statues, waiting for a command.

James returned his gaze to the woman. "Just a few minutes of your time is all I ask, Ms. Algernon, and I promise I won't bother you again."

Perhaps it was his tone, or the pleading on his face, but whatever it was, it reached through her defenses. She turned to the Dobermans. "Warlock. Bruiser. Sit."

Warlock? Bruiser? Lovely.

Though their eyes never left James, the dogs obeyed.

Pagan Algernon crossed her arms over her chest. "What, exactly, do you wish to know, Mr. Morrow?"

How old was she? James fleetingly wondered. Twenty-five? Twenty-six? "You say you are not *directly* descended from Catherine?"

"No. My line is descended from her brother, Sir Antony Algernon."

Collier had mentioned the boy—a rebel sure to die for the cause of the Lancasters. It seemed Antony had made it to maturity after all. "What do you know of Collier Gilchrist?" he asked.

"You really believe you're descended from him?"

"It's not all that implausible. After all, the Gilchrists were vassals of the Morrows." Actually, until that moment, James hadn't even considered the parallel.

"There were never any marriages between the two families," Pagan Algernon said. "Thus, you are either a liar, Mr. Morrow, or very mistaken."

"You know for certain there were not any marriages?"

She smiled. Though it was not genuine, it brightened her pretty face. "I'm a genealogist, Mr. Morrow. Believe me, I know my family history."

James's heart sped. She could be a wealth of information. "And what of the history of the Gilchrists?"

"*That* I am still working on, but I will tell you what I do know." She stepped forward. "And then you will leave?"

Not petite, he thought as he looked down at her, but neither of average height. And there was nothing average about her looks. Even with dark shadows beneath her eyes, she was incredibly lovely. "Yes, I'll leave."

Pagan Algernon stared at him a moment longer, then bent down before the headstone. "He was called the peacemaker—God's man." She smoothed her fingers across Collier's name. "He defended his family with the courage of a lion, but not once in all his years did he take another's life."

No, James couldn't imagine Collier would. "And what was his life like?"

"Good, I think. As you see, he lived to a very old age. And his wife, Catherine as well. I like to think his passing soon after her death was more the result of a broken heart than of age."

The love of Collier's life. Once again, emotion bottled James's throat. He swallowed. "Did he have any children?"

"Three."

"Sons? Daughters?"

She looked over her shoulder. "Not in five hundred years was a daughter born to either the Algernons, or the Gilchrists. Sons only."

Five hundred years? That hardly seemed possible. "But you—"

"I am the first since Catherine."

Strange. Very strange.

The woman stood and walked farther into the small graveyard. "Over here is the grave of Lewis Gilchrist, Collier's eldest son."

Lewis? Named in honor of Catherine's father, then.

Her back to James, Pagan Algernon halted before a granite headstone. "He also lived to a good age, as it seems most of the Gilchrists did—leastwise, from what I am able to tell so far."

"So far?"

She turned back around. "As I mentioned, I am still working on the genealogy of the Gilchrists."

James was intrigued. "And how do you go about that?"

"Archives," she said, retracing her steps, "old journals, diaries—"

"Diaries? Did Collier leave one behind?"

"He did."

Excitement shot through James. "You have read it?"

Suspicion flashed in the woman's eyes. "Parts of it." She frowned. "Strangely enough, though he began it in a hand that appears similar to our modern English—he must have been considered a very poor speller in his time—over the years his writing lends itself more to what we recognize as middle English. Likely, Catherine tutored him."

James realized he was not going to be able to keep his promise to leave this woman alone. He *had* to see the diary. But how was he going to convince her to allow him to take a look at it? "Are there any Gilchrists left?" he asked.

Her laughter was wry. "Most certainly. Men, all of them."

"Then how is it you, an Algernon, are the owner of Toller?"

"I did the same as you, James Morrow. I bought back my ancestral home which, before the Yorks won England from the Lancasters, was to have been Antony Algernon's."

Made sense. "And you live nearby?"

"In the manor house, of course."

Manor house? At Toller? James looked around.

"You can't see it from here," she said. "It's over the rise—built well back from the castle."

Though it seemed there was now a manor house at Toller, James was certain there hadn't been one before. Prior to the purchase of Strivling he had several times flown over Toller. There had been only castle ruins. Was Pagan Algernon from an altered past? he wondered again. Had she not existed four months back?

"That's really all I can tell you," she said. "Now I must ask you to leave."

James looked into her cold eyes. Much as he

wanted to see the diary, now was not the time to ask. "I am indebted."

Her eyebrows arched.

"Truly."

"Good day, Mr. Morrow." She started toward the Dobermans. "Warlock. Bruiser. Come."

"Ms. Algernon?"

Visibly irritated, she looked around. "Mr. Morrow?"

"Would you entertain having dinner with me one of these nights?"

"No."

Not a moment's hesitation. Whoever Pagan Algernon was, and wherever she had come from, she was not very friendly. Or maybe it was just him. Somehow he would get to her, James promised himself as she walked away. Somehow he would get past the defenses of this incredibly attractive woman. Suddenly, it came to him. "Ms. Algernon."

With a heavy sigh, she swung around. "You are not accustomed to keeping your promises, are you, Mr. Morrow?"

"I have something you might be interested in seeing."

Her expression clearly said she doubted that.

"It's a fifteenth-century portrait of Catherine Algernon."

In an instant, her expression changed. At last, he had her attention.

"It's unfinished," he said, "but it has an interesting history. Dinner?"

As if struggling between the desire to see the portrait and a need to tell him where to go, she was a long time in responding. Finally, she said, "I will call you," and set off again.

James smiled. He had gotten to her. But it was time for him to leave—before she sicced Warlock and Bruiser on him.

He looked one last time at his brother's headstone. In spite of the ache inside him, he was happy for Collier. "I'll be back," he said, and turned away.

Epilogue

England, 1468

Catherine looked from her husband's beaming face to the bundled babe he held. Sore from the delivery of their second son early this morning, she eased herself back upon the pillows. "I think he looks like you," she said.

Collier cocked his head, stared hard at little James, then said, "Actually, I think he looks more like Antony. What do you think, Eustace?"

Peering into the swaddling clothes, the boy shrugged. "Mayhap a bit around the eyes?"

Chuckling, Collier looked over his shoulder at the man who hung back. "Come see for yourself."

More than a little uneasy, Antony stepped forward.

Catherine looked long at her brother. In four years, he had more than fulfilled the promise of his boyish good looks. He was tall, broad-shouldered, had a face few maids could resist, and a voice so deep even married women sighed to hear it. But still he was a fugitive, attainted for his acts of treason against Edward's England.

Antony looked over Collier's shoulder, stared at the little face, and finally agreed, "You are right. He does look like me."

"Then he shall be called James Antony Gilchrist," Collier said.

"Two Christian names?" Tilly asked as she stepped into the solar, her arms filled with blankets.

Catherine smiled. Collier had told her of the practice of having both a first and middle name which would not come into its own for at least a couple centuries. Of course, he could not tell the old woman that.

"Don't you think he deserves more than one?" Collier said.

Tilly shrugged. "I suppose . . ."

"He does," Antony said.

"Would you like to hold him?" Collier asked.

Antony looked ready to refuse, but then nodded. He took James in his arms and walked to where the big man stood beside the doorway. "Little Antony looks like me, don't you think, Severn?" There was pride in his voice.

Severn took one look. "Don't see it. Looks like a baby to me—red and wrinkled."

Catherine held back her laughter. Severn had never been tactful, and was not about to change his ways. But for all that, it was good to see him again. Once or twice a year, he and Antony made the crossing from France to England, disguised lest they be recognized. This visit to Toller had coincided with the birth of James, but it was no coincidence. Three years earlier, they had come following Lewis's birth.

Catherine looked to where her three-year-old son lay asleep in his grandmother's lap. It had been a very exciting day for him.

Collier lowered himself to the mattress edge. "How are you feeling?"

"Wonderful," she said.

He pressed her hands between his. "You look wonderful."

Even though she would not care one bit to look upon her reflection, she knew Collier did not lie. He saw with the eyes of a man in love. She leaned toward him. "Methinks you would like to make another son on me, husband."

He grinned. "That I would." He kissed her tenderly. "But I will be content to simply hold you for a while."

As he drew back, Catherine looked into the eyes of the man who had journeyed across time to find her. She had his love. Two beautiful sons. And no more accursed dreams. She sighed.

At last, all was well in their world.